# THE 1898 MOVEMENT IN SPAIN

# THE 1898 MOVEMENT
# IN SPAIN

TOWARDS A REINTERPRETATION
WITH SPECIAL REFERENCE TO
*En torno al casticismo* AND *Idearium español*

by

## H. RAMSDEN

Professor of Spanish Language and Literature
in the University of Manchester

## MANCHESTER
## UNIVERSITY PRESS

ROWMAN AND LITTLEFIELD

© 1974 H. RAMSDEN

Published by the University of Manchester at

THE UNIVERSITY PRESS

Oxford Road, Manchester M13 9PL

UK ISBN 0 7190 0565 3


USA

ROWMAN AND LITTLEFIELD

81 Adams Drive, Totowa, N.J. 07512

US ISBN 0 87471 586 5


Printed in Great Britain by
WESTERN PRINTING SERVICES LTD,
Bristol

# CONTENTS

La ciencia es el carácter dominante de nuestro tiempo. Todo tiende a someterse a ella, desde la industria hasta la milicia. La misma política se reconoce que debiera ser patrimonio de los sociólogos. Y el arte no puede quedar excluido de este movimiento intelectual (Antonio Royo Villanova, in *Alma Española* 16, 21 February 1904).

El principio de unidad y la doctrina de la evolución son hoy las ideas madres en la ciencia (1894; MU, I, 879).

La idea de evolución—madre del pensamiento moderno (1915; Azorín, III, 260).

Nuestro siglo—decía Juan de Mairena, aludiendo al siglo XIX—es, acaso, el que más se ha escuchado a sí mismo, tal vez porque nosotros, los que en él vivimos, tenemos una conciencia marcadamente temporal de nuestro existir [. . .]. Su filosofía típica es el positivismo, un pensar de 'su tiempo', 'venido—según él—a superar una edad metafísica y otra teológica'. En política ha peleado por el progreso y por la tradición, dos fantasmas del tiempo. Su ciencia es biologismo, evolucionismo, un culto a los hechos vitales sometidos a la ley del tiempo (Antonio Machado, *Juan de Mairena*, Madrid 1936, pp. 99–100).

No se pueden violar impunemente las leyes biológicas (Luis Morote, *La moral de la derrota*, Madrid 1900, p. 761).

# INTRODUCTION

## FACTS, PROBLEMS AND AIMS

Unamuno and Ganivet first met in May 1891 when they were both candidates for University Chairs of Greek: Unamuno for the Chair at Salamanca (to which he was appointed), Ganivet for the Chair at Granada (to which he was not appointed). Unamuno was twenty-six and Ganivet a year younger, and after attending one another's *oposiciones* they would go off together and eat ice-cream and talk, though it was apparently Unamuno who did most of the talking. After their *oposiciones* the two men lost touch with one another until 1896 or thereabouts when Unamuno wrote to Ganivet after reading a number of his articles in *El Defensor de Granada*. Thereafter, they were in correspondence with one another for two years, until Ganivet's death in November 1898 (MU, III, 637–9; VIII, 251–5). Unamuno's *En torno al casticismo* first appeared in *La España Moderna* from February to June 1895 and was subsequently published as a book in 1902 (Biblioteca Moderna de Ciencias Sociales, Madrid). Ganivet's *Idearium español* first appeared in August 1897, in book form (Sabatel, Granada). From 12 June 1898 to 14 September 1898 a public exchange of letters between the two writers appeared in *El Defensor de Granada* under the title 'El porvenir de España' (seventeen parts: eight by Unamuno and nine by Ganivet; complete in MU, III, 641–77).[1]

Early commentators indicated Ganivet as a forerunner of Unamuno. There are several possible explanations. In the first place, a number of early studies give 1862 instead of 1865 as Ganivet's date of birth and this, together with his premature death, may well have misled scholars about the respective seniority of the two writers. Moreover, despite the prestige of *La España Moderna, En torno al casticismo* attracted relatively little attention when it first appeared in periodical form, whereas, in consequence of an intensive campaign by personal friends, Ganivet and his *Idearium español* were brought forcibly to the attention of the Spanish reading public in the weeks immediately following the writer's death—at a time when Unamuno was still trying unsuccessfully to have his *En torno al casticismo* essays published in book form. Unamuno objected to the imputation of influence: in an article published in May 1908 (VIII, 251–5), in his 'Aclaraciones previas' to the first book edition of *El porvenir de España* (Renacimiento, Madrid 1912) and, yet again, in a letter of com-

[1] For abbreviations and editions used in this study, see below, pp. 211–12.

plaint to Antonio Gallego Burín, written on receipt of the latter's study, *Angel Ganivet* (Granada 1921). Tradition, it seems, dies hard. In the introduction to his centenary biography, *Angel Ganivet, el excéntrico del 9 8* (Granada 1965), Antonio Gallego Morell took up the point again, with quotation from Unamuno's letter of 1921 and with continuing reluctance to renounce the notion of Ganivet's priority, at least in the general panorama of Spanish literature of the time: 'Es Angel Ganivet quien abre este espléndido Segundo Siglo de Oro de la Literatura Española, aunque tan rotunda afirmación empinase en protesta la protesta del viejo Rector de Salamanca.'

Meanwhile, also in the centenary year, Pedro Rocamora was emphasizing influence in the opposite direction, to the point where Ganivet was held to be merely a pale reflection of Unamuno's genius.[2] But Rocamora's case rests not on a comparative study of *En torno al casticismo* and *Idearium español*. It rests solely on the alleged impact on Ganivet of his meeting with Unamuno during their *oposiciones*:

> ¿Cómo no creer que después de aquellas charlas en el Ateneo matritense—Unamuno escrutaba el mundo enjuizándolo con imponente magisterio—, Ganivet no retornaría a su casa de huéspedes trémulo de emoción ante el descubrimiento de aquel hombre, ansioso de recoger en una cuartilla—el pulso ya febril—alguna de las ideas escuchadas al maestro? (op. cit., p. 7).

The suggestion is interesting, but evidence for it is entirely lacking.

Since *En torno al casticismo* was published in 1895 and *Idearium español* was written in 1896, we can banish immediately any notion that Ganivet's book influenced Unamuno's. Moreover, we can apparently banish also the possibility that Ganivet influenced *En torno al casticismo* through personal contact or correspondence. In the opposite direction the case is less clear. It is certain that Ganivet knew Unamuno's *En torno al casticismo* at the time he was writing *Idearium español*,[3] and it may well be that Unamuno's study prompted Ganivet to write his own. Moreover, it seems probable that on a number of points, at times by acceptance and at times by rejection, he was responding directly to views expressed in *En torno al casticismo*. But a study of Ganivet's development from 1888

[2] 'Ganivet y su *Idearium* desde otro siglo', in *Arbor*, Nos. 237–8 (September–October 1965), 5–17.

[3] NML, 69–70; Gallego Morell, op. cit., 127.

to 1895 shows him to be evolving very clearly to the position we find in *Idearium español* and there is perhaps no point in the work at which it can reasonably be asserted that, in the light of Unamuno's study, Ganivet had modified either his approach to civilization or his view of the problem of Spain.

Nevertheless, no one, reading these two works from the vantage-point of another age, can overlook their fundamental similarities. Nor is the significance of these similarities confined to the two works in question. On 24 May 1899 Unamuno informed Pedro Jiménez Ilundain that, though he thought he had gained in clarity, he suspected that he would never again write anything 'de tanta intensidad de pensamiento como *En torno al casticismo* y *Paz en la guerra*', and three years later, in the prologue to the first book edition of *En torno al casticismo*, he declared, 'En estas páginas están en germen los más de mis trabajos posteriores'. Similarly, according to Ganivet's close friend Nicolás María López *Idearium español* was without doubt the work that Ganivet himself esteemed most highly among his writings; in it, he continues, 'se contienen las bases fundamentales del ganivetismo' (NML, 126).[4] In other words, in comparing *En torno al casticismo* and *Idearium español* we are comparing also fundamental aspects of the thought of their respective authors. It may be possible to go still further than this and say that in studying the characteristics that the two works have in common we are touching on fundamental aspects of Spanish thought, and even of European thought, at the time the works were written. Finally, we may be able to find in those common characteristics pointers to a better understanding of the much debated 1898 Generation. Such, at least, are my hopes and my aims. It is these hopes and aims that have determined the structure of my book.

In Part I ('*En torno al casticismo* and *Idearium español*: A Comparative Study') I compare the two works and seek to demonstrate their most striking similarities and differences. Their similarities, it will be seen, are fundamental. But I do not infer from this that there was any profound influence of one writer on the other. Nor do I believe that a study of their mutual contacts and separate development allows us to make such an inference. My interest lies in the apparently remarkable coincidence that at a particular moment in time two Spanish writers devoted themselves to the

[4] Cf. LSLP, 50–1.

same problem, applied the same methods, diagnosed the same evil and sought to confirm their findings in the same way. In order to demonstrate the relevance of my observations to Unamuno's and Ganivet's thought beyond *En torno al casticismo* and *Idearium español* I shall add brief footnote references to other works by the same authors.

But with Unamuno there are difficulties. During the last twenty years Unamuno studies have made progress in two notable directions: under the influence of Armando Zubizarreta and Antonio Sánchez Barbudo scholars have come to recognize the importance of Unamuno's emotional crisis of March 1897, and under the guidance of Carlos Blanco Aguinaga and Rafael Pérez de la Dehesa scholars are gradually coming to acknowledge the importance of Unamuno's early socialism. These two characteristics of recent Unamuno research have given notable impetus to a third that embraces both and is more important than either: an increasing awareness among Unamuno scholars of the need for close chronological study. But they have also given renewed strength to the notion of two Unamunos: an early Unamuno '[que] trata, por lo general, de lo más fácil y objetivo, y lo trata objetivamente' and a later Unamuno '[que] lanza al público su intimidad como un reto'.[5] The year 1897, it appears, is being seen increasingly as a pivot year in which (as formerly 1610 for Góngora) an angel of light gave way to an angel of darkness or, according to one's political and religious standpoint, an angel of darkness gave way to an angel of diversely estimated light.

My findings in this study, in so far as they are relevant to the problem, tend to play down rather than exalt the importance of 1897, for the characteristics we shall observe in *En torno al casticismo* do not undergo any notable change in that year. On the contrary, they can be seen developing from Unamuno's doctoral thesis of 1884, reaching full expression in 1895 and thereafter, like a personal *roca viva* or intra-historic *yo*, persisting through the crisis year and on into the works of the author's later maturity. 'En rigor,' declared Unamuno in 1916, 'desde que empecé a escribir he venido desarrollando unos pocos y mismos pensamientos cardinales' (I, 873). And in 1924: 'Hombre que haya permanecido más fiel a sí mismo, más uno y más coherente que yo

[5] Carlos Blanco Aguinaga, *Unamuno, teórico del lenguaje*, Mexico 1954, pp. 66–7.

difícilmente se encontrará en las letras españolas' (VIII, 520).
There is perhaps more truth in these statements than is now
commonly believed.

The difficulty has been to suggest this briefly in a study whose
main aim lies elsewhere. In the belief that a wide range of reference
makes it too easy to prove too much I have confined myself almost
entirely in Part I of my study to Unamuno's writings from 1895
to 1902, with special emphasis on those written during the five
years following 1897. This information has been placed in footnotes. The reader will thus have, in the main text, a comparative
study of *En torno al casticismo* and *Idearium español* and, in the
footnotes, evidence to suggest—very briefly for Ganivet, somewhat more fully for Unamuno—that the characteristics noted find
expression also in other works by the same authors. Evidence
from Unamuno's writings after 1902 will in general be reserved
for Part III of my study.

In Part II ('The Intellectual Context: Determinist Thought and
Methods') I aim to probe my earlier reference to the 'apparently
remarkable coincidence' that at a particular moment in time two
Spanish writers devoted themselves to the same problem, applied
the same methods, diagnosed the same evil and sought to confirm
their findings in the same way. As historians of literature we are
reluctant to accept remarkable coincidences. Is there perhaps a
common influence operating on both works? I shall suggest that
there is, for, as we shall see, all the basic similarities of method,
diagnosis and prescription that we find in *En torno al casticismo* and
*Idearium español* are to be found also in the writings of the French
philosopher and historian Hippolyte Taine (1828–93), whose
work Unamuno and Ganivet both admired. But behind Taine
there is a still more fundamental influence that weighs on all three
writers and indeed on a host of thinkers of the later nineteenth
century. I refer to the influence of natural science, exalted and
indeed almost omnipotent for several decades after the publication
of Darwin's *Origin of Species* in 1859. How were the findings of
natural science applied to the study of civilization and to what
effect? What was the appeal of natural history to students of
civilization and, more especially, to Unamuno and Ganivet?
These are some of the questions I shall seek to answer in this
second part of my study. In offering my answers I shall point to
further similarities between *En torno al casticismo* and *Idearium*

*español,* similarities less immediately obvious than those illustrated in Part I.

Finally, in Part III ('Towards the Understanding of the 1898 Movement') I shall consider the influence of *En torno al casticismo* and *Idearium Español,* and of the organic determinism that they exemplify, on subsequent Spanish thought and literature. But, as in Parts I and II, my main aim is not to demonstrate influences; it is to establish parallels and thereby to draw attention to certain notable characteristics in twentieth-century Spanish writing. But they are not merely random characteristics. The basic schema observed in *En torno al casticismo* and *Idearium español*—and in Taine—enables us to see them as complementary elements in a coherent pattern of thought and feeling peculiar to the age. My underlying submission throughout Part III is that, by a careful study of the radiation of those characteristics, one can hope for an eventual re-definition of the 98 Generation. In the meantime, I continue to use the term '98 Generation', with misgivings, as a provisional label. It is a situation well known to the student of literature. On the one hand, he is faced with a series of such labels (often terms of unhelpful or misleading etymology: Romanticism, Impressionism, Decadentism); on the other hand, with the realities of literature at a given period. The banishment of an established label, it seems, is virtually impossible; the most one can do is to change its meaning. I accept this in my approach to the 98 Generation. One may question the relevance both of the '98' and of the 'Generation'; one may also regret some of the critical misconceptions traditionally associated with the Generation. What one cannot reasonably do is to deny the existence in Spanish literature during the first half of the twentieth century—and especially in writings by the most commonly accepted members of the 98 Generation—of a number of characteristics that together constitute an immediately recognizable pattern peculiar to the age. One may create a new name for the pattern (say, Lyrico-determinism, or Determanticism, since it is basically a determinism-guided Romanticism) or one may seek to adapt the term most nearly at hand (98 Generation). In general I have opted for the latter, albeit with an underlying conviction—not always disguised —that as a reasonable compromise between traditional terminology and a totally new label the word Generation (synchronically too broad in meaning, diachronically too narrow) should at least be replaced by the word Movement. My ultimate aim in Part III is to point the way to an eventual re-definition of the 98 'Generation' based on internal, textual evidence.

But in saying this I am pressing for an approach very different from that commonly pursued in comprehensive studies of the Generation, with their emphasis on generational factors. Champions of this approach, who claim to start from scholarly generational criteria and to arrive thereby at a valid generational grouping of authors, are apt to find, for example—as Luis Granjel has found—that Ganivet cannot be included in the 98 Generation because he did not live long enough for the great 'generational event' of 1898 to have the impact on him that it had on the *noventayochistas* and because he did not maintain close personal contacts with his contemporaries in *tertulias*, periodicals and collective acts of homage and protest. It is one of my aims in this study to show that, whatever externally applied generational factors may suggest, internal textual evidence demands that *En torno al casticismo* and *Idearium español* be grouped together in any meaningful survey of Spanish literature of that period. The term 98 Generation may still be inappropriate to *Idearium español*, but if it is, it is inappropriate also to *En torno al casticismo*. Within the Generation or outside the Generation the two works belong together. It is common characteristics in literature that must guide us in our definitions of *literary* generations, not common characteristics in the lives of authors. We have been encouraged to believe that by birth-dates, common formative influences (which in the case of the 98 Generation have been reduced to mere *autodidactismo*), personal contacts, a common generational experience and common leadership we can arrive inductively at a definition of the 98 Generation. In fact, these most commonly emphasized generational factors can do no more than check, control and, somewhat feebly, confirm findings arrived at by the study of the texts themselves.

It is common characteristics in literature, I have said, that must guide us in our definitions of literary generations. But common characteristics in the literature of a generation's formative period, or common characteristics in the literature of its maturity? My question is prompted by the current emphasis on virtually forgotten socialist and anarchist writings published during the 1890's. In many ways this emphasis is fascinating and promises to open up a host of new perspectives on the formative years of the Generation. But unless it can be shown that socialism and anarchism are relevant to the writings for which the Generation is best known, they are, I suggest, a *pis aller* from the point of view of defining the Generation, a tacit admission that one can find no significant positive relationship between the writings that have given the Generation its ultimate fame. Of course it may be, as several scholars have suggested, that by 1905 the Generation ceased to exist as a significant grouping, in which case we shall have to content ourselves with pre-1905 similarities—and socialism or anarchism may then prove to offer the firmest bond. But I am myself reluctant to accept this view. The emphatically non-socialist and non-anarchist works *En torno al casticismo* and *Idearium español*, published in the mid 1890's, contain in essence characteristics that were to imprint themselves on Spanish thought and literature for half a century. The clearest evidence of those characteristics is to be found—both before and after 1905—in writings generally considered to belong to the 98 Generation.[6]

---

[6] For a critical survey of the principal interpretations of the 98 Generation, see HR, 'The Spanish "Generation of 1898": I. The history of a concept', in *Bulletin of the John Rylands University Library of Manchester* 56 (1973–74), 463–91.

# I

*En torno al casticismo* AND *Idearium español*

A COMPARATIVE STUDY

## 1. THE PROBLEM OF SPAIN

Pienso ir aquí agrupando las reflexiones y sugestiones que me han ocurrido pensando en torno a este punto del casticismo, centro sobre que gira torbellino de problemas que suscita el estado mental de nuestra patria (*ETC*, 784).

Se habrá notado que el motivo céntrico de mis ideas es la restauración de la vida espiritual de España (*IE*, 295).

These two extracts, the former from the opening pages of *En torno al casticismo* and the latter from the closing pages of *Idearium español*, remind us immediately of the underlying similarity of aim. Indeed, the similarity is greater than these quotations alone might lead us to expect, for each complements the other and might almost have been written by either author. Both writers are concerned basically with what has come to be called the 'problem of Spain'. Formerly Spain was great; now it is in decline. Why did it fall into decline, how does that decline reveal itself, and by what means can the nation be regenerated? These are their basic questions.

Past, present and future. But both writers are happily free from any nostalgic emphasis on the manifest greatness of Spain's past. Both are concerned primarily to probe the less joyful aspects of the country's past and present and, in the light of their findings, to offer guidance to a better future.

We shall consider later the apparently casual, asystematic approach suggested by the modest 'reflexiones y sugestiones' (and by the titles of the two works). But there is a far more significant resemblance in the expressions 'estado mental' (*ETC*) and 'vida espiritual' (*IE*). They remind us that for both writers the problem of Spain is basically a psychological problem.[1]

---

[1] In view of Carlos Blanco Aguinaga's attack on the traditional interpretation of the 'problem of Spain' (*Juventud del 98*, Madrid 1970, especially pp. 3–38) I must emphasize that I am here not concerned with what a modern historian might consider *was* the problem of Spain, only with what the authors of *En torno al casticismo* and *Idearium español* believed was the problem of Spain. It will subsequently become apparent that I disagree with Blanco Aguinaga in his tendency to equate the two.

## 2. A PSYCHOLOGICAL PROBLEM

Atraviesa la sociedad española honda crisis; hay en su seno reajustes íntimos, vivaz trasiego de elementos, hervor de descomposiciones y recombinaciones, y por de fuera un desesperante marasmo. En esta crisis persisten y se revelan en la vieja casta los caracteres castizos, bien que en descomposición no pocos (*ETC*, 856).

Si yo fuese consultado como médico espiritual para formular el diagnóstico del padecimiento que los españoles sufrimos (porque padecimiento hay y de difícil curación), diría que la enfermedad se designa con el nombre de *no-querer* o, en términos más científicos, por la palabra griega *aboulia*, que significa eso mismo, *extinción o debilitación grave de la voluntad*; y lo sostendría, si necesario fuera, con textos de autoridades y examen de casos clínicos muy detallados (*IE*, 286).

For Unamuno as for Ganivet the problem of Spain reveals itself primarily as a psychological problem. If there are underlying economic factors—and for Unamuno, at least, there are[2]—these are scarcely touched upon. Unamuno's emphasis throughout is on 'el estado mental de nuestra patria' (*ETC*, 784); Ganivet's on 'la vida espiritual de España' (*IE*, 295).[3] From this common emphasis other basic similarities follow.

First, in the approach. Both writers accept as fundamental to their work a probing of the nation's 'conciencia colectiva' (*ETC*, 859; *IE*, 292). Both employ concepts and terminology derived from the study of individual psychology: *percepción, discernimiento, impresiones discretas, tejido conjuntivo intelectual,* etc. (*ETC*, 813–14); *abulia, atáxico, actos* [. . .] *instintivos producidos por sugestión, idea fija,* etc. (*IE*, 287). Both develop and illustrate their findings with frequent references to individual psychology; 'lo mismo un pueblo que un hombre' (*ETC*, 799) and 'los pueblos [. . .] como los artistas' (*IE*, 212) are characteristic expressions in both works. The prober of national destinies is basically a 'médico espiritual':

---

[2] 'La pobreza económica explica nuestra anemia mental' (*ETC*, 861).

[3] External evidence supports this suggestion: *En torno al casticismo*, says Unamuno, is 'un ensayo de estudio del alma castellana' (I, 1289); *Idearium español*, says Ganivet, is an attempt to 'definir y afirmar el espíritu español' (LSLP, 95–6).

El individuo, a su vez, es una reducción fotográfica de la sociedad [. . .]. En este sentido, creo yo que es provechosa la aplicación de la psicología individual a los estados sociales, y la patología del espíritu a la patología política (*IE*, 288).

The principal findings of the two works, also, are remarkably alike. Contemporary Spanish society, it is claimed, is in a state of mental and spiritual crisis, confused, disorientated, unable to find its direction amidst a profusion of often irreconcilable or un-integrated elements, 'vivaz trasiego de elementos, hervor de descomposiciones y recombinaciones' (*ETC*, 856), 'retazos de diferentes colores, como la vestimenta de los mendigos' (*IE*, 267). There is an underlying 'tendencia disociativa', says Unamuno (*ETC*, 858), a 'debilitación del sentido sintético, de la facultad de asociar las representaciones', adds Ganivet (*IE*, 291). In short, Spain lacks a basic guiding principle and the outcome is *atonía* and *abulia* (both writers use the terms), a state of near paralysis of the will and understanding that results in general apathy and inaction disrupted by occasional outbursts of ill-directed energy as one element or another is seized upon, out of context, and made the unconsidered motive of action:

Nos gobierna, ya la voluntariedad del arranque, ya el abandono fatalista [. . .]. Extiéndese y se dilata por toda nuestra actual sociedad española una enorme monotonía, que se resuelve en atonía, la uniformidad mate de una losa de plomo de ingente ramplonería (*ETC*, 857).

Nuestra nación hace ya tiempo que está como distraída en medio del mundo. Nada le interesa, nada le mueve de ordinario; mas de repente una idea se fija, y no pudiendo equilibrarse con otras produce la impulsión arrebatada (*IE*, 289).

Against this background of basic similarity two differences stand out:

1. For Unamuno dissociation is a fundamental Castilian charac-teristic and the elements in confusion within the Spanish mentality are principally elements inherited from the native tradition ('los caracteres castizos, bien que en descomposición no pocos', *ETC*, 856); for Ganivet, on the other hand, the discordant elements are generally elements imported from abroad ('la atención se debilita tanto más cuanto más nuevo o extraño es el objeto sobre el cual hay que fijarla', *IE*, 287).

2. Unamuno emphasizes far more than Ganivet the aridity and stagnation of Spanish contemporary life; Ganivet gives greater place to its lack of direction.

They are only differences of emphasis but they are significant and we shall return to them.[4]

### 3. IN SEARCH OF SPAIN

#### (a) *The need for self-knowledge*

Si vas a saltar una zanja sin conocer previamente cuánto saltas, lo haces con el encojimiento del miedo y caes; mas si ejercitándote en gimnasia habías medido tus fuerzas, saltas con valor, con conocimiento de ti mismo, que éste es el valor verdadero, conocimiento de sí mismo. La misma utilidad que la gimnasia para la vida corporal tiene el examen de conciencia para la espiritual y el estudio sereno de la historia para un pueblo (*ETC*, 799).

Y en tanto que el pensamiento de una nación no está claramente definido, la acción tiene que ser débil, indecisa, transitoria. El sentido sintético es en la sociedad, y en particular en quienes la dirigen, la capacidad para obrar conscientemente, para conocer bien sus propios destinos. Hay naciones en las que se observa, por encima de las divergencias secundarias, una rara y constante unanimidad para *comprender sus intereses*. Esta comprensión parece tan clara como la de un individuo que en un momento cualquiera, recordando su pasado y examinando su situación presente, se da cuenta precisa de lo que es o de lo que representa (*IE*, 292-3).

---

[4] In *El porvenir de España* Unamuno himself was to touch on an aspect of the second difference noted:

No es, por desgracia, ni la insubordinación ni la anarquía lo que, como usted insinúa, domina en nuestras letras; es la ramplonería y la insignificancia que brotan como de manantial de nuestra infilosofía y nuestra irreligión, es el triunfo de todo género que no haga pensar (III, 641-2).

But it must be emphasized again that this is only a difference of emphasis. In *Idearium español* Ganivet, too, had concerned himself with 'nuestra postración intelectual' (269), 'nuestra penuria intelectual' (284), and lamented the lack of 'trabajo constante e inteligente' by which to transform the existing 'charlatanería' into 'pensamientos sanos y útiles' (284-6). Conversely, in *En torno al casticismo* Unamuno, too, had lamented the Spanish 'instinto de los extremos' (858), the admiration for 'los actos de energía anárquica' (857) and the lack of 'un principio asociante y un principio de asociación' (863).

The first and all-important step towards a solution of Spain's national crisis of lost directions is collective self-knowledge. After all, say Unamuno and Ganivet, each nation has its own particular character, its own way of looking at reality and of reacting to it, its own special aptitudes, its own strengths and weaknesses; in short, its own 'conciencia colectiva', its own 'personalidad nacional'. A nation that struggles against or is forced to act against its native character becomes inwardly confused and outwardly ineffectual; a country that lives at one with its character prospers. Consequently, whoever would claim to guide a nation's destinies must start by understanding the national character.[5]

But Spain is singularly lacking in men who study Spanish society 'en su centro' (*ETC*, 859), who base their policies on 'la verdadera realidad de las cosas, la eterna y honda realidad' (*ETC*, 786). 'Se halla, a lo sumo, algún hombre hábil para ejecutar una misión que se le encomiende; pero no encontraremos uno solo que vea y juzgue la política nacional desde un punto de vista elevado o, por lo menos, céntrico' (*IE*, 231–2). It is this gap, this lack of 'fundamentalidad y dirección' (*ETC*, 863), that Unamuno and Ganivet aim to fill. They want to recognize the inevitable in order to exploit it, to arrive at 'la comprensión viva de lo necesario' (*ETC*, 801), 'conociendo la realidad y sometiéndose a ella, no pretendiendo trastrocarla ni burlarla' (*IE*, 243).

'La verdadera realidad de las cosas' (*ETC*, 786), 'la observación consciente de la realidad' (*IE*, 292). But reality is complex and

[5] '*El comienzo de la salud es conocer el hombre la dolencia del enfermo*, dice sentenciosamente Sempronio en *La Celestina*. Y si es, sin duda, el *conócete a ti mismo* principio de regeneración para el individuo, eslo en tan alto o mayor grado aún, para un pueblo' (1900; MU, VII, 416).

'Esta idea, conciencia clara de nuestra vida y perfecta comprensión de nuestros destinos, hemos de buscarla dentro de nosotros, en nuestro suelo, y la hallaremos si lo buscamos' (AG, *PE*, 677).

It may be observed, in passing, that *El porvenir de España* is less helpful than one might at first expect for a comparative study of the type with which we are here concerned, for in it both writers accept almost without comment the underlying premises and method that they have in common with one another and with their age, and concern themselves principally with relatively superficial differences resulting from the application of those common premises and method. From the vantage-point of another age it is the premises and method that strike us especially as characteristic and worthy of attention.

diffuse. Is it possible to find within that complexity and diffuseness
a firm basis for understanding? Both writers believe that it is.

(b) *From complexity to a nucleus*

es entrar en intrincado laberinto el pretender hallar lo característico
y propio de un hombre o de un pueblo, que no son nunca idénticos
en dos sucesivos momentos de su vida. Aun así y todo, he inten-
tado caracterizar nuestro núcleo castizo (*ETC*, 856).

El problema más difícil de resolver en el estudio psicológico, en
el que han encallado los investigadores y observadores más perspi-
cuos, es el de enlazar con rigor lógico la experiencia interna con los
fenómenos exteriores [. . .].

De igual modo, cuando se estudia la extructura psicológica de
un país, no basta representar el mecanismo externo, ni es prudente
explicarlo mediante una ideología fantástica; hay que ir más hondo
y buscar en la realidad misma el núcleo irreducible al que están
adheridas todas las envueltas que van transformando en el tiempo
la fisonomía de ese país (*IE*, 173–5).

The aim is ambitious: nothing less than to embrace Spanish
civilization in all its bewildering complexity and to show it finally
as an evolving, meaningful structure. But where does one start?
With the external manifestations of Spanish civilization or with
the national character that Unamuno and Ganivet believe to
underlie those external manifestations and give them form?
'Estudio sereno de la historia' or 'intuición directa' (*ETC*, 799)?
'Mecanismo externo' or 'ideología fantástica' (*IE*, 175)?
Unamuno clearly advocates the former:

No hay intuición directa de sí mismo que valga; el ojo no se ve si
no es con un espejo, y el espejo del hombre moral son sus obras,
de que es hijo. Al árbol se le conoce por sus frutos; obramos según
somos, y del conocimiento de nuestras obras entramos al de
nosotros mismos (*ETC*, 799).

But he sees the danger of losing oneself in mere facts and emphasizes it in his attack on historians who bury themselves in archives
amidst the lifeless remnants of the past (*ETC*, 795–7, 869). The
study of one's national history, he says, should be 'un implacable
examen de conciencia' (*ETC*, 798), and national conscience,
national character, can best be studied in the living present, in the

lives of ordinary men and women, people without history who day by day go about their ordinary work. It is these people who are the real bond between different historic moments, who are the all-important, unbroken, unconscious, intra-historic element, the bearers of true tradition, eternal tradition, and the substance of progress. Consequently, it is these people whom one should study in order to understand Spain and discover the mainsprings of its role in history:

> En este mundo de los silenciosos, en este fondo del mar, debajo de la historia, es donde vive la verdadera tradición, la eterna, en el presente, no en el pasado, muerto para siempre y enterrado en cosas muertas. En el fondo del presente hay que buscar la tradición eterna, en las entrañas del mar, no en los témpanos del pasado, que al querer darles vida se derriten, revertiendo sus aguas al mar (*ETC*, 794).

The progressive narrowing of Unamuno's field of reference is striking: from 'el estudio sereno de la historia de un pueblo' to 'el examen de la conciencia histórica', thence, with concentration on the present, to 'este mundo de los silenciosos' and on to the underlying 'tradición eterna'. Nor does the process end there, for, narrowing his focus spatially also, Unamuno then concentrates attention on a single area of alleged special significance: Castile. Indeed, it is only at this point, where he needs history to justify his narrowing of focus from Spain as a whole ('la tradición eterna española') to Castile ('el casticismo castellano'), that he advocates a dispassionate, empirical approach to history. Elsewhere in his work historical facts play little part. Where they do appear, they are used not to suggest interpretations but merely to confirm them.[6]

---

[6] I find no notable change in Unamuno's attitude to history during the period under review. 'Es menester estudiar al pueblo en sus manifestaciones, y lo primero es recojer éstas y determinar el objeto del estudio,' he affirms in his doctoral thesis (1884; IV, 88), but even in these early years he is quick to uphold, in a truth-laden partial jest, his own 'inestimable don de la intuición histórica' against the 'menguada verdad histórica' of those 'empedernidos positivistas, ojos sin color y alma sin poesía' (1887; I, 100). Similarly, in his allegedly post-scientific period he writes, 'No hay más que un medio para poner la cuestión de la psicología de los pueblos peninsulares en buen camino, y ese medio es estudiarla objetivamente, en laboratorio, como la ciencia pide' (1902; III, 716). This does not prevent him from seeing

Ganivet's approach is similar. He too emphasizes the need for those 'ideas sanas que nacen del estudio reflexivo y de la observación consciente de la realidad' (*IE*, 292); yet he too, like Unamuno, finds little merit in mere 'archive history':

> El criterio excesivamente positivista en que se inspiran hoy los estudios históricos obliga a los historiadores a colocar todos los hechos sobre un mismo plano y a cifrar todo su orgullo en la exactitud y en la imparcialidad. En vez de cuadros históricos se nos da solamente reducciones de archivo hábilmente hechas y se consigue la imparcialidad por el facilísimo sistema de no decir nunca lo que esos hechos significan. Sin embargo, lo esencial en la historia es el ligamen de los hechos con el espíritu del país donde han tenido lugar; sólo a este precio se puede escribir una historia verdadera, lógica y útil (*IE*, 224).

In other words, historical facts are valuable only when they are considered in the light of national character, when one can show which are in harmony with national character and which are opposed, which are favourable to the 'evolución natural' of the country and which are contrary to it (*IE*, 224). Each territory, together with its inhabitants, constitutes 'una personalidad histórica' (*IE*, 224). It is this 'personalidad histórica' that one must probe in order to arrive at a true understanding of the nation.

But the 'personalidad histórica', like the 'conciencia histórica' that Unamuno sets out to probe, is complex, and Ganivet, like Unamuno, seeks to narrow his field of reference:

> La vida de una nación ofrece siempre una apariencia de integridad de funciones, porque no es posible existir sin el concurso de todas ellas; mas, conforme transcurre el tiempo, se va notando que todas las funciones se rigen por una fuerza dominante y céntrica, donde pudiera decirse que está alojado el ideal de cada raza (*IE*, 211).

We can understand now more clearly the significance of the passage quoted at the beginning of this section, with its declared

---

history, 'la condenada historia', as a great concealer of the all-important underlying national spirit:

> La historia, a la vez que nos ha revelado gran parte de nuestro espíritu en nuestros actos, nos ha impedido ver lo más íntimo de ese espíritu. Hemos atendido más a los *sucesos* históricos que pasan y se pierden, que a los *hechos* sub-históricos, que permanecen y van estratificándose en profundas capas (1898; III, 661–2).

search for a 'núcleo irreducible al que están adheridas todas las envueltas que van transformando en el tiempo la fisonomía de ese país'. Ganivet, like Unamuno, reduces the study of Spanish civilization to the search for a central, structuring nucleus.[7]

In short, Unamuno and Ganivet both aim to understand Spanish civilization and believe that one can best do this by probing national character: 'la vida silenciosa de los millones de hombres sin historia' (*ETC*, 793), 'las clases proletarias, que son el archivo y el depósito de los sentimientos inexplicables, profundos de un país' (*IE*, 203). But national character itself is complex and diffuse, and both writers look for a firm and more easily definable nucleus within that national character: 'nuestro núcleo castizo' (*ETC*, 856), 'lo nativo' as opposed to 'lo adventicio' (*ETC*, 856), 'el núcleo irreducible' (*IE*, 175), 'una fuerza dominante y céntrica, donde pudiera decirse que está alojado el ideal de [la] raza' (*IE*, 211). Unamuno finds it in Castile's 'tradición eterna'; Ganivet finds it in the Peninsula's 'espíritu territorial'.

(c) *Explaining and defining the nucleus*

Allí dentro vive una casta de complexión seca, dura y sarmentosa, tostada por el sol y curtida por el frío, una casta de hombres sobrios, producto de una larga selección por las heladas de crudísimos inviernos y una serie de penurias periódicas, hechos a la inclemencia del cielo y a la pobreza de la vida (*ETC*, 811).

el espíritu permanente, invariable, que el territorio crea, infunde, mantiene en nosotros (*IE*, 176).

In their explanation of the all-important nucleus of Spanish national character Unamuno and Ganivet reveal a basic similarity and a striking difference.

The similarity is revealed clearly in the above quotations: both writers explain the alleged nucleus of Spain's 'conciencia colectiva' as a product of physical conditions.[8] Unamuno emphasizes the

[7] 'No debe satisfacernos la unidad exterior; debemos buscar la unidad fecunda, la que resume aspectos originales de una misma realidad [. . .]. Lo que yo llamo espíritu territorial no es sólo tierra; es también humanidad, es sentimiento de los trabajadores silenciosos de que usted [Unamuno] habla' (1898; AG, *PE*, 650, 671).

[8] '¿No se refleja acaso en el paisanaje el paisaje? Como en su retina, vive en el alma del hombre el paisaje que le rodea' (1901; MU, VIII, 910).

extremes and contrasts of the Castilian climate and landscape and considers the effects of these on the lives and character of the inhabitants; Ganivet emphasizes the influence of Spain's peninsular configuration.

But the difference, too, is striking. Faced with the obvious physical and climatic variety of the Peninsula, Unamuno focuses attention on a single area of alleged special significance, Castile, which occupied the centre of the Peninsula, was the most centralizing in spirit, 'el de instinto más conquistador e imperativo' (ETC, 804), and subsequently infused its spirit into other parts of the Peninsula:

> Castilla, sea como fuere, se puso a la cabeza de la monarquía española, y dio tono y espíritu a toda ella; lo castellano es, en fin de cuenta, lo castizo (ETC, 805).

Ganivet, on the other hand, ignores regional differences, detaches himself from complications of climate and landscape, and views the Peninsula only in its overall peninsular configuration.

In their findings also the two writers differ greatly. Unamuno finds gravity, slowness, tenacity, monotony, uniformity; 'seca rigidez, dura, recortada, lenta y tenaz'; an 'espíritu cortante y seco, pobre en nimbos de ideas'; a mentality that perceives things clear cut, having little capacity for synthesis and a strong tendency to dissociation (ETC, 807–16). Ganivet finds simply the allegedly fundamental, all-important spirit of independence.

In short, both writers view Spanish civilization in the same way and both approach it in the same way. Yet with similar methods they arrive at very different findings on basic Spanish character. We shall consider the implications later. For the moment it is sufficient to note the facts.[9]

---

'He aquí un criterio fijo, inmutable, para proceder cuerdamente en todos los asuntos políticos: agarrarse con fuerza al terruño y golpearlo para que nos diga lo que quiere' (AG, PE, 671).

[9] For maximum accuracy it is necessary to draw attention to two points that might appear to have been overlooked:

1. Ganivet does make a one-line allusion to the influence of climate on Spanish ideas (IE, 211) but does not develop the point.

2. In addition to the spirit of independence Ganivet emphasizes also, elsewhere in Idearium español (151–73), the importance of stoicism evolving to christian fervour. But from the point of view of Spain's alleged

## (d) *Confirming the nucleus*

Y ahora [. . .] entremos de golpe y porrazo a indicar dónde y cómo
se han de buscar las pruebas de que en este clima extremado y sin
tibiezas dulces, de paisaje uniforme en sus contrastes, es el espíritu
también cortante y seco, pobre en nimbos de ideas; pruebas de
cómo generaliza sobre los hechos vistos en bruto, en serie discreta,
en caleidoscopio, no sobre síntesis de un análisis de ellos, viéndolos
en serie continua, en flujo vivo; cómo los ve recortados como las
figuras en su campiña, sin rehacerlos apenas, tomándolos como
aparecen en su vestidura, y cómo, por fin, ha engendrado un
realismo vulgar y tosco y un idealismo seco y formulario, que
caminan juntos, asociados como Don Quijote y Sancho, pero que
nunca se funden en uno. Es socarrón o trágico, a las veces, a la vez,
pero sin identificar la ironía y la austera tragedia humanas (*ETC*,
815–16).

[On war and organization] España es por esencia, porque así lo
exige el espíritu de su territorio, un pueblo guerrero, no un pueblo
militar (*IE*, 187).

[Law] Tenemos, pues, un régimen anómalo, en armonía con
nuestro carácter (*IE*, 206).

[Arts] No se piense que el rasgo señalado [the lack of technical
reflection] es privativo de Velázquez o de Goya; es constante y es
universal en nuestro arte, porque brota espontáneo de nuestro amor
a la independencia (*IE*, 213–14).

Unamuno and Ganivet have purported to find fundamental and
persistent national traits through the examination of fundamental
and persistent physical conditions. Now they both look for confirmation in various spheres of national activity: Unamuno in a

---

'núcleo irreducible', formed by physical conditions, it is something of a
*deus ex machina* and can be left aside.

In this latter respect it is worth noting that Unamuno, too, introduces a
*deus ex machina*, unaccounted for by physical environment, to explain Castile's
rise to preeminence in Spanish history: namely, Castile's 'instinto más
conquistador e imperativo' (*ETC*, 804); 'Castilla, *sea como fuere*, se puso a la
cabeza de la monarquía española' (*ETC*, 805; my italics). Similarly: 'fue el
*destino* apoderándose de la libertad del espíritu colectivo' (*ETC*, 805; my
italics) and, in *Idearium español*, 'la desviación histórica a que la *fatalidad* nos
arrastró' (*IE*, 303; my italics). This is characteristic of the type of thought
that both works exemplify: over-simplist in its basis and therefore, also,
over-dependent on *ad hoc* explanations for phenomena that the basis itself
fails to explain.

review of certain aspects of Spanish thought and literature (Parts III and IV of his study: 'El espíritu castellano' and 'De mística y humanismo'); Ganivet in evidence drawn from three main spheres of national activity: military (187–99), legal (199–208) and artistic (209–22).

The progression is important. Each believes that a given civilization is a geographically localized complex of social, political, religious and artistic phenomena. On the surface are the phenomena themselves, the countless elements of Spanish civilization; behind them, imposing form and structure, is Spanish national character with its own all-pervading 'núcleo irreducible'; behind this is the ultimate formative influence, physical environment. But as we have seen, though Unamuno extols the merits of empirical study, he does not himself practise it. Nor does Ganivet. There is little evidence of any 'inferencia de nuestras obras a nuestro carácter' (*ETC*, 799). Nor are elements from Spain's past presented merely as the source for a provisional working hypothesis. 'Más adelante ejemplificaremos todo esto en la literatura *castiza* castellana,' writes Unamuno in a footnote to his description of the landscape and people of Castile (812). And this in fact is what he does. Ganivet likewise. In both works Spanish civilization is invoked not to suggest an interpretation of Spanish character but simply to confirm one and, as we shall see later, to be judged by that interpretation.[10]

[10] I have elsewhere considered this point more fully with reference to *Idearium español* (HR, 115–24). For whoever wishes to explore the problem with reference to *En torno al casticismo* the following passage will be fundamental:

> Todo cuanto se repita que hay que buscar la tradición eterna en el presente, que es intra-histórica más bien que histórica, que la historia del pasado sólo sirve en cuanto nos lleva a la revelación del presente, todo será poco (*ETC*, 797).

If one must look for eternal tradition in the present (first point), it is difficult to see how history can serve as a means of *revealing* the present (third point), however valuable it might be as a means of *confirming* a given interpretation of the present. Unamuno, it seems, like Ganivet, tends to shift his position according to the exigencies of the moment. His basic emphasis is on probing the present and confirming it by reference to the past, but, as we have seen (above, p. 18), in the first half of his second essay, where he needs to justify his narrowing of focus from 'la tradición eterna española' to 'el casticismo castellano', he is obliged to invoke the aid of history and it is in that part of the book alone that he calls for an empirical approach to history.

In this respect Golden Age literature plays an important role. Thus, for Unamuno, Calderón is 'el símbolo de casta' (817), 'cifra y compendio de los caracteres diferenciales y exclusivos del casticismo castellano' (816), and his theatre reveals characteristics immediately suggestive of those previously noted by Unamuno in his description of the landscape and the people: a kaleidoscopic but monotonous succession of clearly outlined characters and events loosely and superficially juxtaposed with little psychological depth; a mingling of extremes but not the fusion that gives them life; great ideas that fail to take on human form. Moreover, continues Unamuno, the dissociation and polarization that one finds in Calderón's theatre reveals itself also in the vain luxury of words and concepts (*culteranismo* and *conceptismo*) that characterizes other Castilian literature. For Spaniards have little real imagination; fairies and goblins belong to another world; in Spain everything is clear cut. It is a land of observation and intellection: either a jumble of 'hechos tomados en bruto' (the outcome of observed reality) or abstract concepts (with didactic aims); 'sensitivismo e intelectualismo, disociación siempre' (821). 'Y de todo ello resulta un estilo de enorme uniformidad y monotonía en su ampulosa amplitud de estepa, de gravedad sin gracia, de periodos macizos como bloques, o ya seco, duro y recortado' (822).

As Calderón exemplifies the differential and exclusive aspects of Castilian *casticismo*, so the mystics, with their striving to bridge the abyss between aspiration and reality, 'sus esfuerzos [. . .] por armonizar su idealismo quijotesco con su realismo sancho-pancino' (816), represent its underlying 'humanidad eterna'. Oppressed by external law, they sought to penetrate the life of the universe in order to make it the living law of their own conscience, to make it part of themselves in the depths of their souls and thus find no burden in their obedience to it. And Fray Luis de León, saving it from its excesses, found cosmic peace and harmony 'en la solidaridad universal, en el concierto universal, en la Razón hecha Humanidad, Amor y Salud' (850).[11]

[11] The following extract from an article published more than two years after the crisis of 1897 assumes all the stages of thought so far noted in this first part of my study and could well have been incorporated into *En torno al casticismo*:

Todo lo que el castellano toca se cristaliza al punto; todo lo que él dice se hace dogma. Como en los vastos páramos castellanos o como en

Ganivet's approach is similar, though somewhat less sophisticated: a masterpiece of literature, he says, throws light on the spirit of the nation's history, with which it is inevitably in harmony:

Y cuanto más estrecha sea la concordancia, el mérito de la obra será mayor, porque el artista saca sus fuerzas invisiblemente de la confusión de sus ideas con las ideas de su territorio, obrando como un reflector en el que estas ideas se cruzan y se mezclan y adquieren, al cruzarse y mezclarse, la luz de que separadas carecían (*IE*, 278)

Thereupon he proceeds to show how in *La vida es sueño* Calderón

los cuadros de Ribera, no hay en él medias tintas; todo es claroscuro, todo adquiere ese relieve duro que da el sol al separar, con las sombras que les hace proyectar, a los objetos. Cada uno de éstos adquiere una individualidad decisiva y firme; no hay envolvente nimbo que los una y armonice en superior conjunto.

Y así es la concepcíon castellana, todo *en discreto*, todo en orden social. Léanse nuestros romances y se verá cómo desfilan los sucesos que narran perfectamente definidos y distintos, destacándose cada uno de ellos del precedente y del subsiguiente.

Es como la música de nuestro popular género chico, música de notas martilleantes, sin continuidad real, música en que el ritmo se sacrifica a la cadencia. Y así es el verso entre nosotros, tamborilesco, machacón, intermitente.

De este modo de ser de nuestro idioma nacen como de común raíz el gongorismo y el conceptismo, vicios que lleva en potencia la lengua castellana en sus entrañas mismas (1899; IV, 332).

Moreover, since I have referred, above, to Unamuno's view of Calderón as a representative of differentiating, exclusive *casticismo*, it is worth noting here his later but similar treatment of Echegaray:

No cabe negar que Echegaray es profundamente castizo y que es su casticismo que está más en el fondo que en la forma de sus producciones, lo que le ha valido popularidad.

Echegaray representa en nuestra literatura el elemento diferencialmente español, lo que distingue a nuestra literatura de las demás de Europa.

Cabría que dijese de él un casticista, en son de elogio, que es forzoso ser español para entusiasmarse con sus obras [. . .].

Los pueblos se envanecen y glorían, por lo común, de lo que tienen de distintivo y excluyente, que suelen ser sus defectos (1905; VIII, 228–9).

With the last sentence one can compare the almost identical view expressed in *En torno al casticismo*:

Hay pueblos que se vanaglorian de sus defectos. Los caracteres nacionales de que se envanece cada nación europea son muy de ordinario sus defectos (*ETC*, 795).

'nos da [. . .] una explicación clara, lúcida y profética de nuestra historia' (278). In similar fashion, Velázquez and Goya and Lope de Vega and the author of the *Celestina* are seen to exemplify the fundamental Spanish spirit of independence (212–16). And Seneca, he says, simply gave expression to the stoicism he found around him, 'obrando como obran los verdaderos hombres de genio' (152). And the *Romancero* contains Spain's '*Summa* teológica y filosófica' (160). And the mysticism and fanaticism born of the Reconquest found expression both in the mystics and in the *autos de fe* (161). And Cervantes and the *Quijote* are repeatedly invoked by Ganivet for the light they throw on fundamental Spanish character: Cervantes was the greatest of the *conquistadores*, the *Quijote* is 'nuestra obra típica', and the Manchegan knight represents the characteristic Spanish attitude to justice.

> Todos los pueblos tienen un tipo real o imaginario en quien encarnan sus propias cualidades; en todas las literaturas encontraremos una obra maestra en la que ese hombre típico figura entrar en acción, ponerse en contacto con la sociedad de su tiempo y atravesar una larga serie de pruebas donde se aquilata el temple de su espíritu, que es el espíritu propio de su raza (303).

It is Don Quixote who fulfils this role in Spain, like Ulysses in Greece, like Robinson Crusoe in England, like Dante in Italy, like Faust in Germany.[12]

But one is here faced with a problem. Unamuno and Ganivet each describe a different basic national psychology, yet they each seek—and find—confirmation in similar, and often identical, texts and authors: the *Romancero*, the *Celestina*, the mystics, the *Quijote*, Lope de Vega, Calderón. One may perhaps be forgiven for feeling a slight unease about a method that allows such apparently ready confirmation of very different findings.

Nor is this sense of unease mitigated by evidence that on occasion both authors confuse national and temporal characteristics in the evidence they adduce. Thus Unamuno, after describing the landscape and people of Castile, finds confirmation of his findings in Castilian painting:

> Si estáis en ciudad, y hay en ella algunos cuadros de la vieja y castiza escuela castellana, id a verlos, porque esta casta creó en

[12] On Ganivet's search for confirmation in other aspects of Spanish civilization, see HR, 101–5.

los buenos tiempos de su expansión una escuela de pintura realista, de un realismo pobre en matices, simplicista, vigoroso y rudo, de que sale la vista como de una ducha. Tal vez topéis con algún viejo lienzo de Ribera o de Zurbarán, en que os salte a los ojos un austero anacoreta de huesosa complexión, en que se dibujan los músculos tendinosos en claros vivos sobre sombras fuertes, un lienzo de gran pobreza de tintas y matices, en que los objetos aparecen recortados (812).

But the style of painting that Unamuno here alludes to can hardly be adduced as evidence of eternal Castilian tradition. It belongs very clearly to the late sixteenth and the seventeenth centuries and it is in no way peculiar to Castile. Indeed, the very names mentioned press the point. Ribera, a Valencian who perhaps did not know the Castilian meseta, left his native land while still in his early twenties and spent the rest of his life in Italy. Caravaggio and the *tenebrosi* painters of seventeenth-century Naples were manifestly more relevant to his 'claros vivos sobre sombras fuertes' than anything in the Castilian landscape.[13] Nor was Zurbarán a Castilian. Born in Extremadura, trained in Seville, he too bears clearly, through the Sevillian school, the imprint of the Italian *tenebrosi*. He may conceivably have been influenced also, later, by the Castilian landscape, but I know of no evidence for this stronger than the attractiveness of Unamuno's argument. And in this, precisely, lies the danger of the method.

In *Idearium español* Ganivet is guilty of a similar confusion between national and temporal characteristics. Stoicism, he claims, is fundamental in Spain's 'constitución ideal' (151). It arose at a particular moment in time as the natural response to the exhaustion of Graeco-Roman philosophy. But it lacked positive goals and therefore prepared the way for man's acceptance of a new faith, which was to be Christianity. Stoicism, then, by Ganivet's own admission, was not peculiar to Spain; it was common to all those parts of the world that inherited the Classical tradition. Moreover, it marked only a stage in Spain's development: 'esa solución [el senequismo] es transitoria' (154). But in admitting this Ganivet has clearly undermined his own emphasis on the special relevance of stoicism to Spain's later development.

[13] For Blasco Ibáñez, it may be noted, Ribera was one of the principal initiators of the Valencian artistic tradition ('Alma valenciana', in *Alma Española* 11, 17 January 1904).

Like Unamuno he has confused a temporal phenomenon, something common to different peoples at a given moment in time, with a national phenomenon, something characteristic of a particular people throughout their history.

## 4. JUDGES AND GUIDES

### (a) The 'living rock'

La tradición eterna es lo que deben buscar los videntes de todo pueblo, para elevarse a la luz, haciendo conciente en ellos lo que en el pueblo es inconciente, para guiarle así mejor (ETC, 794).

El sentido sintético es en la sociedad, y en particular en quienes la dirigen, la capacidad para obrar conscientemente, para conocer bien sus propios destinos (IE, 293).

It is evident that for Unamuno and Ganivet the probing of national character is no mere academic exercise. It has profound practical consequences. In the recognition and revitalizing of the fundamental national spirit lies the way out of Spain's psychological dilemma of lost directions. Awareness of national character can give a rallying-point for hitherto disparate and diffused energies, a 'roca viva' on which to construct a more appropriate future and, since national action can thrive only when it is in harmony with fundamental national character, a more successful future too. Consequently, it must be the basic aim of the nation's leaders to recognize the national character and to ensure that national action is consistent with that character: 'es deber de cada cual ayudar a la naturaleza y no meterse a poner carriles al progreso' (ETC, 855), 'porque caminar a ciegas no puede conducir más que a triunfos azarosos y efímeros y a ciertos y definitivos desastres' (IE, 258).[14]

---

[14] The aim of the nation's leaders, wrote Unamuno in the month of the Paris Peace Treaty, must be to 'apartar obstáculos' and, by studying the people, to 'sacarle su inconciente ideal de vida' (III, 699–701):

El deber de los intelectuales y de las clases directoras estriba ahora, más que en el empeño de modelar al pueblo bajo este o el otro plan, casi siempre jacobino, en estudiarle por dentro, tratando de descubrir las raíces de su espíritu (1898; III, 699).

They are significant words, completely in harmony with the views expressed in En torno al casticismo—and earlier—, and they contain the key, I suggest, to

But knowledge of national character serves not only as a guide to the future; it serves also as a firm basis from which to judge the past and the present. Both writers apply their findings in all three directions.

### (b) *Past, present and future*

Fue grande el alma castellana cuando se abrió a los cuatro vientos y se derramó por el mundo; luego cerró sus valvas y aún no hemos despertado. Mientras fue la casta fecunda no se conoció como tal en sus diferencias, su ruina empezó el día en que gritando: 'Mi yo, que me arrancan mi yo', se quiso encerrar en sí (*ETC*, 866).

La miseria mental de España arranca del aislamiento en que nos puso toda una conducta cifrada en el proteccionismo inquisitorial que ahogó en su cuna la Reforma castiza e impidió la entrada a la europea [. . .]; sólo abriendo las ventanas a vientos europeos, empapándonos en el ambiente continental, teniendo fe en que no perderemos nuestra personalidad al hacerlo, europeizándonos para hacer España y chapuzándonos en pueblo, regeneraremos esta estepa moral (*ETC*, 869).

Apenas constituida la nación, nuestro espíritu se sale del cauce que le estaba marcado y se derrama por todo el mundo en busca de glorias exteriores y vanas, quedando la nación convertida en un cuartel de reserva, en un hospital de inválidos, en un semillero de mendigos (*IE*, 219).

El origen de nuestra decadencia y actual postración se halla en nuestro exceso de acción, en haber acometido empresas enormemente desproporcionadas con nuestro poder (*IE*, 294).

Una restauración de la vida entera de España no puede tener otro punto de arranque que la concentración de todas nuestras energías dentro de nuestro territorio. Hay que cerrar con cerrojos, llaves y candados todas las puertas por donde el espíritu español se escapó de España para derramarse por los cuatro puntos del horizonte (*IE*, 276–7).

---

Unamuno's ever-present reservations about Marxism. Emphasis on eternal tradition precludes the notion of social revolution. Moreover, against scholars' current emphasis on the impact of socialist thought on the formative years of the 98 Generation, one may usefully recall, apart from Baroja's own declared 'antipatía profunda por esa doctrina y por ese partido' (1904; V, 17), his later, more general observation:

Yo creo que no había entre los escritores que figuraron en la supuesta generación del 98 ninguno que fuera republicano ni socialista (1944; VII, 446).

Here, it seems, one must speak of contrasts rather than similarities. According to Unamuno, Spain found greatness by opening itself to the four winds and pouring forth its energies on the world; according to Ganivet Spain destroyed its nascent greatness by giving itself up to a political 'Rosa de los vientos' (223) and squandering its energies on the world. For Unamuno, who is here in line with liberal thought of the Spanish nineteenth century, the stagnation and disorientation of the present stem from a policy of inquisitorial isolationism; for Ganivet, in line with more conservative thought, they stem from a policy of world involvement. For Unamuno national regeneration depends on the opening up of Spain to invigorating currents from abroad; for Ganivet it depends on the closing of national frontiers to prevent the escape of native energies. 'No dentro, fuera nos hemos de encontrar' (*ETC*, 852); 'Noli foras ire; in interiore Hispaniae habitat veritas' (*IE*, 277).

But despite these manifest differences in the interpretation of Spain's past, present and future, the underlying similarity of approach remains: Spain, it is argued, has been great in the past in so far as the fundamental national spirit has been allowed free expression; it is in decline in the present because that spirit has been obstructed in some way; it can be made great again in the future by revitalizing the native spirit and accepting it as the necessary basis of national action.[15]

To demonstrate the relevance of these statements to *En torno al casticismo*, however, it is necessary to supplement what was said earlier about Unamuno's concept of 'tradición eterna'. With Unamuno's own determinist assumptions one is tempted to believe that if a given collective character (in this case, the landscape-formed Castilian character) reveals certain persistent, distinctive characteristics, those characteristics will continue to be present however deeply one probes that character in search of an underlying 'intrahistoria' or 'tradición eterna'. But this is not Unamuno's view. On the contrary, he believes that by reaching

---

[15] 'No podrá haber sana vida pública, amigo Ganivet, mientras no se ponga de acuerdo lo íntimo de nuestro pueblo con su exteriorización, mientras no se acomode la adaptación a la herencia. Esta, que es la idea capital de usted, es también la mía' (MU, *PE*, 661).

'Todo cuanto viene de fuera a un país ha de acomodarse al espíritu del territorio si quiere ejercer una influencia real' (AG, *PE*, 650).

down to the 'tradición eterna' one escapes from the exclusive elements of *casticismo* and discovers common humanity: 'el fondo del ser del hombre mismo' (794), '[la] tradición universal, cosmopolita' (797). He accepts, then, a duality of national character: on the one hand, 'el casticismo castellano', which represents the allegedly differential and exclusive, landscape-formed aspects of Castilian character, 'cortante y seco, pobre en nimbos de ideas', perceiving facts clear cut and manifesting itself accordingly in 'un realismo vulgar y tosco y un idealismo seco y formulario' (815–16); on the other hand, 'la tradición eterna', which represents the allegedly underlying common humanity, 'la tradición eterna española, que al ser eterna es más bien humana que española' (794). According to Unamuno Spanish society in the seventeenth century was no longer able to resolve the tensions of the native spirit because the Inquisition had closed the nation to foreign contacts and thereby prevented its harmonious development. As the distinctive, exclusive aspects of the Castilian spirit ('el casticismo castellano') came to predominate over its eternal humanity ('la tradición eterna'), so the nation fell into decline. Moreover, the influence of the Inquisition still persists, he believes, with predominance of the historic over the intra-historic. But it is the intra-historic that is important as a guide to national destinies, and it lives on still, unchanged, in the common people, waiting to be awakened by winds from Europe. The spirit that must be revitalized and accepted as a guide to national destinies, then, is not the superficial restrictive spirit of Castilian *casticismo* which at present predominates; it is the allegedly underlying, fundamentally human spirit of Spain's eternal tradition. 'Para hallar lo humano eterno hay que romper lo castizo temporal' (798); 'lo castizo eterno sólo obrará olvidando lo castizo histórico en cuanto excluye' (854):

> ¡Gran locura la de querer despojarnos del fondo común a todos, de la masa idéntica sobre que se moldean las formas diferenciales, de lo que nos asemeja y une, de lo que hace que seamos *prójimos*, de la madre del amor, de la humanidad, en fin, del hombre, del verdadero hombre, del legado de la especie! (*ETC*, 794–5).

We shall return to the duality in a later section. For the moment I merely ask again whether, by reaching down to the 'tradición eterna', one can really escape from the exclusive elements of *casticismo* and discover an abstracted common humanity. Or does one perhaps merely escape from material limitations and discover a realm of unsullied ideals? Is there perhaps a conflict here between Unamuno the enthusiast for natural science and Unamuno the admirer of Hegel?

In *Idearium español* the case is straightforward and can be presented more briefly. The peninsular spirit of independence, says Ganivet, was diverted from its proper path, 'del cauce que le estaba marcado' (219), by the discovery of the New World and by the accession of Charles I, a continental monarch who imposed a continental policy foreign to Spanish character and Spanish interests. Charles I himself, because he was continental, could make it effective, but Philip II was a Spaniard who saw everything with Spanish eyes, 'con independencia y exclusivismo' (229), and the outcome was national disaster. 'Con Felipe II desaparece de nuestra nación el sentido sintético, esto es, la facultad de apreciar en su totalidad nuestros varios intereses políticos' (231). It is to this lack of synthesis that Ganivet attributes Spain's contemporary disorientation. The future, however, is promising—provided the nation conforms to its peninsular spirit of independence:

> Hay que tener una organización, y para que ésta no sea de puro artificio, para que cuaje y se afirme, ha de acomodarse a nuestra constitución natural (*IE*, 197).

> La fábrica española ha estado parada durante largos años por falta de motor; hoy empieza a moverse porque hemos aligerado, o nos han aligerado, el artefacto, y ya hay quien desea volver a las antiguas complicaciones, en vez de trabajar por aumentar la escasa fuerza motriz de que hoy disponemos. De aquí la necesidad perentoria de destruir las ilusiones nacionales; y el destruirlas no es obra de desesperados, es obra de noble y legítima ambición, por la cual comenzamos a fundar nuestro positivo engrandecimiento (*IE*, 271).

At this point one may recall the two differences of emphasis observed in the diagnosis of Spain's contemporary psychological condition (above, pp. 14–15). Both writers diagnosed mental and spiritual disintegration: loss of direction, aboulia and occasional ill-directed outbursts of energy. But we can see now that each interpreted his findings in the light of a different case history: Unamuno, looking back on three centuries or more of the alleged inquisitorial repression of Spain's 'tradición eterna', found the elements in confusion in modern Spain to be primarily national and emphasized the resulting stagnation; Ganivet, looking back on almost four centuries of debilitating foreign involvement, believed the confusion of modern Spain to stem largely from undigested foreign influences and emphasized the resulting lack of direction. The same system of thought has served to justify different political standpoints.

### (c) *Spain and Europe*

Lo mismo los que piden que cerremos o pocos menos las fronteras y pongamos puertas al campo, que los que piden más o menos explícitamente que nos conquisten, se salen de la verdadera realidad de las cosas, de la eterna y honda realidad (*ETC*, 786).

En cuanto a la restauración ideal, nadie pondrá en duda que debe ser obra nuestra exclusiva; podremos recibir influencias extrañas, orientarnos estudiando lo que hacen y dicen otras naciones; pero mientras no españolicemos nuestra obra, mientras lo extraño no esté sometido a lo español y vivamos en la incertidumbre en que hoy vivimos, no levantaremos cabeza (*IE*, 267).

Writing at the end of a century of civil strife in which Spain had been torn between upholders of the national tradition and advocates of Europeanization, Unamuno and Ganivet both see Spain's crisis of lost directions in terms of a conflict between tradition and Europeanization. The question is, where should Spain take its stand?

Given their common insistence on the need for national action to be in harmony with the permanent national spirit, they clearly cannot advocate a complete cutting off from the past. Nor can a nation isolate itself from the surrounding present, they believe. The extremes of Right and Left, then, must be rejected. Neither native tradition nor European modernity is alone sufficient. There must be some form of reconciliation tending to national modernity, a recognition of what is fundamental in Spain's native tradition and, upon this basis, the acceptance of foreign influences in so far as these serve to stimulate the native tradition. But how far is this? How much emphasis should be placed on tradition and how much on Europeanization? At this point the two writers give rather different answers.

Unamuno's attitude is the more clearly defined. Since in his view Spain was great when its frontiers were open to Europe and fell into decline because of an inquisitorial policy of isolationism, it follows that Spain must again open its frontiers to invigorating contacts from abroad. But potentially Europe already lies within Spain, in the common humanity of the nation's hitherto suppressed eternal tradition, in the 'vida difusa intrahistórica que languidece por falta de ventilación' (867). Europe, for Unamuno, is freedom, energy, personality, youth, sympathy, '[un] remolino de escuelas, sectas y agrupaciones que se hacen y deshacen [. . .], una vida potente' (862)—all those things that are at present stifled in Spain. Contact with Europe will help Spain to discover its own potential vitality. 'Cosquilleos de fuera despiertan lo que duerme en el seno de nuestra conciencia' (853); 'hay que mantenerse en equilibrio con el ambiente asimilándose lo de fuera' (853); 'España está por descubrir, y sólo la descubrirán españoles europeizados' (866); 'tenemos que europeizarnos y chapuzarnos en pueblo' (867).[16] Again and again he makes the point: in order for Spain to find itself again and to realize its potential, there must be probing within and free acceptance without. Nor is there any danger, he insists, that immersion in European currents would cause any loss of fundamental Spanish character; on the contrary, the national spirit would thereby be given new life and energy. '¡Pobre temor el de que perdiéramos nuestro carácter al abandonarnos a la corriente!' (853), '¡Fe, fe en la espontaneidad propia, fe en que siempre seremos nosotros, y venga la inundación de fuera, la ducha!' (867). Education is important ('Hay abulia para

[16] Beyond the crisis of 1897 Unamuno continues to see himself as a Europeanizer in the sense in which he employs the term in *En torno al casticismo*. The Spanish people, he declares, need culture, 'cultura impuesta, y tal como la entendemos nosotros, los europeos, los que nos debemos constituir en directores por santo derecho divino' (MU–JA, 12 December 1900). Emphasis on Unamuno's post-1897 anti-Europeanization, it seems, stems often from a failure to distinguish between Europeanization in the sense in which the word is used in *En torno al casticismo* (above; intimately related to what Unamuno elsewhere refers to as *renovación*) and Europeanization in the sense of material progress (dismissed by Unamuno as mere *regeneración*). Nevertheless, we cannot entirely disregard statements like the following:

Y, ¡a luchar! Otros, a europeizar a España. Yo, a ver si un día españolizo a Europa. Dios me dé fuerzas (MU–PJI, 9 May 1905).

I shall return to the point in a later section.

el trabajo modesto y la investigación *directa*, lenta y sosegada', 864), but he places little emphasis on economic remedies, either in the Costa sense or in the Iglesias sense. Here as elsewhere in the work Unamuno's main emphasis is psychological. Spain should find its true self—its truly *traditional* self—by immersion in varied experience. Europe, unrepressed, can offer that experience:

> sólo abriendo las ventanas a vientos europeos, empapándonos en el ambiente continental, teniendo fe en que no perderemos nuestra personalidad al hacerlo, europeizándonos para hacer España y chapuzándonos en pueblo, regeneraremos esta estepa moral. Con el aire de fuera regenero *mi sangre*, no respirando el que exhalo (*ETC*, 869).

Ganivet's attitude is more ambiguous and more cautious and has frequently been misinterpreted. Whereas for Unamuno Europe already exists potentially within Spain, for Ganivet, with his emphasis on Arabic influence (160–2, 302),[17] Spain and Europe are fundamentally different: on the one hand, there is Spain, religious and artistic, a land of high ideals and individual, often impulsive, actions, at present exhausted materially, intellectually and spiritually; on the other hand, there is Europe north of the Pyrenees, materialistic and scientifically minded, the home of practical aims and collective enterprises, where powerful nations exert economic and intellectual influence on other parts of the world, including Latin America. For a determinist who believes that national policy must be in harmony with national character and yet wants his country to prosper in the modern world, the choice is clearly a difficult one.

In probing Ganivet's proposed solution one must distinguish initially between the advocated radius of Spain's material involvement abroad and the advocated extent of foreign influence on Spain. In the former case his attitude is clear: Spain should concentrate its weakened energies completely within the confines of its own frontiers (see previous section). In the latter case there is some ambiguity and even inconsistency, and any brief account must necessarily leave a number of loose ends. Basically, Ganivet,

[17] With Ganivet's emphasis on Arabic influence one can contrast Unamuno's view:

> De los árabes no quiero decir nada, les profeso una profunda antipatía, apenas creo en eso que llaman civilización arábiga y considero su paso por España como la mayor calamidad que hemos padecido (*PE*, 646).

like Unamuno, opposes the extremes of Right and Left: 'un rompimiento con el pasado sería una violación de las leyes naturales' (281); on the other hand, when the national tradition has lost its creative force 'se hace necesario introducir levadura fresca' (284), 'echarle ideas, para que no ande en seco' (286).[18] In a nation that is disorientated as Spain is disorientated, he says, national action is necessarily weak and uneven:

> Unas veces el móvil será la tradición, que jamás puede producir, aunque otra cosa se crea, un impulso enérgico, porque en la vida intelectual lo pasado, así como es centro poderoso de resistencia, es principio débil de actividad; otras veces se obedecerá a una fuerza extraña, pues las sociedades débiles, como los artistas de pobre ingenio, suplen con las imitaciones la falta de propia inspiración (IE, 293).

Similarly, neither 'exclusivist' (that is, traditional) education nor 'free' education (education strongly influenced from abroad) is wholly good: the former maintains national unity of thought and actions but is narrow and lacks drive; the latter gives the impulse of free choice and original thought but encourages an intellectual imbalance. Ganivet, like Unamuno, advocates a form of reconciliation. With reference to religion he even suggests that Spain needs a dissident minority in order to make the majority react with a new consciousness of their true native tradition. But there is no expansive, Unamuno-like suggestion that Spain should immerse itself wholeheartedly in a flood of Europeanization. Ganivet lacks his contemporary's faith that national character

---

[18] The problem is complicated for Ganivet by his insistence on the need for Spain to become the intellectual and spiritual mentor of the Hispanic world. To influence other nations, he says, one must fuse foreign and national ideas, but we, 'por nuestra propia constitución, somos inhábiles para esas manipulaciones, y nuestro espíritu no ha podido triunfar más que por la violencia' (230–1). However, since Latin America has undergone the 'escarlatina de las ideas francesas', Spain, if it wishes to regain its position of prestige there, must open its own frontiers to foreign ideas in the same way that it opened its frontiers to foreign construction materials for the building of its railways (251). In other words, the ideal of spiritual leadership in Latin America makes it necessary to overcome 'la escasa fuerza expansiva de nuestra producción intelectual' (250) by foreign importation, and causes Ganivet to argue at moments for rather more European influence than he might otherwise wish. For a fuller account of Ganivet's views on the problem of tradition and Europeanization, see HR, 43–56, 59–60.

would survive—and indeed benefit from—such an immersion. Under the Bourbons, says Ganivet, the Spanish spirit lacked the necessary '*mano fuerte que lo obligara* a buscar la salvación donde únicamente podía hallarla, en la restauración de las energías nacionales' (233; my italics), and today, 'para que los esfuerzos individuales ejerzan un influjo benéfico en la nación, *hay que encaminarlos con mano firme*' (296; my italics). For Ganivet, it seems, the 'fuerzas espontáneas' of national character need authoritarian supervision.

There is clearly a basic similarity, then, between the recommendations of the two writers. But there is also, equally clearly, a difference of emphasis. Unamuno's emphasis is on the need to throw open Spain's frontiers to influences from abroad, in the belief that beneath *casticismo* in its exclusiveness lies *casticismo* in its common humanity, 'la masa idéntica sobre que se moldean las formas diferenciales' (794), 'el fondo común' from which it is folly to cut Spain off (794): 'No dentro, fuera nos hemos de encontrar' (852). Ganivet's emphasis, on the other hand, is on the allegedly fundamental national spirit of independence and he therefore advocates only a necessary minimum of foreign contacts: 'Noli foras ire: in interiore Hispaniae habitat veritas' (277). Both conclusions, it seems, follow from the respective writers' interpretations of the impact of physical environment on national character.

But do these conclusions follow *necessarily*? I suggest that they do not. I shall consider in a later section Unamuno's distinction between *casticismo* in its exclusiveness and *casticismo* in its essential humanity. For the moment I propose something different: I wish to show how, starting from Unamuno's description of Castile, it is possible to arrive at Ganivet's emphasis on the need for independence, and how, starting from Ganivet's evocation of Spain's peninsular configuration, it is possible to arrive at Unamuno's emphasis on cosmopolitanism.[19]

I start from a passage in Unamuno's description of Castile:

El caserío de los pueblos es compacto y recortadamente demarcado, sin que vaya perdiéndose y difuminándose en la llanura con casas

[19] Unamuno was later to reject the term 'cosmopolita' in favour of the terms 'universal' and 'internacional'. In *En torno al casticismo*, however, he makes no distinction: 'Y la tradición eterna es tradición universal, cosmopolita' (797).

aisladas que le rodean, sin matices de población intermedia, como si las viviendas se apretaran en derredor de la iglesia para prestarse calor y defenderse del rigor de la naturaleza, como si las familias buscaran una segunda capa, en cuyo ambiente aislarse de la crueldad del clima y la tristeza del paisaje (*ETC*, 810).

Because of the rigorous climate—and the Castilian's total immersion in an environment of contrasts—Castilian villages are compact and clearly separated from the surrounding countryside. The observation is manifestly justified, but it could serve as a basis for conclusions very different from those arrived at by Unamuno. It could be argued, for example, that the very compactness of each village encouraged an inward-looking, isolationist psychology ('las viviendas *se* aprietan en derredor de la iglesia para prestar*se* calor [y para] aislar*se*') and that this is confirmed by the inter-village rivalry that immediately strikes the traveller in Castile.[20] Transposed to the realm of national psychology, these findings could then be used to argue that, in order to be in harmony with the fundamental character-forming Castilian nucleus, Spanish policy should be basically one of independence and isolationism, as Ganivet maintained.[21]

Conversely, Ganivet's observations on what he takes to be the all-important character-forming peninsular environment can all too easily be used to arrive at conclusions completely opposed to those that he himself affirms. For Spain, as Ganivet points out, is 'una isla colocada en la conjunción de dos continentes [. . .], una especie de parque internacional, donde todos los pueblos y razas han venido a distraerse cuando les ha parecido oportuno' (181), and in *El porvenir de España* he emphasizes still further the importance of these invading peoples:

Si usted suprime a los romanos y a los árabes, no queda de mí quizá más que las piernas; me mata usted sin querer, amigo

[20] Cf. 'Difícil será que haya nación alguna de Europa donde los habitantes de unas comarcas se burlen con más dureza de los de otras' (Lucas Mallada, *Los males de la patria*, Madrid 1890, p. 38).

[21] 'Ofrécesenos, en general, este pueblo [the Castilian people] como pueblo urbano y guerrero, sin clara conciencia de la hermosa soledad de la austera llanura que lo sustenta. Recogido en ciudades y poblados donde se defendía y amparaba de las incursiones del moro y de los contrapuestos rigores de la intemperie, desarrolló en su espíritu sentimientos sociales *de viril independencia y de anárquica altivez* (1902; MU, I, 58; my italics).

Unamuno. Pero lo importante es que usted, aunque sea a regaña-
dientes, reconozca la realidad de las influencias que han obrado
sobre el espíritu originario de España [. . .]. La transformación
psicológica de una nación por los hechos de su historia, es tan
inevitable como la evolución de las ideas del hombre, merced a las
sensaciones que va ofreciéndole la vida (*PE*, 648).

Even if one accepts Ganivet's argument that a peninsular configuration produces a character of independence—and his argument is, to say the least, not entirely convincing—one could still
argue that the incursion of successive peoples formed by non-
peninsular environments, together with the alleged ease with
which such peoples amalgamated with the existing inhabitants
(*IE*, 178), endowed the Spanish people with a richer, more
multi-faceted, more international psychology than other peoples.
This, together with Spain's position at the cross-roads of Europe
and Africa and of the Mediterranean and the New World, would
then offer a basis for urging not a policy of independence and even
isolationism, as Ganivet does, but a policy of open frontiers and
closer contact with other peoples, as Unamuno urges.

Unamuno's basis of argument, then, could be used to support
Ganivet's emphasis on the need for national independence, and
Ganivet's basis of argument could be used to support Unamuno's
emphasis on the need for cosmopolitanism. The inference would
appear to be that neither basis of argument offers a very sure
pointer to anything—except, perhaps, to the fallibility of geographical determinism as exemplified in both works. And at this
point one must perhaps consider more critically a statement made
earlier: namely, that Unamuno's and Ganivet's different attitudes
to Europeanization follow, *it seems*, from their different interpretations of the impact of physical environment on national
character (above, p. 37). It would now appear more accurate to
invert the terms and suggest that their different interpretations of
geographical causality are prompted by their different views of
what constitutes a desirable national response to Europeanization.
Geographical determinism as handled by Unamuno and Ganivet,
like historical interpretation, seems to adapt itself rather too
readily to desired conclusions.

# II

## THE INTELLECTUAL CONTEXT

### DETERMINIST THOUGHT AND METHODS

## I. INTRODUCTION

Pocas convicciones han sido más arraigadas y hondas en mí que la convicción del determinismo volitivo (MU-PJI, 3 January 1898).

creo que la suma sabiduría está en las cosas y en dejaɪ que las cosas obren, incluyendo en las cosas a las personas, siempre que funcionen normalmente y sin intención de enmendar la plana a las fuerzas naturales (1894; AG, II, 985).

pour moi, je suis absolument déterministe, et j'appuie mon opinion sur l'observation psychologique autant que sur l'expérience physique. Je ne puis là-dessus que vous renvoyer à la *Logique* et surtout à l'*Examen* de Stuart Mill; c'est un chef-d'œuvre de bon sens, de force et de netteté (Taine, *VC*, II, 345).

In Part I we have noted two basic similarities between *En torno al casticismo* and *Idearium español*: a similarity in the object of study (Section 1) and a similarity in the method of study (Sections 2–4). As we have observed, there is also considerable similarity in the findings of the two works, but since this is largely a consequence of the method it has not been felt necessary to consider it separately. What we shall have to explain, in a later section, are the differences that appear despite the common method.

Traditionally, students of the 1898 Generation, in so far as they have concerned themselves with common *internal* characteristics, have placed their main emphasis on the object of study, Spain, or, with some slight concession also to method, on Spain as a problem.[1] Under the impact of the Disaster of 1898, it is said, a new generation of writers awoke to the recognition of Spain as a problem. Ortega y Gasset, Azorín and Maeztu pointed the way to this interpretation and gave the initial impetus: 'Al cabo,' commented Maeztu in 1913, 'España no se nos aparece como una afirmación ni como una negación, sino como un problema' (I, 88).

But, as has been amply demonstrated during the last half cen-

[1] I find the following statement to be generally characteristic:
El problema de España es el vínculo—el único por cierto—que da cohesión a los dispares valores y mentalidades de la generación del 98 (Alberto Sánchez, in the Introduction to his edition of Maeztu's *Don Quijote o el amor*, Anaya, Salamanca 1964, p. 22).

tury, the consideration of Spain as a problem was in no way peculiar to the men of 98:

> parece por todo extremo evidente que desde 1812 hasta 1936 esa cultura [Spanish culture] ha venido siendo un problema para todos sus protagonistas y consideradores. Lo fue para Alberto Lista y Jaime Balmes, para Pi y Margall y Menéndez Pelayo, para Cajal y Unamuno, para Valera y Ganivet, para Giner de los Ríos y Ramiro de Maeztu; y lo ha seguido siendo para Menéndez Pidal, Ortega y Gasset, Eugenio d'Ors, Américo Castro, Sánchez Albornoz, Marañón, Rey Pastor, Ledesma Ramos y José Antonio Primo de Rivera. Es decir: para todos los españoles que no han querido limitarse a un candoroso arbitrismo de cenáculo o de gabinete, y se han propuesto de veras hacer algo eficaz en o por la cultura de España (Pedro Laín Entralgo, *España como problema*, I, Madrid 1956, p. 18).

Concern with the problem of Spain, then, however fundamental and recurrent a characteristic it may have been in writers of the 98 Generation, does not suggest itself as a distinctive, distinguishing characteristic. Nor is the notion of 'disaster' more helpful, for the Spanish nineteenth century offered every generation its own disaster: from the Napoleonic occupation and colonial losses of the beginning of the century, via civil wars and constitutional crises, to the loss of Cuba, Puerto Rico and the Philippines at the end. Besides, evidence of the impact of the 1898 disaster on alleged members of the Generation is not strong. 'Con 1898, época del desastre colonial español,' declared Baroja, 'yo no me encuentro tener relación alguna' (1924; V, 496). 'Para hablar de la generación del 98,' observed Maeztu, 'sería necesario empezar por demostrar que los sucesos transcendentales de aquel año ejercieron sobre los hombres incluidos en la aludida "generación" alguna influencia decisiva. ¿Quiere decir alguien dónde está la influencia de la pérdida de las colonias sobre los señores Baroja, Valle-Inclán y Azorín?' (1935; I, 65). 'La idea de la palingenesia de España estaba en el aire,' commented Azorín. 'La corriente de doctrinas regeneradoras no la motivó la catástrofe colonial. No hizo más que avivarla. Venía el noble anhelo desde antiguo' (1941; VI, 224). *En torno al casticismo* and *Idearium español* are themselves invaluable evidence. The former was written, at least in part, before the Cuban rising began; the latter was published before it reached its crisis. Their common concern with the problem of Spain places them within an immediately recognizable tradition.[2] What it does not do is to place them significantly within their age.

Emphasis on the method of study, it seems, might prove more helpful, for what I have been illustrating in Part I, Sections 2–4, are in fact basic aspects of an approach to civilization that one associates immediately with the later nineteenth century: a determinist approach consisting in the application to men and their institutions of methods and concepts derived from the study of natural history. Not that those methods and concepts were entirely new, either among scientists or among students of civilization.[3] But in the same way that Copernicus's heliocentric concept of the universe did not make its full impact on human thought until it was confirmed by Newton a century and a half later, so also eighteenth- and nineteenth-century notions of organic evolution and physical determinism were confined to a minority of intellectuals until they were brought together by Darwin into a coherent and unified theory (*On the Origin of Species . . .*, 1859). Thereafter, for half a century, the biological sciences were to dominate human thought. Dislodged by the physical sciences from his exalted position at the centre of the universe, man was now to find it increasingly difficult, in the light of biological discoveries, to see himself as the outcome of an act of special creation. The emphasis, henceforth, it seemed, was to be on man as a product of physical environment and natural selection. It is in this context that we must consider *En torno al casticismo* and *Idearium español*.

The available range of comparison is wide, especially in the works of writers born 1820–34: Spencer (1820–1903), Buckle (1821–62), Renan (1823–92), T. H. Huxley (1825–95), Taine (1828–93), Lilienfeld (1829–1903), Schäffle (1831–1903), Haeckel

[2] For further evidence on this point see the extensive bibliography appended by Pedro Sainz Rodríguez to his *Evolución de las ideas sobre la decadencia española*, Madrid 1962; especially Section C of the bibliography, pp. 171–231.

[3] Professor G. G. Simpson has surveyed the scientific field in *The Meaning of Evolution* (Yale University Press, 1949, Ch. XVI). Among students of civilization Montesquieu (*L'Esprit des lois*, 1748) and Herder (*Ideen zur Philosophie der Menschengeschichte*, 1784–91) are probably the most notable eighteenth-century forerunners of the approach with which we are here concerned. August Comte (1798–1857) and John Stuart Mill (1806–73) added important elements during the first half of the nineteenth century.

(1834-1919)—and all these names appear frequently in Spanish books and periodicals during the late 1890's.[4] In the sixth number of *Germinal* (11 June 1897), for example, an article on Darwin prompts references to Spencer, Haeckel, and Huxley; another article in the same number, 'Estadística social', refers to Comte, Spencer, Schäffle and Lilienfeld. 'La teoría transformista,' writes Joaquín Dicenta with evident approval a few weeks later, is 'la doctrina revolucionaria por excelencia',[5] and Enrique Lluria, in a characteristic attempt of the period to reconcile evolutionism and Marxism, proclaims: 'La ley de la evolución ha permitido a Darwin explicar la historia natural, a Spencer la filosofía, a Marx la evolución económica de la historia'. He continues: 'el mundo orgánico, que empieza en el amibo, no termina en los simios, ni aun en el hombre, sino que termina y se complementa en el mundo social, que obedece en un todo a la ley de la evolución [. . .]. En la teoría de la evolución está la solución biológica del problema social [. . .]; el hombre debe regirse por leyes naturales, y no por las leyes falsas y artificiales que hoy tiene.'[6] José de Laugi makes a similar point: 'Darwin, Huxley, Haeckel y demás naturalistas en sus originales ideas evolucionistas' are champions of a new spirit that must be accepted in Spain as it has gradually come to be accepted elsewhere.[7]

As Laugi's words indicate, evolutionism, with its frequently accompanying attacks on 'religiones positivas, herencias ridículas, desigualdades absurdas . . ., todos los cimientos sobre que descansa esta sociedad moribunda',[8] was still not generally accepted in Spain. Menéndez y Pelayo, for example, wishing to dissociate himself from the 'campañas anticlericales' of *Vida Nueva*, protested at the unauthorized inclusion of an extract from one of his works. His letter prompted a long, ironic reply from the editors. The following paragraph is characteristic:

¡Qué pícaro mundo éste! Mil veces oímos tachar al señor Pelayo de egoísta con las cosas vivientes, y de crítico arqueológico, que por

---

[4] It is known that evolutionism and its associated methodology reached Spain in the 1870's. I have found little evidence of any great impact, however, before the 1890's. The subject calls for further study.

[5] In *Germinal* 19, 10 September 1897.

[6] In *Vida Nueva* 21, 30 October 1898.

[7] In *Vida Nueva* 55, 24 June 1899.

[8] In *Germinal* 19, 10 September 1897.

comodidad de su persona y de sus ideas, rechazaba por sistema cuanto críticos insignificantes, como Taine, Renan, Macaulay, Spencer, Max Nordau, y otros aceptaron como digno de su censura, es decir, de lo viviente, moderno, palpitante, de aquello, en fin, que refresca la pluma del escritor y le lanza heroicamente a la lucha, al circo literario en que pelean los Zola, los Anatole France, los Lemaître y tantos otros. Oímos decir que el señor Menéndez se preocupaba más de un tal Osio, obispo de Córdoba, que del último libro lleno de esperanzas que publica cualquier joven indefenso. Y al tacharle de egoísta y de desempolvador eminente, atribuimos a mala fe esos ataques y protestamos de ellos.

But we were apparently mistaken, the editors continue:

Discutir hoy a Macaulay, a Taine, por si fueron reaccionarios o liberales, sería poner a los dos genios al nivel de Sagasta o de Villaverde [. . .]. ¡Menéndez y Pelayo es ya un recuerdo glorioso para los amantes del libre espíritu; una renovada esperanza para los explotadores del sentimiento católico de la nación! (In *Vida Nueva* 32, 15 January 1899).

Taine and Spencer then—names to which we shall return—are among the foremost representatives of 'lo viviente, moderno, palpitante'; Menéndez y Pelayo, a 'desempolvador eminente', rejects their ideas. For the editors of *Vida Nueva* the acceptance or non-acceptance of evolutionism and its application to human institutions was clearly a basic criterion by which to distinguish *lo nuevo* from *lo viejo*.

It is in this context, as manifestations of *lo nuevo*, that I propose to study *En torno al casticismo* and *Idearium español*. But it is not sufficient to ascribe them vaguely to an allegedly significant intellectual context. We must seek to establish clear and irrefutable parallels. Herbert Spencer, whose Synthetic Philosophy represents the most grandiose effort of the age to transform evolutionary theory into a comprehensive speculative synthesis, has a special relevance and his influence on Spanish thought of the later nineteenth century is traditionally much emphasized, especially with reference to Unamuno. A wholly convincing case, however, has still to be made and in my own view the closest resemblances to the two works with which we are here concerned are to be found not in Spencer's writings but in those of the French historian and philosopher Hippolyte Taine, referred to with approval both in *En torno al casticismo* (796) and in *Idearium español* (180). I do not infer from this that other scholars' suggested parallels with Spencer, Buckle, Carlyle and, as we shall see, with an earlier thinker, Hegel, are therefore mistaken. I seek simply to affirm yet another series of significant resemblances and thereby to place both *En torno al casticismo* and *Idearium español* a degree more firmly than hitherto in the context of their age.

I shall make my case on internal evidence, establishing parallels between what we have noted in *En torno al casticismo* and *Idearium español* and what we find in Taine's writings. But external evidence is not lacking. Too much emphasis has been placed on Unamuno's later view of Taine as 'el gran falsificador francés'.[9] But in the 1890's his enthusiasm for Taine was clear:

> ¡Taine! El coloso francés, el pensador fuerte y rudo, la verdadera cabeza de genio que tienen en Francia; su 'Histoire de la Littérature Anglaise', su obra 'L'Intelligence', y sobre todo sus 'Origines de la France contemporaine', una historia de la revolución francesa, es de lo más grande, de lo más serio, de lo más hondo que se ha hecho; la verdad pura duela a quien duela (MU-PM, July 1890).

Taine, he declares in a later letter, is 'una maravilla [. . .], uno de mis favoritos' (MU-PM, 1 May 1891), one of the most profound of all contemporary thinkers (MU-PM, 23 November 1891) and one whose accessibility he himself aspires to (MU-JA, 17 June 1892). Years later, in a letter to Marcel Bataillon who was at that time preparing a French translation of *En torno al casticismo*, Unamuno referred as follows to the period at which the work was written:

> Era una época en que atravesaba yo por un agnosticismo rígido, no sin algo de desesperación. Me duraba el influjo de Spencer y del positivismo. Pero sin duda lo que influyó más algunas páginas de esos ensayos [*En torno al casticismo*] fue Taine. Toda aquella descripción de Castilla, paisaje, etc., responde a las de Taine de los Países Bajos. Leía yo mucho a Taine entonces. Y a Carlyle. Por cierto que después he visto ese mismo procedimiento aplicado con más fuerza en Oliveira Martins. No sabe usted bien el efecto que me hizo *Les origines de la France contemporaine*. Sólo después he comprendido su endeblez íntima. Pero como arte es excelente, aunque libresco. Hasta en el paisaje (1922; I, 27).

In fact, as we shall see—and as is suggested by Unamuno's

[9] MU-JA, 12 December 1900; also MU, I, 1024-5 (1902), III, 590-4 (1907).

reference to the impact on him of the landscape-free *Origines*—similarities with Taine are by no means confined to the few pages in which he describes the physical aspects of Castile. They are evident on all the points examined above in Part I, Sections 2–4. The same can be said of Ganivet's *Idearium español*, and again the author himself gives us a pointer, referring frequently to Taine in his writings and declaring, on the occasion of local celebrations in Antwerp:

> Esta feria de aquí es como todas, aunque tiene algunos rasgos característicos de la raza, que decía Taine, cuyas obras estoy leyendo de cabo a rabo, con bastante más satisfacción que las de Renán (1893; II, 829).

From 1893 to 1896 one can trace clearly the growing influence of Taine on Ganivet's thought and writings.

But I am not much concerned in what follows to demonstrate influences. I start from the view that influences are accepted by a significant thinker only as a response to pre-existent needs and that it is the needs rather than the influences that determine the character and stature of the thinker. My prime aim in establishing parallels between what we have noted in Unamuno and Ganivet and what we find in Taine is to set the Spanish writers in the main intellectual current of their age as represented by one of the most influential and most characteristic writers of the time: for Nietzsche, 'der erste lebende Historiker';[10] for Giraud, 'la conscience intellectuelle de son temps';[11] for Rosca, 'le directeur intellectuel, le maître le plus autorisé, ou encore, le véritable éducateur des générations qui sont arrivées à la vie de l'esprit entre 1860 et 1890'.[12] 'Et c'est justement à cause de la relation étroite que l'œuvre de Taine tout entière a eue avec l'esprit de l'époque,' adds Rosca, 'qu'on a pu dire d'elle, avec raison, qu'elle en a été la plus complète et la plus juste expression'.[13] For a final balanced contemporary judgement of Taine's influence, one can perhaps best consult Gustave Lanson's *Histoire de la littérature française*, first

---

[10] Friedrich Nietzsche, *Jenseits von Gut und Böse*, Leipzig 1886, p. 217.

[11] Victor Giraud, *Essai sur Taine, son œuvre et son influence*, 6th ed., Paris n.d., p. 52. See also pp. 170–6, where Giraud offers impressive evidence on the number of re-editions and reprints of Taine's publications up to 1901.

[12] D. D. Rosca, *L'influence de Hegel sur Taine théoricien de la connaissance et de l'art*, Paris 1928, p. 24.

[13] Op. cit., pp. 22–3.

published in 1894, the year after Taine died and the year before *En torno al casticismo* appeared in *La España Moderna*. Lanson was critical of Taine's method but of his influence he had no doubt: 'Toutes les générations arrivées à maturité depuis 1865 lui doivent plus qu'à personne, sauf (pour une minorité) à Renan!' (p. 1032).

In Spain, too, Taine's authority was well recognized. From 1893 to 1900 'La España Moderna' published fifteen volumes of his works in translation. Enthusiastic references to Taine and his writings are frequent in books and periodicals of the time and continue well into the twentieth century.[14] 'La influencia directa de Taine sobre los intelectuales ha sido enorme,' wrote Pompeyo Gener in 1898; 'él es quien ha hecho positivistas a casi todos los pensadores y artistas de Europa que hoy tienen de treinta a cuarenta años; él, más que Darwin y Spencer, ya que éstos son más técnicos, más complicados, más abstrusos, menos artistas.'[15] 'La literatura contemporánea está saturada de su pensamiento,' declared J. Uña Sarthou in 1901; 'ninguno de sus contemporáneos poseyó en tan alto grado el espíritu sintético [. . .]. No hay para qué entrar a detallar las ideas de Taine: todo el mundo las sabe.'[16] Unamuno and Ganivet, we have seen, both acknowledged their own debt to Taine, and Baroja, we are informed, had several of Taine's works in his library.[17] In an article on Asturian character

[14] 'el inimitable Hipólito Taine' (A. de Santaclara, in *Germinal* 12, 23 July 1897); 'este Santo que no creía ni en el Cielo, ni en la otra vida' (Pompeyo Gener, *Amigos y maestros* [1898], 2nd ed., Barcelona 1915, p. 126); 'la labor maravillosa de Hipólito Taine' (J. Martínez Ruiz, *Evolución de la crítica* [1899]; I, 422); 'Taine, el gran filósofo Taine' (Luis Morote, *La moral de la derrota*, Madrid 1900, p. 538); 'la obra admirable de Taine' (Miguel S. Oliver, 'La potencia nacional' [1904], in *Entre dos Españas*, Barcelona 1906, p. 82) . . .

[15] *Amigos y maestros*, 2nd ed., Barcelona 1915, pp. 125–6.

[16] In *La Lectura*, June 1901, p. 112.

[17] José Alberich, *Los ingleses y otros temas de Pío Baroja*, Madrid–Barcelona 1966, pp. 52, 55. Alberich notes the presence of Taine's two most substantial works, *Histoire de la littérature anglaise* and *Les Origines de la France contemporaine*, together with his two-volume *Philosophie de l'art* 'y algunos ensayos' —all apparently in Spanish translation. Unfortunately no indication is given of the dates of these various editions. Perhaps they are the translations published by 'La España Moderna' in the 1890's, for these bore no date. Alberich notes also the presence in Baroja's library of '[obras] dedicadas a un tema tan finisecular como el de la "patología del genio"', as well as works on his 'favorita preocupación por las razas' and others on biology and psychology, including works by Darwin, Broca and Haeckel (pp. 51–2). These are

Ramón Pérez de Ayala paid his own tribute to the French thinker:

> Yo, que le admiro casi tanto como *Fray Candil*, opino que en sus indagaciones críticas de carácter histórico, literario y sociológico, júntase la extraordinaria perspicacia observadora con un raro sentido filosófico y especulativo. Sólo él ha fundido en un todo completo y armónico el análisis minucioso con la síntesis total y sistemática. Su teoría de la *faculté maîtresse*, de la *raza*, del *momento*, del *medio*, de las *dependencias* y *condiciones*, depurada de exageraciones accidentales y de influencias momentáneas, ha quedado como método de investigación ineludible en trabajos de la índole de este mío (In *Alma Española* 7, 20 December 1903).

Three weeks later the future Azorín observed in an article on Taine:

> No, no fue ministro; pero ha ejercido Taine en su patria y en el mundo entero una prepotencia enorme. No hay en los tiempos modernos otro ejemplo de una vida intelectual más intensa, más perseverante, más noble y más sincera. Nosotros hemos encontrado en Taine un fervoroso amor a los grandes problemas del espíritu, un desinterés exquisito, un hondo patriotismo que le lleva a no sacrificar ni un átomo de la verdad a los prejuicios de las masas (In *Alma Española* 10, 10 January 1904; VII, 465).

In May 1908 Ortega y Gasset published a review of Aulard's extremely critical study, *Taine, historien de la Révolution française.* Perhaps overlooking Taine's influence on his own thought, he began his review in characteristic fashion:

> Hace pocos días un amigo mío, catalán y aun catalanista, me escribía estas palabras: 'Ya sabe usted cómo fue educada la generación de la cual salieron los que hoy gobiernan en este caos desdichado que se llama política catalana: se les ha enseñado el prólogo de la obra de Taine y . . . nada más.'
>
> Pero no ha ocurrido esto en Cataluña únicamente. Toda la generación española que ahora llega a las preocupaciones intelectuales ha sido educada, mal educada, por Hipólito Taine (I, 86).[18]

---

all relevant to the sort of guidance that writers of around 1900 were finding also in Taine.

[18] The following characteristic lines will serve as a pointer to Taine's possible influence on Ortega:

> Tandis qu'en Allemagne et en Angleterre le régime féodal conservé ou transformé compose encore une société vivante, en France son cadre mécanique n'enserre qu'une poussière d'hommes. On trouve encore

But despite growing minority objections—including Unamuno's —Taine's influence, I repeat, continued well into the twentieth century. As late as 1927 the Espasa-Calpe Encyclopaedia devoted a six-page article to him, slightly more than that allowed in other volumes of the period (1926–28) to Rousseau, Spencer and Tolstoy.

In short, in establishing parallels between Taine's writings and *En torno al casticismo* and *Idearium español* we are not only placing these latter works in their contemporary European context; we are also pointing the way to the study of an important and somewhat neglected aspect of Spanish intellectual life at the end of the nineteenth century and the beginning of the twentieth. I shall subsequently suggest that in the underlying common approach to the study of civilization lies the basis for a better understanding of important aspects of the 1898 Generation.

### 2. SIMILARITIES IN TAINE

Sur la seconde question [historical determinism], je ne diffère de vous qu'en partie. Certainement, nul historien ou psychologue ne peut se flatter d'épuiser le total infini des idées, sentiments, passions, circonstances et conditions qui composent la vie d'une nation donnée à une époque donnée. Mais, dans les choses morales comme dans les choses physiques, il y a des valeurs de différents ordres; certains caractères ont une valeur supérieure et décisive, parce qu'ils entraînent après eux et forcément une masse énorme d'autres caractères; je les appelle *générateurs*; vous les trouverez dans l'histoire humaine comme dans l'histoire naturelle. Mon ambition est de saisir ceux de la France contemporaine; j'ai tâché de les dégager dans l'Ancien Régime, je tâche de les suivre dans la Révolution, et je tâcherai de les mettre en lumière dans le Régime nouveau, en tenant compte des grandes influences qui viennent se surajouter à eux pour retarder ou accélérer leur effet [. . .]. En histoire, comme dans toute autre science, il me semble qu'il faut d'abord dégager, définir, mesurer autant que possible les grandes

---

l'ordre matériel; on ne trouve plus l'ordre moral. Une lente et profonde révolution a détruit la hiérarchie intime des suprématies acceptées et des déférences volontaires (*OFC*, I, 131).

Here, it seems, and in several similar passages, one finds already in essence the argument that Ortega was to develop and apply to Spain in *España invertebrada*.

forces agissantes et permanentes, puis ajouter l'étude des données plus ou moins accidentelles et perturbatrices. Par ce procédé seulement on pourra déterminer l'effet total et final, et prévoir jusqu'à un certain point les grandes lignes de l'avenir (*VC*, IV, 128–9).

We have seen that for Unamuno and Ganivet the problem of Spain reveals itself basically as a psychological problem. Taine views civilization in the same way: 'l'histoire au fond est un *problème de psychologie*' (*HLA*, I, xlv). As in *En torno al casticismo* and *Idearium español* so also in Taine's writings the use of concepts, terminology and comparisons derived from the study of individual psychology is both frequent and characteristic, to such an extent that in the last years of his life Taine could justifiably write, 'je n'ai jamais fait que de la psychologie appliquée ou de la psychologie pure, chacune des deux aidant l'autre' (*VC*, IV, 317). Moreover, drawn to the study of French history by the twin disasters of 1870–71, the Franco-Prussian war and the Commune, Taine—parallel to Unamuno and Ganivet in their own works—sees himself as 'un médecin consultant' (*OFC*, XI, xvii), diagnoses present disintegration, the inability of individuals to 's'associer spontanément autour d'un intérêt commun' (*OFC*, XI, ii–iii), and attributes this to the disruptive influence of the Revolution of 1789:

La structure de la France est une anomalie dans l'Europe; elle a manqué, en 1789, la transformation qu'ont réussie les nations voisines; il lui en est resté une sorte de luxation de la colonne vertébrale, et une telle lésion ne peut se guérir que très lentement, par une infinité de précautions.

Si je ne me trompe, quand un malade est dans cet état, la première condition pour qu'il guérisse, c'est qu'il sache sa maladie; cette connaissance le rendra sage, lui ôtera l'envie de faire des mouvements précipités, violents et faux (*VC*, IV, 39–40).

The first step towards a cure, says Taine, is a knowledge of the illness and, beyond that, knowledge of ourselves as a nation. It is not a matter of creating a constitution; it is a matter of *discovering* (that is, *un*covering) the one that is suited to us. He continues:

A cet égard, nos préférences seraient vaines; d'avance la nature et l'historie ont choisi pour nous; c'est à nous de nous accommoder à elles, car il est sûr qu'elles ne s'accommoderont pas à nous. La forme sociale et politique dans laquelle un peuple peut entrer et *rester* n'est pas livrée à son arbitraire, mais déterminée par son caractère et son passé. Il faut que, jusque dans ses moindres traits, elle se moule sur les traits vivants auxquels on l'applique; sinon elle crèvera et tombera en morceaux. C'est pourquoi, si nous parvenons à trouver la nôtre, ce ne sera qu'en nous étudiant nous-mêmes, et plus nous saurons précisément ce que nous sommes, plus nous démêlerons sûrement ce qui nous convient (*OFC*, I, iv).

At present France is without adequate direction:

A mon sens, la France, depuis 1789, est un cheval vicieux monté par de mauvais cavaliers; dans les accidents la faute principale est tantôt au cheval, comme en 1789 et en 1848, tantôt au cavalier comme en 1830 et en 1877. La classe supérieure ne se rend jamais un compte exact des dispositions de la nation (*VC*, IV, 31-2).

Alsace and Lorraine have been lost to us, says Taine, and unless we pursue 'prudemment et rigoureusement' 'le régime indispensable', it is to be feared that worse will follow; 'mon livre sera une consultation de médecins' (*VC*, IV, 45), 'une mémoire à consulter par les hommes qui sont ou qui peuvent devenir des hommes d'Etat' (*VC*, IV, 40-1). For Taine, then, as for Unamuno and Ganivet, collective self-knowledge (the 'conócete colectivo' by which Unamuno was later to characterize the writers of 98) is seen as the necessary means of arriving at appropriate and therefore adequate national policies, 'car le vrai gouvernement est celui qui est approprié à la civilisation du peuple' (*VC*, I, 86).

But, as Unamuno and Ganivet noted, civilization is complex:

*Une société humaine, surtout une société moderne, est une chose vaste et compliquée.* Par suite, il est difficile de la connaître et de la comprendre. C'est pourquoi il est difficile de la bien manier (*OFC*, V, 'Préface').

Difficult to understand and therefore difficult to manage (One notes again the practical aim). It is not enough to collect mere 'datos [de] archivo' (*ETC*, 795), 'coloca[ndo] todos los hechos sobre un mismo plan' (*IE*, 224), said the Spanish writers. In order to arrive at an adequate understanding of a civilization one must discover, behind the civilization's external manifestations ('el mecanismo externo', 'las envueltas'), a hidden psychology ('la conciencia colectiva', 'una personalidad histórica') and, within that psychology, the all-pervading, all-structuring nucleus ('nuestro núcleo castizo', 'una fuerza dominante y céntrica'). Taine's view was no different: Niebuhr, he believed, was to be criticized for his 'recherche immodérée des détails'; 'en histoire, les vérités de détail ne servent qu'à établir les vérités générales' (*ETL*, 102); 'la difficulté pour moi, dans une recherche, est de trouver un trait caractéristique et dominant duquel tout peut se déduire géométriquement, en un mot d'avoir la formule de la chose' (*VC*, II, 7). Indeed, it was here especially that Taine made his own special contribution to the study of civilization: in his emphasis on explanatory as opposed to descriptive study, in his insistence that 'les choses morales ont, comme les choses physiques, *des dépendances et des conditions*' (*ECH*, viii), and in his constant attempt to identify a central, structuring 'faculté maîtresse'. In the self-confessed manifesto of method that prefaces his *Histoire de la littérature anglaise* he considers briefly the historian's use of sources in a way that immediately reminds us of Unamuno (*ETC*, 795–7)[19] and thereafter, like both Spanish writers, invites us to proceed, step by step, from external complexity to an internal nucleus. First, he says, we must make the transition from external facts to the psychology beneath them:

> Quand vous observez avec vos yeux l'homme visible, qu'y cherchez-vous? L'homme invisible. Ces paroles qui arrivent à votre oreille, ces gestes, ces airs de tête, ces vêtements, ces actions et ces œuvres sensibles de tout genre, ne sont pour vous que des expressions; quelque chose s'y exprime, une âme. Il y a un homme intérieur caché sous l'homme extérieur, et le second ne fait que manifester le premier [. . .]. Tous ces dehors ne sont que des avenues qui se réunissent en un centre, et vous ne vous y engagez que pour arriver à ce centre; là est l'homme véritable, j'entends le groupe de facultés et de sentiments que produit le reste [. . .]. C'est ce monde souterrain qui est le second objet, l'objet propre de l'historien (*HLA*, I, ix–xi).

Then we must look for a comprehensible structure in that psychology:

---

[19] 'La coquille et le document sont des débris morts, et ne valent que comme indices de l'être entier et vivant [. . .]; la véritable histoire s'élève seulement quand l'historien commence à démêler à travers la distance des temps, l'homme vivant [. . .]. Une langue, une législation, un catéchisme n'est jamais qu'une chose abstraite; la chose complète, c'est l'homme agissant, l'homme corporel et visible, qui mange, qui marche, qui se bat, qui travaille' (*HLA*, I, iv–viii).

Est-ce une psychologie qu'un cahier de remarques? Ce n'est pas une psychologie, et, ici comme ailleurs, la recherche des causes doit venir après la collection des faits (*HLA*, I, xv).

This, Taine continues, will guide us to the discovery of a basic driving force:

Il y a donc un système dans les sentiments et dans les idées humaines, et ce système a pour moteur premier certains traits généraux, certains caractères d'esprit et de cœur communs aux hommes d'une race, d'un siècle ou d'un pays (*HLA*, I, xviii).

Here, he believes, lies the key to our understanding:

Là s'arrête la recherche; on est tombé sur quelque disposition primitive, sur quelque trait propre à toutes les sensations, à toutes les conceptions d'un siècle ou d'une race, sur quelque particularité inséparable de toutes les démarches de son esprit et de son cœur (*HLA*, I, xvii).

In the following passage Taine sums up his view and invites us to look for an explanation of the alleged central nucleus of national character:

En tout cas, le mécanisme de l'histoire humaine est pareil. Toujours on rencontre, pour ressort primitif quelque disposition très-générale de l'esprit et de l'âme, soit innée et attachée naturellement à la race, soit acquise et produite par quelque circonstance appliquée sur la race (*HLA*, I, xxii–xxiii).

A few pages later he explains his view more fully:

dès qu'un animal vit, il faut qu'il s'accommode à son milieu; il respire autrement, il se renouvelle autrement, il est ébranlé autrement, selon que l'air, les aliments, la température sont autres. Un climat et une situation différente amènent chez lui des besoins différents, par suite un système d'actions différentes, par suite encore un système d'habitudes différentes, par suite enfin un système d'aptitudes et d'instincts différents. L'homme, forcé de se mettre en équilibre avec les circonstances, contracte un tempérament et un caractère qui leur correspond, et son caractère comme son tempérament sont des acquisitions d'autant plus stables que l'impression extérieure s'est enfoncée en lui par des répétitions plus nombreuses et s'est transmise à sa progéniture par une plus ancienne hérédité [. . .]. Telle est la première et la plus riche source de ces facultés maîtresses d'où dérivent les événements historiques (*HLA*, I, xxv–xxvi).

Taine's subsequent account of English character as a mingling of Saxon and Norman elements is well known. On the one hand, the Saxons: 'la sève du pays humide, grossière et puissante, qui coule dans l'homme comme dans les plantes, et par la respiration, la nourriture, les sensations et les habitudes, fait ses aptitudes et son corps'; transplanted 'dans ce pays de marécages et de brumes', 'il leur fallait vivre en chasseurs et en porchers, devenir, comme auparavant, athlétiques, féroces et sombres' (HLA, I, 3, 6). On the other hand, the Normans: 'une bande scandinave, mais grossie par tous les coquins courageux et par tous les malheureux désespérés qui vaguaient dans le pays conquis', 'allégés par leur transplantation et leur mélange [in France], sent[ant] déjà se développer en eux les besoins de l'esprit' (HLA, I, 75–6, 77). Well known, too, is Taine's account of the Flemish character to which Unamuno refers in the passage quoted earlier (above, p. 47): a coming together of 'caractère inné' (Germanic race: coarse mannered, heavy eaters and drinkers, slow in movements and impressions, mentally well organized) and 'caractère acquis' (ten centuries of adaptation to the physical environment of the Low Countries: 'Impossible, en semblable pays, de rêver, de philosopher à l'allemande, de voyager parmi les chimères de la fantaisie et les systèmes de la métaphysique. On est tout de suite ramené sur terre; l'appel à l'action est trop universel, trop urgent et trop incessant; si l'on pense, c'est pour agir. Sous cette pression séculaire, le caractère se fait; ce qui était habitude devient instinct', PhA, I, 249).[20]

But despite Unamuno's special reference to Taine's account of Flemish character, it is perhaps Taine's treatment of French character, in La Fontaine et ses fables, that offers the closest parallel to Unamuno's presentation of Spanish character. Taine, like Unamuno, invites us to accompany him on a journey: up the Rhine from the North Sea and then westwards across the Vosges mountains:

Vous quittez le pays à demi allemand qui n'est à nous que depuis un siècle. Un air nouveau moins froid vous souffle aux joues; le ciel change et le sol aussi. Vous êtes entré dans la véritable France, celle qui a conquis et façonné le reste. Il semble que de tous

[20] The comprehensive references for the above are: (1) on the formation of English character (HLA, I, 1–164); (2) on the formation of Flemish character (PhA, I, 227–62).

côtés les sensations et les idées affluent pour vous expliquer ce que c'est que le Français (*LFF*, 4).

One notes especially the words 'la véritable France, celle qui a conquis et façonné le reste', with their reminder that Taine, like Unamuno, generalizes outwards from an area of alleged special significance; then, a few lines later, one continues:

> Plus de grandeur ni de puissance; l'air sauvage ou triste s'efface; la monotonie et la poésie s'en vont; la variété et la gaieté commencent. Point trop de plaines ni de montagnes; point trop de soleil ni d'humidité. Nul excès et nulle énergie. Tout y semblait maniable et civilisé; tout y était sur un petit modèle, en proportions commodes, avec un air de finesse et d'agrément (*LFF*, 4).

We must pass over a page of lyrical evocation of the landscape and climate of Champagne (corresponding to *ETC*, 808–9) and come to its proclaimed effect on man:

> On peut sortir en toute saison, vivre dehors sans trop pâtir; les impressions extrêmes ni viennent point émousser les sens ou concentrer la sensibilité; l'homme n'est point alourdi ni exalté; pour sentir, il n'a pas besoin de violentes secousses et il n'est pas propre aux grandes émotions. Tout est moyen ici, tempéré, plutôt tourné vers la délicatesse que vers la force. La nature qui est clémente n'est point prodigue; elle n'empâte pas ses nourrissons d'une abondance brutale; ils mangent sobrement, et leurs aliments ne sont point pesants (*LFF*, 6).

One is tempted to lengthen the quotation, but one must desist, drawing attention only to the subsequent evocation of Flanders and Germany to emphasize the characteristics of Champagne (in the same way that Unamuno evokes northern landscapes to emphasize the special qualities of the Castilian environment). Thereafter Taine continues:

> Ici, et à cinquante lieues alentour de Paris, la beauté manque, mais l'intelligence brille, non pas la verve pétulante et la gaieté bavarde des méridionaux, mais l'esprit leste, juste, avisé, malin, prompt à l'ironie, qui trouve son amusement dans les mécomptes d'autrui (*LFF*, 7).

People wink at each other behind our backs, and when we go into a local workshop we are somewhat apprehensive. Doubtless we shall later become objects of amusement, for such is the character of the people. 'Ce sont là des raisonnements de voyageur,' comments Taine, 'tels qu'on en fait en errant à l'aventure dans des rues inconnues ou en tournant le soir dans sa chambre d'auberge' (7). How close we are, here, to the 98 Generation that we love! Azorín is scarcely a step away.[21]

But we must continue with Taine: 'il ne faut pas trop se hasarder en conjectures' (9); we need confirmation of our 'raisonnements de voyageurs'. Let us see 'dónde y cómo se han de buscar las pruebas', says Unamuno, who thereupon looks for confirmation in various aspects of Spanish literature. Taine proceeds in the same way:

> En tout cas, il y a un moyen de s'assurer de ce caractère que nous prêtons à la race. La première bibliothèque va vous montrer s'il est en effet primitif et naturel. Il suffit d'écouter ce que dit ce peuple, au moment où sa langue se délie, lorsque la réflexion ou l'imitation n'ont pas encore altéré l'accent originel. Et savez-vous ce que dit le peuple? Ce que La Fontaine, sans s'en douter, redira plus tard. Quelle opposition entre notre littérature du douzième siècle et celle des nations voisines! Quel contraste entre nos fabliaux, nos romans du Renard et de la Rose, nos chansons de Gestes, et les Niebelungen, le Romancero, Dante et les vieux

[21] A single example will serve to illustrate the similarity further:

> On n'entre jamais ici dans un atelier sans inquiétude; fussiez-vous prince et bordé d'or, ces gamins en manches sales vous auront pesé en une minute, tout gros monsieur que vous êtes, et il est presque sûr que vous leur servirez de marionnette à la sortie du soir (loc. cit).

This gently ironic view of oneself as the self-important but unintegrated and ultimately deflated city-dweller ('tout gros monsieur que vous êtes') is very much what we later find in Azorín:

> El se quedado mirándome un momento en silencio; indudablemente, yo era un hombre colocado fuera de la realidad [. . .]. Vosotros sois ministros; ocupáis los gobiernos civiles de las provincias; estáis al frente de los grandes organismos burocráticos; redactáis los periódicos; escribís libros; pronunciáis discursos; pintáis cuadros; hacéis estatuas . . ., y un día os metéis en el tren, os sentáis en los duros bancos de un coche de tercera y descubrís—profundamente sorprendidos—que *todos* no sois vosotros (que no sabéis que Cinco Casas da lo mismo que Argamasilla), sino que *todos* son Juan, Ricardo, Pedro, Roque, Alberto, Luis, Antonio, Rafael, Tomás, es decir, el pequeño labriego, el carpintero, el herrero, el comerciante, el industrial, el artesano (1905; II, 250–1).

For evidence of Taine's influence on Azorín see HR, *Azorín's 'La ruta de Don Quijote'*, Manchester U.P., 1966, 123–39. For a fuller treatment than is offered above of his influence on Ganivet see HR, 93–124.

poëmes saxons? Au lieu des grandes conceptions tragiques, des rêveries sentimentales et voluptueuses, des générosités et des tendresses du vieux poëme allemand; au lieu de l'âpreté pittoresque, de l'éclat, de l'action, du nerf des récits espagnols; au lieu de la farouche énergie, de la profondeur lugubre des hymnes saxonnes, vous rencontrez des épopées prosaïques et des contes frondeurs. Leur style n'a pas de couleur et ne donne pas de secousses (*LFF*, 9–10).

One serves one's case badly by quoting no further, but the main point has been made: that having described the national character in terms of physical environment, Taine, like Unamuno and Ganivet, seeks to confirm his findings by reference to literature.

In his *Histoire de la littérature anglaise* the process is similar, and in an early study Giraud noted how in 1856, at the beginning of the seven years that he was to devote to the study of English literature, Taine already had a clear idea of the essential spirit that he was to find there. Giraud comments:

Il me semble que nous surprenons ici sur le fait les procédés de conception et de composition de Taine. Un sujet étant donné, il commence par l'étudier sommairement, et par s'en faire une première idée aussi exacte, aussi précise que possible. Cette vue générale, au lieu de la retenir uniquement à titre d'idée directrice, d'hypothèse à vérifier, à son insu il la considère comme un programme à développer, comme une sorte de théorème à démontrer. Elle exerce un tel empire sur sa pensée qu'il devient presque incapable de voir les faits qui la démentent ou qui l'infirment. Ainsi s'expliquent, je crois, la plupart des erreurs ou des inexactitudes qu'il a commises (*Essai sur Taine*, Paris, n.d., p. 52 n.).[22]

Unamuno perhaps had a similar point in mind in his article 'Taine caricaturista' of 1907:

Puede un hombre ser estudioso, sincero y amante de la verdad y ser falsificador y caricaturista. Su genio mismo le impulsaba a ello (III, 593).

[22] There is ample support for Giraud's suggestion in Taine's own references to his method, and against pointers to an inductive approach (e.g. *HLA*, I, ix–xi; cit. above p. 54 are to be set the author's own indications of a deductive process (e.g. 'La difficulté pour moi, dans une recherche, est de trouver un trait caractéristique et dominant *duquel tout peut se déduire géométriquement*', *VC*, II, 7; my italics). Unamuno and Ganivet, it will be recalled, reveal similar shifts of position (above, pp. 17–21).

But the same observation can be made with at least equal justification of Unamuno himself and of Ganivet. We shall return to this point in a later section.

For Taine, then, as for Unamuno and Ganivet, the arts—literature in *La Fontaine et ses fables* and in *Histoire de la littérature anglaise*; painting and sculpture in *Philosophie de l'art*—serve primarily as psychological documents: 'Vous n'étudiez le document ['un poëme, un code, un symbole de foi'],' says Taine, 'qu'afin de connaître l'homme' (*HLA*, I, iv) and thereby to arrive at the essential spirit of his race and his age, 'quelque disposition primitive, quelque trait propre à toutes les conceptions d'un siècle ou d'une race' (*HLA*, I, xvii):

> quand ce document [littéraire] est riche et qu'on sait l'interpréter, on y trouve la psychologie d'une âme, souvent celle d'un siècle, et parfois celle d'une race (*HLA*, I, 54–5).

> Quand un drame original et national s'élève, les poëtes qui l'établissent portent en eux-mêmes les sentiments qu'il représente. Ils manifestent mieux que les autres hommes l'esprit public, parce que l'esprit public est plus fort chez eux que chez les autres hommes (*HLA*, II, 27).

It is in this sense that Unamuno presents Calderón as 'el símbolo de casta' (*ETC*, 817), 'cifra y compendio de los caracteres diferenciales y exclusivos del casticismo castellano' (*ETC*, 816), and that Ganivet finds in *La vida es sueño* 'una explicación clara, lúcida y profética de nuestra historia' (*IE*, 278).

Having probed a given civilization, discovered the underlying national character, identified its central motive force, explained it in terms of physical environment and confirmed one's findings by reference to various aspects of the nation's civilization, one can proceed to sit in judgement on the past and the present and to make recommendations for the future. In Taine one finds this most clearly in *Les Origines de la France contemporaine*, the work to which he devoted the last twenty-two years of his life:

> Personnellement, dans les *Origines de la France contemporaine*, j'ai toujours accolé la qualification morale à l'explication psychologique; dans le portrait des Jacobins, de Robespierre, de Bonaparte, mon analyse préalable est toujours rigoureusement déterministe, et ma conclusion terminale est rigoureusement judiciaire (*VC*, IV, 292).

In the human will, he says, there are two layers: one superficial and conscious, fragile and vacillating, the other profound and unconscious, 'stable et fixe comme une roche' (*OFC*, IV, 59). It is the latter that, like Unamuno's 'roca viva', determines the character of a given civilization and must serve as the necessary basis for one's judgement of a nation's past and present and for one's recommendations for its future. 'Plus nous saurons précisément ce que nous sommes,' Taine wrote in the preface to the first volume of his *Origines*, 'plus nous démêlerons sûrement ce qui nous convient' (*OFC*, I, iv). The prime aim of the historian, he declared fifteen years later, is 'de démêler les lois générales et de fournir un jour aux gouvernements et aux peuples des préceptes d'hygiène sociale, analogues aux prescriptions d'hygiène physique que les physiologistes et les médecins introduisent aujourd'hui dans les hôpitaux' (*VC*, IV, 306).

We return, then, to Taine's likening of the historian to a doctor. And, of course, just as a doctor, by reason of his studies, is better qualified than his patient to diagnose that patient's illness and prescribe a course of cure, so also the historian (or the serious politician) is better qualified than ordinary people to diagnose national maladies and to indicate the necessary remedy. Taine is impatient with democracy, 'cette épaisse démocratie où nous étouffons', 'l'ascendant, l'autorité, la dictature des imbéciles' in which 'les souverains, rois, parlements et ministres exécuteront les volontés de *P.P.C. Clerk of the Parish*, de M. Homais, de M. Prudhomme, de l'illustre Gaudissart et de Jean Hiroux' (*VC*, IV, 184). The views of Unamuno and Ganivet are not significantly different. One must study and base one's recommendations on 'la vida silenciosa de los millones de hombres sin historia' (*ETC*, 793), on 'las clases proletarias, que son el archivo y el depósito de los sentimientos inexplicables, profundos, de un país' (*IE*, 203). But it is the serious student who must do this, not the people themselves:

> Pedirle al pueblo que resuelva por el voto la orientación política que le conviene, es pretender que sepa fisiología de la digestión todo el que digiere (MU, *PE*, 662).[23]

[23] 'Yo soy anti-demócrata,' wrote Unamuno in 1890 (MU–PM, 16 December), and ten years later, beyond the crisis:

No, libertad, no. Nuestro pueblo ni la merece, ni la necesita, ni le conviene; cultura, cultura, cultura. Cultura impuesta, y tal como la entende-

Y el principio fundamental del arte político ha de ser la fijación exacta del punto a que ha llegado el espíritu nacional. Esto es lo que se pregunta de vez en cuando al pueblo en los comicios, sin que el pueblo conteste nunca, por la razón concluyente de que no lo sabe ni es posible que lo sepa. Quien lo debe saber es quien gobierna, quien por esto mismo conviene que sea más psicólogo que orador, más hábil para ahondar en el pueblo que para atraérselo con discursos sonoros (AG, *PE*, 648–9).

'Des passions avides comme celles de la démocratie contemporaine (*VI*, I, 385); 'democracia concupiscente' (MU, IV, 283, 284); 'la inmunda democracia' (AG, II, 886)—Ganivet expresses their common standpoint in words from Ibsen's *The Enemy of the People*:

En política es verdad inconcusa la de Ibsen en *El enemigo del pueblo*: 'que, estando compuesta de imbéciles la mayoría, la minoría es la que debe gobernar' (II, 927).

Taine died before he could fully formulate his own recommendations, but, as André Chevrillon pointed out in the preface to the last, posthumous volume of *Les Origines de la France contemporaine*, his views were already clear: because of the Revolution France had broken with its racial traditions, was out of step with the rest of Europe, and denied to its people a sense of common purpose; there was, 'en somme, un appauvrissement organique de toutes les facultés de cohésion, aboutissant à la destruction des centres de groupement naturels et, par suite, à l'instabilité politique' (*OFC*, XI, ii–iv). His aim, Taine maintained, was a middle path between the extremes of clerical reaction and Jacobin radicalism,[24] and it appears probable, says Chevrillon, that he

---

mos nosotros, los europeos, los que nos debemos constituir en directores por santo derecho divino [. . .]. Joaquín Costa ha hecho un daño horrible adulando a este pueblo español que tiene siempre gobiernos mejores de los que se merece, por malos que éstos sean. Hay que convencerle de que es muy bruto y de que para no caer bajo el cura que le embrutece más aún tiene que dejarse guiar por nosotros y se le convencerá . . . ¡Vaya si se le convencerá! (MU–JA, 12 December 1900).

[24] At one moment he finds the radicals to be the greater evil ('en France, quoique les cléricaux ne valent rien, les radicaux sont pires, étant aussi bêtes et plus violents', *VC*, III, 210); at another moment, the clericals ('S'il faut opter entre le radicalisme et le cléricalisme, c'est triste; le premier est la gale et le second la peste. J'aime mieux la gale', *VC*, III, 233). Basically

would have based his recommendations for the future of France on the one firm bond that remained, the family, 'le seul remède à la Mort', working outwards from that point (*OFC*, XI, iv–xx).

But Taine was ever modest in his task. In 1885 Jules Sauzay wrote to him: 'Après avoir diagnostiqué le mal, achevez l'œuvre du médecin en indiquant le remède avec l'autorité qui vous appartient.' Taine's reply is characteristic:

> J'essaie de faire dans un cinquième volume ce que vous me deman-dez. Mais je ne suis pas sûr de pouvoir le bien faire. Il faudrait être plus instruit, plus compétent, avoir touché de près, par la pratique, par l'exercice de fonctions administratives, les hommes et les choses. J'essaie depuis plusieurs années de me mettre au courant (*VC*, IV, 203–4).

This, after fourteen years of intensive work in the field. The contrast with Unamuno's and Ganivet's somewhat easier con-fidence and slighter documentation is too obvious to require development.

In drawing the present section to a close, we may recall Unamuno's description of *En torno al casticismo* as a bringing together of 'reflexiones y sugestiones' on the subject of *casticismo* (*ETC*, 784). We may recall, too, the frequent references by critics to the 'espíritu genuinamente asistemático' that is said to underlie Ganivet's own 'ideario' on the problem of Spain.[25] But it is clear from what precedes that the basic thought of both writers is in fact extremely systematic, almost naïvely systematic, with a system that we recognize unfailingly as characteristic of the age in which the works were written. Certainly neither work is very accurately described as 'una serie de notas sueltas, especie de sarta sin cuerda' (*ETC*, 869). Indeed, it is perhaps more in the system than in the ideas incorporated into that system (at times 'cosas sabidas de sobra', as Unamuno himself insists repeatedly) that we recognize the real originality of the works within the context of Spanish thought and letters. Moreover, as I shall show in Part III of my study, it is the system of thought rather than any

---

he suspects that both the 'esprit révolutionnaire' and the 'esprit clérical' reveal common characteristics: 'le goût des principes admis d'avance, l'obéissance aux phrases toutes faites, l'instinct de la tyrannie, l'aptitude à l'esclavage; on en conclurait qu'on ne peut combattre l'un par l'autre, mais qu'il faut les combattre tous les deux' (*VC*, III, 215).

[25] Melchor Fernández Almagro, in *El Libro Español* VIII, 1965, 129.

'notas sueltas' that enables us to see both works as corner-stones of the so-called 1898 Generation.

But before considering the impact of the works it is necessary to carry our exploration of similarities between Taine, Unamuno and Ganivet a stage further.

### 3. FROM REALITY TO THE IDEAL

j'ai fait là [in HLA] ce que font les zoologistes lorsque, prenant les poissons et les mammifères par exemple, ils extraient de toute la classe et de ses innombrables espèces un type idéal, une forme abstraite commune à tous, persistante en tous, dont tous les traits sont liés (VC, II, 301).

Toda la labor del maestro se reduce a fijar bien los hechos y ordenarlos, alinearlos, para que se expliquen a sí mismos. Basta escribir en el encerado series de formas convenientemente dispuestas para que surja la ley (1894; MU, I, 888).

Por los cuerpos advino almas, y las almas me resultan cuerpos [. . .]. El alma de la metafísica te he dicho mil veces, no es la observación; es la abstracción que obra sobre las formas reales exteriores e intenta reducirlas a la forma una. En cuanto cogemos el microscopio. la unidad se fue a freír morcilla (1896; AG, in Helios II, 1903, 550-1).

'Innombrables espèces' and 'type idéal', 'hechos' and 'ley'' 'formas reales exteriores' and 'la forma una', and, to express the duality in terms that are already familiar to us, 'intrincado laberinto' and 'núcleo castizo', 'mecanismo externo' and 'núcleo irreducible', 'vérités de détails' and 'faculté maîtresse'. On the one hand, the complexity of real-life phenomena; on the other hand, the underlying law and ideal form. It is a duality characteristic of the age: 'first, ascertaining facts; secondly, framing laws'.[26] In the present section I aim, firstly, to explain the duality

[26] R. G. Collingwood, The Idea of History, Oxford 1961, 126-7. Cf.

Hamon es un obrero intelectual de una laboriosidad extraordinaria; positivista convencido, trabaja sobre los hechos, y de ellos saca todas sus conclusiones, y por ellos formula la ley, la regla media, general, que rige y gobierna las relaciones sociales (1897; Azorín, I, 286; Martínez Ruiz's italics).

It will be noted that, in the type of thought we are here examining, ideal form (Ganivet's 'forma una') and law (Unamuno's 'ley') are virtually synonymous. 'De même qu'il y a des rapports fixes, mais non mesurables quantita-

by reference to Taine and, secondly, to show how the duality reveals itself in *En torno al casticismo* and *Idearium español*.

The key to understanding lies initially in the influence of natural science:

> La structure morale d'un peuple et d'un âge est aussi particulière et aussi distincte que la structure physique d'une famille de plantes ou d'un ordre d'animaux. Aujourd'hui, l'histoire comme la zoologie a trouvé son anatomie (*HLA*, I, xii).

Whether it be in the study of human intelligence (*De l'Intelligence*) or of an individual writer (*Essai sur Tite-Live, La Fontaine et ses fables*) or of a nation's literature (*Histoire de la littérature anglaise*) or of a nation's art (*Philosophie de l'art*) or of a nation's history (*Les Origines de la France contemporaine*) Taine's aim is basically the same:

> Je fais de la physiologie en matières morales, rien de plus. J'ai emprunté à la philosophie et aux sciences positives des méthodes qui m'ont semblé puissantes, et je les ai appliquées dans les sciences psychologiques. Je traite des sentiments et des idées comme on fait des fonctions et des organes (*VC*, II, 183).

> J'ose déclarer ici que je n'ai point d'autre but; on permettra à un historien d'agir en naturaliste: j'étais devant mon sujet comme devant la métamorphose d'un insecte (*OFC*, I, viii).

But alongside Taine the would-be 'naturaliste', for whom 'les physiologistes et les anatomistes sont nos maîtres à tous' (*VC*, II, 320), is also Taine the self-confessed 'idéaliste', for whom Hegel is, 'de tous les philosophes, celui qui s'est le plus rapproché de la vérité' (*VC*, II, 257–8):

> J'ai lu Hegel, tous les jours, pendant une année entière, en province; il est probable que je ne retrouverai jamais des impressions égales à celles qu'il m'a données. De tous les philosophes, il n'en est aucun qui soit monté à des hauteurs pareilles, ou dont le génie approche de cette prodigieuse immensité (*PhC*, 132–3).

---

tivement, entre les organes et les fonctions d'un corps vivant, de même il y a des rapports précis, mais non susceptibles d'évaluation numérique, entre les groupes de faits qui composent la vie sociale et morale' (*VC*, II, 300). It is these 'rapports précis', 'ces relations générales nécessaires', that Taine calls 'lois'—like Montesquieu in the eighteenth century and like zoologists and botanists in the later nineteenth century. In arriving at the 'type idéal', he believes, one is arriving also at the essential 'loi' (*VC*, II, 300–1).

As D. D. Rosca has shown in an extensive study, Taine's under-lying notion of universal determinism comes directly from Hegel and Spinoza. Hegelian, too, albeit with modifications, is his notion of the 'faculté maîtresse'.[27] Hegelian, too—and anti-positivist—his belief that isolated facts are without value and indeed unreal. But Taine was apparently ill at ease with the third volume of Hegel's *Logik*, with its exaltation of reason (*Vernunft*) over understanding (*Verstand*). 'Les spiritualistes,' he comments, 'veulent toujours avoir une raison, une intuition sublime séparée de toutes les facultés; et ils voient dans les choses une substance, une force, un arrière-fond tout à fait séparé, distinct des faits, ce qui est parfaitment faux' (*VC*, II, 258). For Taine, it is not by Hegelian reason (which he finds extra-logical and equates with intuition, revelation and illumination) that one aspires to the essence; it is by the understanding operating on facts:

> mon effort est d'atteindre l'essence, comme disent les Allemands, non de prime assaut, mais par une grande route unie, carrossable. Remplacer l'intuition (*insight*), l'abstraction subite (*Geist, Vernunft*), par l'analyse oratoire. Mais cette route est dure à creuser (*VC*, II, 259).

In the following key passage from his study of John Stuart Mill, Taine juxtaposes the English emphasis on facts and the German emphasis on abstraction and indicates clearly his own position:

> A mon avis, ces deux grandes opérations, l'expérience telle que vous l'avez décrite et l'abstraction telle que j'ai essayé de la définir, font à elles deux toutes les ressources de l'esprit humain. L'une est la direction pratique, l'autre la direction spéculative. La première conduit à considérer la nature comme une rencontre de faits, la seconde comme un système de lois; employée seule, la première est anglaise; employée seule, la seconde est allemande. S'il y a une place entre les deux nations, c'est la nôtre. Nous avons élargi les idées anglaises au dix-huitième siècle: nous pouvons, au dix-neuvième siècle, préciser les idées allemandes. Notre affaire est de tempérer, de corriger, de compléter les deux esprits l'un par l'autre, de les fondre en un seul, de les exprimer dans un style que tout le monde entende, et d'en faire ainsi l'esprit universel (*HLA*, V, 416).

[27] But Schlegel's 'vorherrschendes und überwiegendes Seelenvermögen' (rendered as 'l'élément intellectuel ou la *faculté souveraine*' in the French translation of 1836) is doubtless relevant too. See Giraud, *Essai sur Taine*, Paris n.d., p. 41 n.

Neither English positivism ('rencontre de faits') nor German idealism ('système de lois'), then, but a fusion of the two.

And, of course, it was a means of arriving at such a fusion that Taine found in the methods of natural science: facts ('innombrables espèces') for the would-be naturalist; laws ('rapports précis', 'type idéal') for the self-confessed idealist. First ascertain facts; then frame laws. As the zoologist looks for a basic structure within the complexity of organic forms, so the philosopher and the psychologist and the historian must look for a basic structure within the complexity of their own fields of study. In this respect, the 1866 preface to Taine's *Essais de critique et d'histoire* is a key document, with its proposed parallels between what Cuvier, Richard Owen, Saint-Hilaire and Darwin had found in organic life and what Taine invites the historian to find in the study of civilization. He concludes:

> Il suit de là qu'une carrière semblable à celle des sciences naturelles est ouverte aux sciences morales; que l'histoire, la dernière venue, peut découvrir des lois comme ses aînées; qu'elle peut, comme elles et dans sa province, gouverner les conceptions et guider les efforts des hommes (*ECH*, xxxi).

Beneath the complex, confused and ever-changing manifestations of a given civilization one can henceforth hope to discover, like the zoologist, an essential, persistent structure. Hegel's *a priori* philosophy of history, it seems, can be given a scientific basis. Scholarly concern for facts and Hegelian hunger for the ideal can apparently be reconciled. But to what extent and at what cost? It is these questions that I propose to consider with reference to *En torno al casticismo* and *Idearium español*.

I start with *En torno al casticismo* and the basic duality: on the one hand, a profusion of biological terms and comparisons suggesting faithful adherence to the naturalist's insistence on observation; on the other hand, an abundance of terms indicating purification, ideals and eternal truths. The former, for Unamuno, represents a world of distasteful limitation (*cuerpo, carne, pecado original, individual, vulgar, histórico, muerto*); the latter, a desirable realm of vastness, permanence and unsullied form (*hondo, continuo, universal, absoluto, esencia, ideal, eterno*). And there, as a bridge between the one and the other, are the author's characteristic indications of the need to probe deeply (*entrañas, raíces, fondo*) and to free oneself from undesirable ties (*purificarse, despojarse, desligarse*). One must follow the natural law in society, he says, but 'más que ley natural es ésta sobrenatural, porque eleva la naturaleza al ideal naturalizándola más y más' (786); 'lo accidental, lo pasajero, lo temporal, lo castizo, de puro sublimarse y exaltarse se purifica destruyéndose' (798). 'Volviendo a sí, haciendo examen de conciencia, estudiándose y buscando en su historia la raíz de los males que sufren, [los pueblos] se purifican de sí mismos, se anegan en la humanidad eterna. Por el examen de su conciencia histórica penetran en su intrahistoria y se hallan de veras' (798).

Superficial, changing reality and the eternal, hidden essence. Like Taine, Unamuno invokes evolutionist thought to justify his transition from the one to the other. History, he says, is part of sociology which itself is part of biology. Like palaeontology, history can serve to establish permanent features and fundamental relationships. Thus, as the palaeontologist, by identifying common structures, demonstrates both temporal continuity ('la continuidad zoológica') and species relationship ('enlaza a nuestros ojos las especies vivas hoy [viéndose así] la comunidad de la pezuña del caballo y el ala del águila'), so also the historian, by arriving at the 'roca viva' of national existence, can demonstrate both the nation's continuity in time and its affinity with related nations (*ETC*, 799–800). It is in this context, equating Unamuno's emphasis on 'tradición eterna' with the evolutionist's emphasis on homologous structures, that one must understand the following characteristic argument:

> Y la tradición eterna es tradición universal, cosmopolita. Es combatir contra ella, es querer destruir la humanidad en nosotros, es ir a la muerte, empeñarnos en distinguirnos de los demás, en evitar o retardar nuestra absorción en el espíritu general europeo moderno (*ETC*, 797).

In arriving at Spain's fundamental national morphology, Unamuno believes, one is arriving also at its basic affinity with other European peoples. He infers from this that such affinities should be encouraged.

Indeed, he had already anticipated this finding in the opening paragraphs of his work and there, too, biology was offered as a guide:

> es cosa probada, por ensayos en *castas* de animales domésticos y por

la historia además, que si bien es dañoso y hasta infecundo a la larga todo cruzamiento de razas muy diferentes, es, sin embargo, fuente de nuevo vigor y de progreso todo cruce de castas donde las diferencias no preponderen demasiado sobre el fondo de común analogía (*ETC*, 783).

On the one hand, the 'fondo de común analogía', which we can liken to the 'tradición eterna'; on the other hand, the 'diferencias', which we can equate with historical events, the 'islands' of history, the 'cosas muertas' in which the 'desenterradores de osamentas' take such delight (795–6). Similarly, in the sciences—and for Unamuno 'todo tiene entrañas, todo tiene un dentro, incluso la ciencia' (790)—we are invited to find a 'fondo formado y eterno' and a 'proceso de cambio' (787): 'mientras pasan sistemas, escuelas y teorías [corresponding to the biologist's 'diferencias' and the historian's 'cosas muertas'], va formándose el sedimento de las verdades eternas de la eterna esencia' [corresponding to the biologist's 'fondo de común analogía' and the historian's 'tradición eterna'] (792). Similarly again, in the working of the mind: 'En la sucesión de impresiones discretas hay un fondo de continuidad [. . .]; la vida de la mente es como un mar eterno sobre que ruedan y se suceden las olas' (813).

Again and again Unamuno establishes a duality of change and permanence, of superficial 'diferencias' and basic 'comunidad', of natural complexity and confusion and ideal essence and harmony. But he would doubtless object to my final duality, maintaining that the ideal, too, lies within nature, that, as evolutionism has shown, it is sufficient to establish 'series de formas convenientemente dispuestas para que surja la ley' (I, 888) and that what I refer to as the 'ideal' is neither more nor less than the 'ley' demanded by the facts. One cannot disprove this without an exhaustive study that is no part of my present aim. One can, however, take away Unamuno's principal support by showing that, to arrive at his conclusions, he misapplies a basic evolutionary concept: that of homologous structures. To demonstrate this I take Unamuno's own example of 'la comunidad de la pezuña del caballo y el ala del águila' (800).

It is well known that in related animal species one finds significant similarities of structure. Thus, in the fore-limbs of vertebrates there is a basic pattern—whether it be in frog, reptile, bird or mammal—consisting typically of one bone in the upper leg or arm, two in the lower leg or fore-arm, several in the ankle or wrist, five in the instep or palm, and a number of attached toes or fingers. It is a structure, then, that suggests common descent and thereby indicates both diachronic relationship ('la continuidad zoológica') and synchronic relationship ('enlaza a nuestros ojos las especies vivas hoy'). Applying this notion to the study of civilization, Unamuno finds, temporally, 'algo que sirve de sustento al perpetuo flujo de las cosas' (792) and, spatially, 'el fondo común a todos [los pueblos], la masa idéntica sobre que se moldean las formas diferenciales' (794). From the evolutionist notion of common structures, then, he has proceeded to the notion of a firm basis ('algo que sirve de sustento', 'el fondo') persistent beneath a complex of temporal and spatial differences ('perpetuo flujo de las cosas', 'formas diferenciales').

But in making this transition he has committed an error. Nowhere in the evolutionist notion of homologous structure is there any suggestion that a given structure (for example, the fore-limb pattern of vertebrates) remains constant while associated organisms change. On the contrary, the doctrine of evolution presupposes a total, interdependent, evolving complex in which every part of the whole is subject to change. Thus, within the fore-limb structure of the horse ('la pezuña del caballo') the first and fifth digits have completely disappeared and only the third remains functional—unlike the bird ('el ala del águila') in which there has been a near-fusion of metacarpals and three digits which together carry the primary feathers.[28] There is therefore no justification in evolutionary theory for Unamuno's proposed duality of permanent basis and changing superstructure. For the evolutionist, change permeates the whole organism.

And this is surely true also of civilization for the modern historian. Unamuno, guided by his misinterpretation of evolutionary theory, presents, on the one hand, a basis of permanence, 'la tradición eterna', and on the other hand, a superstructure of

[28] Cf. 'For instance the basic fore-limb of the land vertebrates, five-toed and adapted for walking, has undergone remarkable radiations among later animals. Among other things, it has become a one-toed, tip-toe running apparatus (in proterotheres and horses), an arm and hand (in you and me), a webbed paddle (in duck-bill dinosaurs, otters and others), a flipper (in ichthyosaurs, whales, etc.), a wing (in pterodactyls, birds, and bats), and so on' (G. G. Simpson, *The Meaning of Evolution*, Yale University Press, 1966, p. 180).

transience, 'datos [de] archivo [. . .], papeles [. . .], cosas muertas'. The 'tradición eterna', he believes, like a basic homologous structure, persists across time, thereby establishing a fundamental diachronic relationship between the different moments of Spanish history. Also, like a homologous structure in related species, it points to a fundamental synchronic relationship between different peoples. Unamuno's equation, therefore, follows almost inevitably: 'La tradición eterna es tradición universal, cosmopolita' (797). But his own determinism, with its proclaimed 'inferencia de nuestras obras a nuestro carácter' (799), should have shown him that this was manifestly mistaken. If a given nation's civilization reveals certain persistent characteristics that serve to distinguish it from other civilizations, those differences will surely continue to be present however deeply one probes into national character or national tradition (cf. above, pp. 30–1).

Unamuno is mistaken, then, to infer from the homologous structures of comparative anatomy, a 'fondo común' or 'masa idéntica' of different civilizations. He is mistaken also in two further inferences which carry him directly to his two principal findings in *En torno al casticismo*: firstly, that the persistence of a given 'tradición' throughout Spanish civilization is a guarantee of its continuing importance and, secondly, that a pseudo-morphological resemblance between peoples is a valid reason for advocating a closer practical relationship. The beliefs themselves may be correct in so far as they pertain to civilization, but evolutionary doctrine does not give them the support that Unamuno assumes.

In the first place, it is clear that, in the context of evolutionary theory, the persistence of a given anatomical structure is not necessarily a guarantee of its continuing functional importance. In the snake, for example, the fore-limb pattern referred to earlier has evolved to a merely vestigial organ incapable of carrying out its original functions. Thus, with Unamuno's own evolutionary premises one *could* argue that Spain's persistent features (its so-called 'tradición eterna') may be functionally no longer valid and should therefore be disregarded.

In the second place, the fact that a bird's fore-limbs are related to a horse's is surely no sufficient reason for suggesting that some form of practical approximation of the two should now be attempted. It could more appropriately be argued that each should be encouraged to develop in its differences: the bird's for more efficient flying, the horse's for more efficient running. And a corresponding argument *could* be set against Unamuno's belief that Spain's 'tradición eterna' reveals its essential humanity and should therefore bring it into closer communion with other peoples. If Spain has developed differently from other nations, perhaps these differences are prompted by millennia of different environment and different needs and should therefore be encouraged rather than discouraged.

'El principio de unidad y la doctrina de la evolución,' said Unamuno in 1894, 'son hoy las ideas madres en la ciencia' (I, 879). From our study in the preceding pages it would appear that, in order to arrive at 'el principio de unidad', Unamuno has ridden somewhat roughshod over 'la doctrina de la evolución'. Doubtless, if one is convinced of the importance of national tradition one *can* find apparent support for this conviction in morphological conservatism, and if one feels strongly the need for Spain to open up its gates to currents from abroad one *can* convince oneself that comparative anatomy shows the way. But the critical reader of today can hardly be persuaded by Unamuno's analogies. More probably he will recall Bradley's definition of philosophy as the finding of bad reasons for what one believes by instinct. And here, perhaps, we are touching on the key to the problem. I shall return to the subject in a later section.

But for the present it is sufficient to have noted how evolutionism, and in particular the concept of homologous structures, has been used by Unamuno to justify his repeated transitions from a real world of distasteful limitation to an ideal realm of vastness, permanence and unsullied essence.[29] 'Lo accidental, lo pasajero,

[29] In considering the influence of evolutionism on Unamuno's thought I have confined myself to the basic problem of his biological concept of history and made no reference to such more obvious evidence as his characteristic biological imagery and his presentation of the Castilian people as '*producto de una larga selección* por las heladas de crudísimos inviernos y una serie de penurias periódicas, *hechos a* la inclemencia del cielo y a la pobreza de la vida' (811; my italics). This and similar evidence has been studied by Peter G. Earle (in 'El evolucionismo en el pensamiento de Unamuno', *CCMU* XIV–XV, 1964–5, 19–28). José Alberich has made relevant observations on Unamuno's admiration for Darwin (in 'Sobre el positivismo de Unamuno', *CCMU* IX, 1959, 61–75).

Also relevant to the above—though in a different way—is the more general question of Unamuno's tendency to argue by imagery and similarly

lo temporal, lo castizo, de puro sublimarse y exaltarse se purifica destruyéndose' (798). And at this point we are clearly brought close to Hegel, that 'Quijote de la filosofía' who in Unamuno's own words sought to write 'el álgebra del universo [. . .], aspiración a la ciencia absoluta [. . .], y quiso levantarnos al cenit del cielo de nuestra razón y desde la forma suprema hacernos descender a *la realidad, que iría purificándose y abriéndose a nuestros ojos, racionalizándose'* (790; my italics). For however Unamuno may, like Antaeus, take 'el *ahora* y el *aqui* como puntos de apoyo', his aspiration, like Hegel's, is to 'lo eterno y universal' (791).[30] Evolutionism serves merely as an apparently justified means of making the transition. 'No, nunca estuve enamorado de la ciencia,' Unamuno was to declare later, 'siempre busqué algo detrás de ella' (1906; III, 926). Even the limitations of art—limitations that constitute its very essence—are for Unamuno a cause of regret: 'El arte no puede desligarse de la lengua tanto como la ciencia, ¡ojalá pudiera!' (791).

With *Idearium español* I can be briefer, for elsewhere I have made the case at length.[31] Like Unamuno, Ganivet too establishes, on the one hand, a distasteful realm of coarse realism, practical empiricism and superficial change (*experimental, práctico, externo, accidental, realista, vulgar*) and, on the other hand, an ideal world of permanence and unsullied form (*ideal*—which appears more than fifty times—*permanente, invariable, hondo, esencial*). Moreover, as in *En torno al casticismo* so also in *Idearium español* biological imagery is both frequent and characteristic:

> La síntesis espiritual de un país es su arte. Pudiera decirse que el espíritu territorial es la medula; la religión, el cerebro; el espíritu guerrero, el corazón; el espíritu jurídico, la musculatura, y el espíritu artístico, como una red nerviosa que todo lo enlaza y lo unifica y lo mueve (*IE*, 209).

---

doubtful analogies: islands and the sea-bed, clouds on a mountain crag, superimposed family photographs, alluvion deposits, etc. On argument by imagery in *Idearium español* see HR, 164–6.

[30] One may usefully recall here Unamuno's later definition of faith as 'una serena confianza en que concurren a un fin mismo la naturaleza y el espíritu, en que naturalizando al espíritu lo sobreespiritualizamos y espiritualizando a la naturaleza la sobrenaturalizamos' (1899; VII, 368). 'Spirit' has taken over from 'reason', but the underlying desire to establish a bridge between reality and the ideal is not notably different. Nor is the absence of 'serena confianza'.

[31] HR, 93–124 (especially 97–9, 115–24).

A given civilization is an organism of interdependent parts. Underlying it is a basic principle of 'conservación' that manifests itself differently in different physical environments (176–7). The student of a given civilization must therefore determine the relevant physical environment, discover thereby the nation's underlying 'fuerza natural y efectiva' (257–8), consider its position in the process of 'natural evolución' (281) and ensure that the future organization of the country is in harmony with its 'constitución natural' (197). One recalls Taine on the type of constitution suited to France: 'nos préférences seraient vaines; d'avance la nature et l'histoire ont choisi pour nous; c'est à nous de nous accommoder à elles, car il est sûr qu'elles ne s'accommoderont pas à nous' (*OFC*, I, iv).

But despite this evidence—and it is of course by no means exhaustive—the natural sciences appear to have made a far slighter impact on the *Idearium* than on *En torno al casticismo*. There is less biological imagery and, as in the passage quoted above, what there is tends to be used crudely and with little evidence of real understanding. Certainly one has no feeling, as one does with Unamuno, that the author has himself looked into the writings of evolutionists. Nor can one follow closely, as one can with Unamuno's use of homologous structures, the role of natural science in the author's transition from natural complexity to ideal essence. Ganivet, it seems, accepts the polarity of 'formas reales exteriores' and 'la forma *una*' but proceeds from the one to the other not, as he claims, by 'abstracción', but by an obviously intuitive leap, with little attempt to justify his idealism by close reference to evolutionist theory. In this respect he is more Hegelian than Unamuno himself and his tripartite division of civilizations into island, peninsular and continental reminds one of the German philosopher's corresponding establishment of three basic historically relevant land-types: meseta, valley and coast.

Like Hegel, then, like Taine, like Unamuno, Ganivet is intoxicated by the ideal. I have summed up my findings elsewhere:

> For Ganivet, 'purely objective observations' yield up only the 'external mechanism', the 'wrappings' (174–5). He is impatient with the 'impureza inseparable de lo material' and he despises the realistic, experimental, practical approach to knowledge. He is driven on, in his studies as in his daily life, by the 'fuerza perenne del ideal' (166). And so, despite his view of civilization as an

organism of interdependent parts and despite his use of evolution-ist and psychological terminology, in fact Ganivet scorns the natur-alist's and psychologist's submission to observed facts. Hence my earlier expression, 'biological *pretence*', for Ganivet's own prime aim is not to observe but to interpret, not to study but to explain. With the facile assurance of a café *raconteur*—and with a similar disregard for facts—Ganivet places himself triumphantly, with a single bound, at the 'ideal' centre of his subject and there-upon proceeds to select, from the limitless complexity of Spanish civilization, a number of facts that appear to support his view, and to present unavoidable contrary evidence as signs of a devia-tion from the nation's proper path. It is the point at which Gani-vet's various uses of the word *ideal* come together and are seen in their proper perspective: *ideal*, pertaining to the idea; *ideal*, per-taining to the essence; *ideal*, pertaining to the desirable. What Ganivet conceives 'limpia y sin mancha entre las espumas del pensamiento' (with both restriction and extension of the term *ideal*) is projected outwards on to Spain and presented to us as the essence of Spanish civilization, 'un ideal bien cimentado' (258) after which Spaniards must strive (HR, 120–1).

For Ganivet, then, the world of facts is unworthy; 'lo que realmente vive son las ideas' (221), with the human species as a necessary but apparently subordinate repository of those ideas ('en cuanto necesaria para servir de asilo a las ideas', 221). One recalls Taine's related view: 'Il n'y a rien de réel dans la nature, sauf des trames d'événements liés entre eux et à d'autres, et il n'y a rien de plus en nous-mêmes ni en autre chose' (*Int*, II, 5). One may recall, too, Unamuno's delight in Greek words 'que per-diendo el peso de la tradición permitan el vuelo de la idea' (*ETC*, 789) and his regret at the limiting effect of environment, 'el verdadero misterio del pecado original, la condenación de la idea al tiempo y al espacio, al cuerpo' (*ETC*, 788). Despite their empha-sis on physical conditions, despite their proclaimed respect for historical facts, despite their frequent use of terminology derived from natural science, all three writers seek ultimately to convert physical conditions, historical facts, and natural science into handmaidens of a vast, unsullied, Hegelian ideal. As Unamuno himself was to observe, '¡qué inexhausto fondo de idealismo hay en el tan decantado positivismo de nuestro tiempo!' (1902; I, 1017).[32]

[32] Unamuno does not here admit the relevance of the observation to his

## 4. THE PERSONAL ELEMENT

In *En torno al casticismo* and *Idearium español*, it seems, two currents converge: a national current of preoccupation with Spain and its decline (object of study) and a European current of determinism (method of study). In the present section I aim, firstly, to point to a personal element in the choice of the *method* of study and, secondly, to demonstrate a personal element in the authors' treatment of the *object* of study.

own writings and perhaps did not see it. Nevertheless, ten years earlier he had admitted, 'Tomo la filología como una gimnástica espiritual que contra-balancee mi tendencia, acaso excesiva, a las generalizaciones y abstracciones, mis instintos metafísicos' (MU–PM, 5 April 1892). This observation becomes especially significant when one recalls that for Unamuno one of the most beneficial effects of philology on the 'cultura y gimnasia del espíritu' lay in its teaching by example of the 'principios de la evolución orgánica': 'Con un encerado y una colección de textos basta para las experimentaciones y observaciones que conducen a conocer en vivo la ley de evolución' (1894; I, 883). Unamuno's whole mental and emotive life, it seems, evolves from a struggle (at times an anguished struggle) to reconcile the infinity of Hegelian idealism with the factual demands of nineteenth-century positivism. Thus, as early as 1884 he writes of Schleicher: 'al querer hacer objetiva una ley lógica del conocer, cayó en las dificultades mayores, achaque común a la escuela hegeliana, que buscó fuera del sujeto y del objeto, fuera del ideante y el ideado, en la idea lo absoluto incondicionado' (IV, 99). Unamuno's aim, of course, will be to find his laws within.

In view of this and of the evidence presented in the above section one should perhaps reconsider Unamuno's still unpublished *Filosofía lógica* of 1886, in which, according to Zubizarreta, 'Unamuno logra romper las estrechas barreras del cientificismo y positivismo del siglo, para lanzarse a la captación de la existencia' (*Tras las huellas de Unamuno*, Madrid 1960, p. 16). At the age of twenty-one, continues the Peruvian critic, Unamuno 'condensa en noventa y cuatro páginas una pequeña aventura filosófica que reproduce, en cierto modo, el camino que había de seguir la filosofía occidental desde el positivismo hasta Ortega y Heidegger. En esta pequeña aventura, su primera navegación filosófica, el método de Unamuno se acerca, en alguna manera, a la descripción fenomenológica de Husserl' (p. 17). In fact, it would appear from the extracts quoted by Zubizarreta that here too Unamuno's chief aim was to reconcile positivism and Hegelian idealism. Thus, to Zubizarreta's finding of 'presupuestos positivistas claramente puestos de manifiesto' (p. 17) one can usefully juxtapose Manuel Pizán's claim: 'Desde el título de la obrita, *Filosofía lógica*, hasta su estructura general dialéctica y las continuas citas a Hegel, la influencia de éste es manifiesta. Su pretensión e intento de reducir la metafísica a lógica me parece una prueba definitiva de ello' (*El joven Unamuno: influencia hegeliana y marxista*, Madrid 1970, p. 51).

## (a) *The appeal of determinism*

Tant que sur ta table tu n'auras pas ce bréviaire invincible, je
veux dire la géométrie des choses, je ne réponds ni de toi, ni de
moi, ni de personne! La science est une ancre qui fixe l'homme;
qui ne l'a pas, peut être poussé aux écueils qu'il redoute le moins
(*VC*, I, 82–3).

A medida que se pierde la fe cristiana en la realidad eterna, búscase
un remedo de inmortalidad en la Historia (1898; MU, I, 946).

Es preciso tener fe en la ciencia (1893; AG, II, 926).

Civilization is complex and confused; man looks for form and
structure and direction. In the later nineteenth century natural
science appeared to point the way. Under the impact of natural
history men were becoming aware that the naturalist, like the
historian, was concerned with a world of changing forms. Perhaps
because of this there was a rapprochement between the sciences
of nature which had become historical and the study of history
which it now seemed possible to make scientific. Beneath the
complexity and apparent formlessness of civilization one could
henceforth hope to find, like the palaeontologist in his own studies,
a significant evolving structure. The notion was not entirely new,
but until the publication of Darwin's *Origin of Species* in 1859 it
lacked the appearance of scientific authority. Thereafter, for
almost half a century the biological sciences were to dominate
human thought. Transposed to the realm of civilization, Darwin's
notion of 'hidden bonds of connection' gave new authority to
attempts to discover, amidst the complexity and confusion of a
given national history, 'quelque élément commun [. . .], le
caractère et l'esprit propre à la race' (*ECH*, xvi–xvii), a central,
structuring 'faculté maîtresse'. 'Tous ces dehors,' said Taine, 'ne
sont que des avenues qui se réunissent en un centre, et vous ne
vous y engagez que pour arriver à ce centre' (*HLA*, I, x).

We are reminded, of course, of Unamuno's aim to study
Spanish society 'en su centro' (*ETC*, 859) and of Ganivet's search
for a national 'fuerza dominante y céntrica' (*IE*, 211)—unlike
Spain's leading politicians, none of whom, according to Ganivet,
judged national policy 'desde un punto elevado o, por lo menos,
céntrico' (*IE*, 231–2). We may be reminded, too, of Maeztu's

earlier mentioned article on the 98 Generation. Until the appearance of the Generation, he says, men could not agree about what was wrong with Spain. At times they lamented simply the lack of glory, of strength, of material prosperity; at other times, the lack of merit, of natural wealth, of great men. At one moment it was tradition that was blamed; at another moment, the inheritors of that tradition. 'Faltaba un criterio de discernimiento,' he continues; 'faltaba la pregunta de: ¿qué es lo central, qué es lo primero, qué es lo más importante?'[33] It was the findings and hypotheses of natural science, I suggest, that had at last encouraged a number of writers to ask these questions and that guided them in their search for the answers.

Natural science, then, offered an exciting and apparently firmly based method of studying a given civilization as an evolving structure. Moreover, the theory of adaptation to environment gave weight to the belief that the central, all-pervading 'faculté maîtresse' could be explained in terms of physical conditions. In other words, environment, people and the various manifestations of their civilization could henceforth be viewed as interdependent elements in a total, quasi-organic structure. At the centre of that structure was the all-important nucleus of national character. Discover that nucleus and the civilization as a whole becomes comprehensible; ignore it and the object of one's study appears formless and without direction. 'Hay algo que sirve de sustento al perpetuo flujo de las cosas,' says Unamuno (*ETC*, 792): 'no basta representar al mecanismo externo,' adds Ganivet; 'hay que ir más hondo y buscar en la realidad misma el núcleo al que están adheridas todas las envueltas que van transformando en el tiempo la fisonomía de ese páis' (*IE*, 175). Here, too, natural science was seen to point the way.

But Unamuno himself has taught us to look for something more than a merely intellectual appeal in such cases:

> Nuestra filosofía, esto es, nuestro modo de comprender o de no comprender el mundo y la vida brota de nuestro sentimiento respecto a la vida misma. Y ésta, como todo lo afectivo, tiene raíces subconcientes, inconcientes tal vez (1913; VII, 110).

Indeed, even on the internal evidence of *En torno al casticismo* and *Idearium español* one suspects that both authors found in evolu-

[33] In *Nuevo Mundo*, 13 March 1913; I, 88.

tionary determinism something more than an intellectually convincing approach to the problem of Spain. Their recurring insistence on the need to find permanence beneath change, essence beneath existence, structure beneath confusion—this does not suggest a merely intellectual response, especially since their observations reach out far beyond the immediately relevant question of Spanish civilization. Unamuno's view of philosophy as an aspiration to 'la ciencia una' (839), his belief that in discovering the 'tradición eterna' of Spain one is discovering 'el fondo del ser del hombre mismo' (794), his insistence on 'la fe viva que no consiste en creer lo que no vimos, sino en crear lo que no vemos' (797)[34]—these are but a few of the points by which one is led to suspect, behind the search for a meaningful structure in Spanish civilization, a quest for a meaningful structure in life itself. Similarly in *Idearium español*: on the one hand, 'esa perplejidad de espíritu', that state of near paralysis of will and body that besets us when we lack a guiding 'idea dominante' (286–7) and, on the other hand, the thrill of seeing phenomena take on significant structure where formerly they had appeared confused and incomprehensible:

> Cuando yo, siendo estudiante, leí las obras de Séneca, me quedé aturdido y asombrado, como quien, perdida la vista o el oído, los recobrara repentina e inesperadamente y viera los objetos, que con sus colores y sonidos ideales se agitaban antes confusos en su interior, salir ahora en tropel y tomar la consistencia de objetos reales y tangibles (*IE*, 152–3).

It was just such form and structure, I suggest, that Ganivet, like Unamuno, like Taine, looked for in evolutionary determinism.

When one considers evidence from outside *En torno al casticismo* and *Idearium español* this emotive appeal of determinism becomes clearer. Unamuno and Ganivet had both been brought up in the Catholic faith and in an age of increasing scepticism both had apparently lost that faith during their student years.[35] '¡Ah, qué

---

[34] A clear anticipation, this last quotation, of a notion much repeated in Unamuno's later writings. The seeds of *Del sentimiento trágico* . . . are clearly present in *En torno al casticismo*.

[35] See A. Sánchez Barbudo, *Estudios sobre Galdós, Unamuno y Machado*, 2nd ed., Madrid 1968, pp. 71–2; C. Mª Abad, 'Angel Ganivet', in *Razón y Fe* LXXII (May–August 1925), 18–30, 190–207; A. Castro Villacañas, 'Angel Ganivet, hombre sin fe', in *Arriba*, 7 March 1965.

triste es después de una niñez y juventud de fe sencilla haberla perdido en vida ultraterrena, y buscar en nombre, fama y vanagloria un miserable remedo de ella!' (MU–LA, 9 May 1900). But it is not only in personal fame that we find Unamuno seeking a sense of direction during the years to 1900. '¡Con qué razón escribía Martínez Ruiz que yo no sabía a dónde iba!' Unamuno confessed in his *Diario íntimo* (VIII, 837). And earlier, at a time when he was much preoccupied with his own alleged aboulia (MU–PM, 1 September 1890): 'Proponerse un objeto, una tarea larga, es atarse a la vida por el trabajo' (MU–PM, 29 April 1890). Indeed, the range of his proposed 'objetos' is considerable: science, rationalism, socialism, marriage, attempted returns to the faith of his childhood; sometimes with optimism ('Pedid el reino de la ciencia y su justicia y todo lo demás se os dará por añadidura'),[36] at other times with anguished uncertainty ('y sus energías y sentimientos morales van desfalleciendo, y siente cansancio y que el mundo le devora el alma', MU–LA, 31 May 1895). And always, the desire to belong, the search for roots, the need for a vision of order and direction amidst the confusion and apparent pointlessness of human existence.[37]

[36] Cit. Armando F. Zubizarreta, *Tras las huellas de Unamuno*, Madrid 1960, p. 17.

[37] It is commonly argued that the prestige of positivist science sowed doubts in certain undergraduate minds, thus drawing them away from their religious faith (cf. Alberich on Unamuno, in *CCMU* IX, 1959, 61 and 68). But as the very word indicates, positivism did not sow doubts; it offered the certainties of a new religion. And men do not accept a new religion merely because it is there; they accept it also because their old religion no longer satisfies. In this respect Alvar Ellegård's extremely well-documented study of the reception of Darwin's theory of evolution in the British periodical press from 1859 to 1872 ('Darwin and the General Reader', in *Göteborgs Universitets Årsskrift* LXIV, 1958, VII, 1–394) establishes a fascinating correlation between religious beliefs and attitudes to Darwinism. 'The scientists' attitudes towards the Darwinian theory,' he observes, 'like the general public's, were to a large extent determined by ideological factors' (p. 8), and later: 'It was no coincidence that the leading Darwinians of the time—Darwin, Huxley and Hooker—were all agnostics (a term invented by Huxley), while the leading anti-Darwinians, Owen and Mivart, were decidedly religious men' (p. 337).

In other words, it seems necessary to distinguish between two interacting elements in a transference of faith such as we find in Unamuno and Ganivet: on the one hand, questionings about one's traditional faith (already heralded in Unamuno's pre-university 'ansia devoradora de esclarecer los eternos

Ganivet's own case, it seems, was similar, and I have studied elsewhere 'his desperate and ultimately futile search for an *idea directiva*': first in science and empirical study, then increasingly in *ideas, ideales* and *imaginaciones*.[38] It is in this context, surely, that one must consider the personal appeal of the determinist approach, with its offer of a vision of structure, aim and direction. Taine himself, who likewise lost his religious faith at an early age under the impact of rationalist probing (*VC*, I, 21), had observed:

> La seule chose qui puisse déprendre l'esprit de lui-même et l'absorber, c'est un système. Un coup de volonté isolé peut chasser un instant la peine, elle revient. La consolation n'arrive que lorsqu'on se met à son travail involontairement, par attrait; et le système produit seul cette disposition (*VC*, II, 250);

and again, fifteen years later, after an enthusiastic reading of the newly published first volume of Spencer's *Principles of Sociology*:

> Et puis, mon cher ami, il n'y a que ces grandes généralités pour vous verser l'opium nécessaire; sans cela les malheurs domestiques, les prévisions politiques nous donneraient trop souvent l'envie de nous noyer (*VC*, IV, 30).

Determinism, then, offered the required system and pointed the way to the suicide-saving 'grandes généralités'. Moreover, by bringing together man, civilization and physical environment, it made of national probing a search by the author for the roots of his own personal being:

> la seule chose qui puisse combler un esprit complet, ce sont les grandes vues qui embrassent l'ensemble et les grandes sympathies *qui nous font participer à la vie de l'ensemble* (*VC*, II, 252; my italics).

'¡Motivo de vivir! ¡Motivo de vivir para el individuo y para el pueblo, y el motivo de vivir del pueblo, raíz y médula del patriotismo individual!' (MU, I, 765). In probing the historical destiny

---

problemas', VIII, 144, 'aquellas agonías de la vela de mi espíritu mozo', VIII, 476) and, on the other hand, the attraction of a new faith which thus appears as an opportune response to a threatening void. The Romantic, at one in this with Rousseau, 'au fond de l'abîme, pauvre mortel infortuné, mais impassible comme Dieu même', had already attempted to fill such a void with the deification of his own tormented ego. The determinist, as we shall see in the next sub-section, did not react very differently, despite his scientific pretensions.

[38] HR, especially pp. 138–50 (quotation, p. 138).

of Spain, Unamuno and Ganivet, I suggest—like Taine in his probings of France—were seeking also to discover their own context and destiny.[39] The method of study (determinism) had given a new relevance and a new urgency to the object of study (Spain). The prober of national destinies is no longer a mere observer; the subject and object of study are fused; knowledge henceforth is involvement, necessity, anguish. Evolutionary determinism is one of several nineteenth-century ideologies that sought to give sense and direction to a world from which God and the notion of special creation were increasingly banned.

## (b) *The interpretation of Spain*

La sociedad en que vive y de que se nutre mi espíritu, su hijo, no puede ser mi patria si en ella no caben mis sentimientos y mis ideas (1899; MU, I, 765).

En las sombras que deja lo material, nuestro espíritu dibuja todo un universo (1891; AG, in *Helios* III, 1904, 166).

'Tout se tient,' said the Romantic[40] and showed it by creating a self-centred world of emotion of which he was the very microcosm; 'tout se tient,' says the Determinist[41] and seeks to demonstrate it rationally in his grandiose surveys of civilization. But is there as much difference between the two approaches as this distinction seems to indicate? The determinist of the later nineteenth century, I have suggested, is no mere observer; knowledge has become personal, anguished involvement. Moreover, determinism, with its interplay of natural and ideal findings, allows more room for subjectivity than it might at first appear. Nor is it simply a matter of the personal appeal of the method, referred to under the previous heading. In his findings, too, the determinist reveals much of his own inner, personal concerns. For he not

[39] 'Cada uno de nosotros [los que hace veinte años partimos a la conquista de una patria] buscaba salvarse como hombre, como personalidad; buscaba afirmar en sí al Hombre. En aquel naufragio de la civilidad, esto es, de la humanidad de España, cada uno de nosotros buscaba salvarse como hombre. Pero ¿hombre y sin patria? Por eso partimos a la conquista de una' (1918; MU, VIII, 408).
[40] Victor Hugo, *La Préface de Cromwell*, ed. Maurice Souriau, 6th ed., Paris n.d., p. 191.
[41] *HLA*, IV, 424; *OFC*, VII, 93.

only reasons; he rationalizes, too, and at the centre of his rationalizing is his own particular crisis of lost directions, his need for a
personal 'roca viva' or 'eje diamantino'. In *En torno al casticismo*
and *Idearium español*, it seems, the case is clear.

It was perhaps in 1892, says Sánchez Barbudo, that Unamuno,
observing a valley from the top of a mountain, had a sort of
illumination, 'un momento de dramático entusiasmo que, como
veremos, parece relacionado con la idea que es germen de gran
parte de su obra toda: que hay un hondo silencio, eterna quietud,
bajo la agitación pasajera, bajo las externas apariencias'.[42] This,
continues the critic, is at the heart of *Paz en la guerra* and, under
the form of 'intrahistoria', is the central theme of *En torno al
casticismo*. Sánchez Barbudo's comparison is obviously justified:
on the one hand, in the autobiographical novel, the quest for 'paz
en la guerra misma y bajo la guerra inacabable, sustentándola y
coronándola' (*PG*, II, 300); on the other hand, in the study of
Spain, the search for 'el silencio augusto del mar eterno [. . .], la
tradición eterna, en las entrañas del mar [. . .], debajo de la
historia' (*ETC*, 794). Moreover, the parallel becomes even more
significant if one compares the lines that immediately follow each
of these quotations:

> Así como la tradición es la sustancia de la historia, la eternidad lo
> es del tiempo, la historia es la forma de la tradición como el tiempo
> la de la eternidad (*ETC*, 794).

> Es la guerra a la paz lo que a la eternidad el tiempo: su forma
> pasajera (*PG*; II, 300).

Time is the fleeting form of eternity (*ETC*, *PG*), history the
fleeting form of tradition (*ETC*), war the fleeting form of peace
(*PG*). Pachico, then, looks for peace in war in the same way that
Unamuno looks for tradition in history. Basically, both are concerned to preserve eternity from the ravages of passing time.

These dualities recall others noted in the previous section:
change and permanence, superficial 'diferencias' and basic
'comunidad', natural complexity and confusion and ideal essence
and harmony. And to justify these dualities, Unamuno, I have
suggested, misapplied his basic evolutionary premises. Perhaps
one can see this as an example of how reason and emotion may
interact in a creative writer: evolutionism, with its emphasis on

---

[42] *Estudios sobre Galdós, Unamuno y Machado*, 2nd ed., Madrid 1968, p. 84.

common structures, offers Unamuno a glimpse of permanence amidst a world of diverse and changing forms, whereupon already existent spiritual needs take over and carry him across into a realm of personal illumination, in defiance of science, logic and his own basic determinism.[43]

Moreover, as Unamuno himself in *En torno al casticismo* oscillates between 'entrañas' and 'pureza', 'formas diferenciales' and 'fondo común', scholarly concern for facts and Hegelian hunger for the ideal, so also the Castilian is claimed to oscillate between observation ('hechos tomados en bruto') and intellection ('la inteligencia abstractiva'), 'sensitivismo e intelectualismo' (821), between 'un realismo apegado a sus sentidos' and 'un idealismo ligado a sus conceptos' (838). Indeed, the basic aim of the third and fourth essays is to show how different characteristic figures of the Spanish Golden Age responded to this duality: on the one hand, Calderón, 'cifra y compendio de los caracteres diferenciales y exclusivos del casticismo castellano' (816), who failed to bridge the gap and therefore reveals a fundamental 'disociación'; on the other hand, the mystics, 'el fruto más granado del espíritu castellano', '[quienes se esforzaron] por llegar a lo eterno de su conciencia, por armonizar su idealismo quijotesco con su realismo sancho-pancino' (816). I do not suggest that the distinction is totally unjustified; I do suggest, however, that the emphasis that Unamuno places on it is not purely fortuitous, that it stems less from empirical observation than from the author's own haunting obsession with reality and the ideal. To deny this is to attribute to mere coincidence the coexistence, both in the author and in the object of his study, of the same basic duality.[44]

Similarly, we are informed that the mystics, oppressed by law, sought to penetrate the life of the universe in order to make it the

---

[43] In this respect compare the interplay of reason ('The intellectual basis: determinism') and emotion ('The true basis: personal obsessions') studied in my edition of Azorín's *La ruta de Don Quijote* (Manchester University Press, 1966, pp. 123–76).

[44] The Castilian mystics, says Unamuno, 'no fueron al misticismo por hastío de razón ni desengaño de ciencia, sino más bien por el doloroso efecto entre lo desmesurado de sus aspiraciones y lo pequeño de la realidad' (*ETC*, 841). What a fascinating subject to discuss in its relevance to Unamuno's own quest for faith! 'El sentimiento primordial del hombre,' he wrote in 1892, 'es el dolor, la molestia, la sensación de obstáculo y estorbo que experimenta su voluntad al chocar con el mundo' (IV, 294–5).

living law of their own conscience, to make it part of themselves in the depths of their own souls and thus find no burden in their obedience to it. Unamuno comments:

> La ley moral es, en efecto, la misma de la naturaleza, y quien lograra acabada comprensión del organismo universal viendo su propio engranaje y oficio en él, su verdadera valía y la infinita irradiación de cada uno de sus actos en la trama infinita del mundo, querría siempre lo que debiera querer (*ETC*, 843).

One is reminded, perhaps, of Hegel's view of freedom as a willing acceptance of necessary laws; one is reminded, too, of Unamuno's own emphasis on the 'doctrina del pacto', 'pacto hondamente libre, esto es, aceptado con la verdadera libertad, la que nace de la comprensión viva de lo necesario, con la libertad que da el hacer de las leyes de las cosas leyes de nuestra mente, con la que nos acerca a una como omnipotencia humana' (801). Again, then, Unamuno interprets the mystics in terms of his own attempt to reconcile reality (in this case, determinist necessity) with an aspect of the ideal ('omnipotencia humana'). And again his interpretation may well be justified. But it is again significantly related to his own inner concerns. In the fourth section of the essay 'De mística y humanismo' the author progresses from the mystic's submergence of individual differences in the search for personal completeness to the need for a given people to open its frontiers wide to the world around: 'Sólo así se llega a ser un mundo perfecto, plenitud que no se alcanza poniendo portillos al ambiente, sino abandonándose a él, abriéndose lleno de fe al progreso, que es la gracia humana' (851). The response of Spain to its national problem, then, must be akin to that of the mystics to their individual problem. Akin because dispassionate study shows it to be so? Or akin because Unamuno is the writer? We are touching here on yet another aspect of the work's subjectivity.

I turn now to Unamuno's description of the Castilian as a product of physical environment (*ETC*, 809–15). The climate is extreme and the landscape bare:

> No es una naturaleza que recree al espíritu. Nos desase más bien del pobre suelo, envolviéndonos en el cielo puro, desnudo y uniforme. No hay aquí comunión con la Naturaleza, ni nos absorbe ésta en sus espléndidas exuberancias; es, si cabe decirlo, más que panteístico, un paisaje monoteístico este campo infinito en que,

sin perderse, se achica el hombre, y en que siente en medio de la
sequía de los campos sequedades del alma.

Moreover, as climate and landscape are composed of extreme,
clear-cut, unintegrated elements, so also the Castilian character:
'en este clima extremado y sin tibiezas dulces, de paisaje uniforme
en sus contrastes, es el espíritu también cortante y seco, pobre en
nimbos de ideas'. Under the influence of climate and landscape the
Castilian is slow but tenacious, 'silencioso y taciturno mientras no
se le desata la lengua', like Pero Mudo in the *Cantar de mio Cid*,
slow to speak but then eager to turn speech into action: '*Lengua
sin manos ¿cómo osas fablar?* Todo Pero Mudo se vierte es este
apóstrofe'.

One may well be convinced by Unamuno's case—until one
recalls an earlier delving by him into the relationship between
character and physical environment: in his lecture 'Espíritu de
la raza vasca' (1887). 'Si algo influye en la raza es el medio ambiente,' he claimed, and thereupon proceeded to present the Basque
people as 'un pueblo montañés y costero; las montañas que se
elevan macizas al cielo sin despegarse de la tierra y el mar que bate
incesante nuestras costas han formado nuestro espíritu'. The
Andalusian environment is very different, he continued; the clear
sky ('el cielo sereno y limpio'), the rich farmlands ('el suelo
fertilísimo'), the distant views ('se perdía la vista en aquella
floreciente llanura'). So is its impact on man: 'Allí [in Andalusia]
el cielo aplasta al hombre, la naturaleza le ahoga, su alma se
ensancha, esfuma y pierde en la inmensidad'; on the other hand,
'el cielo brumoso y la tierra ingrata han hecho al vasco tardo, pero
seguro; poco imaginativo, pero de grande sentimiento; mediano
poeta, pero inmenso corazón'. One has to add only one more
quotation to make the confusion complete:

> Nuestro espíritu [the Basque spirit] tiene ancla, si le levantan por
> un momento, luego cae de las nubes de la abstracción y viene al
> suelo. Por eso somos tardos en concebir y convencernos, prontos
> en ejecutar.[45]

The grey skies of coast and mountain, then, have had the same
effect on the Basques as the clear blue skies of the meseta on the
Castilians: they have made them slow to accept new ideas, more
given to action than to thought. Moreover, the luxuriant country-

---

[45] All references are to IV, 157–8.

side of Andalusia stifles man with its abundance and causes his soul to take flight—just as the barren meseta of Castile rejects man and causes his soul to take flight. From a determinist point of view each case undermines the other. Their juxtaposition is nevertheless extremely suggestive. Unamuno has a high regard for silent men not easily swayed but, once swayed, prepared to act, 'hombres enteros, de una pieza, rudos y decididos' (*ETC*, 812); he is also extremely responsive to souls that take flight towards a mystic, Hegelian or Quixotic infinity. Unamuno's personal likings, it seems, have again influenced his case for determinist causality.

We have noted in a previous section that from the evidence adduced by Unamuno one could argue for Ganivet's insistence on national independence and even isolationism (above, pp. 37–9). Yet no one sensitive to the dynamic, expansive, exuberant tone of *En torno al casticismo* could seriously imagine its author making such a recommendation. The characteristic vocabulary of unplumbed depths and uncharted space, the scant respect for semantic tradition and syntactical conciseness, the impatience with any simple 'fila lógica' of rational argument, the delight in exploring extreme points of view and relatively tangential problems and illustrations—all these things stem directly from Unamuno's manifest impatience with any form of restriction on his own titanic, exuberant personality.[46] 'Mi obligación,' he informed his friend Pedro Jiménez Ilundain, 'es trasladar mi personalidad a mis escritos' (MU–PJI, 1897). And as his own personality is confident

---

[46] Of the above points, perhaps only the reference to Unamuno's scant respect for semantic tradition is not immediately apparent. The word *original* will serve as an illustration:

> Y hay, sin embargo, un verdadero furor por buscar en sí lo menos humano; llega la ceguera a tal punto, que llamamos original a lo menos original. Porque lo original no es la mueca, ni el gesto, ni la *distinción* ni lo *original*; lo verdaderamente original es lo originario, la humanidad en nosotros (*ETC*, 794).

Cf.

> Hay que llegar a originalidades, sin advertir que lo hondo, lo verdaderamente original, es lo originario, lo común a todos, lo humano (1896; I, 974).

By semantic contorsion Unamuno has characteristically transferred the word *original* from one pole of his world (that of 'formas diferenciales') to the other (that of the 'fondo común a todos').

and exuberant, so also is his recommendation that Spain should throw open its frontiers to outside influences. 'El que se mete en su concha, ni se conoce ni se posee' (853); '¡Fe, fe en la espontaneidad propia, fe en que siempre seremos nosotros!' (867). In both cases Unamuno is referring to Spain; in both cases the words seem to epitomize also his personal attitude to life.

Not that I mean with this to underplay his crisis of personality. On the contrary, I take Unamuno's 'desenfrenado yoísmo', which he applies also to Spain ('¡Mi yo, que me arrancan mi yo!', 785), to be a reaction against the threatening abyss of annihilation—and fundamental to his repeated dualities of permanence and transience.[47] And it is in this respect, I suggest, that one must consider his description of the Castilian landscape (807–10), with its superb —and dangerous—fusion of rational argument and lyrical evocation: the vastness, the solitude, the austere beauty, the tacit lament at transience: 'alguna procesión monótona y grave de pardas encinas [. . .] que pasan lentamente espaciadas', 'la carretera [que] se pierde', 'el sol [que] se hincha al tocar el horizonte como si quisiera gozar de más tierra y se hunde';[48] then the proclaimed effect of the landscape on man, with a significant switch to the first person: 'Nos desase [. . .] del pobre suelo, envolviéndonos en el cielo puro, desnudo y uniforme'; 'se achica el hombre y [. . .] siente en medio de la sequía de los campos sequedades del alma', and the characteristic recollection of Leopardi's wandering shepherd 'que, en las estepas asiáticas, interroga a la luna por su destino'. Here, he believes, one can find the living soul of Castile (813). It may well be so. But who will doubt that beneath the determinist reasoning one finds also the anguished soul of the admirer of Leopardi and Senancour?

When one turns to *Idearium español* one becomes conscious that with *En torno al casticismo* one has perhaps exaggerated the autobiographical element. For despite considerable subjectivity in Unamuno's approach, findings and recommendations, *En torno al casticismo* still preserves much of the solidity and close reference

[47] Cf. Unamuno's re-quotation of Michelet's words in the *Diario íntimo* with the observation, 'No vio acaso él mismo toda la horrible profundidad de ese grito' (VIII, 822).

[48] 'Una puesta serena de sol en medio del campo, entre las montañas buriladas en el cielo, un vislumbre de su calma. ¿Cuántas veces no deseamos prolongar aquel estado?' (*Diario íntimo*; VIII, 785). See also 'Fantasía crepuscular' (1898; I, 77–9) and 'Puesta del sol' (1899; I, 73–6).

and even apparent detachment of scholarly study, notably in the essays on Calderón's theatre and on Spanish mysticism. This is less clearly the case with Ganivet's *Idearium español* and I have felt justified in describing the work elsewhere as a spiritual auto-biography (HR, 125–53). For in the alleged basic malady of Spain, as in the 'fuerzas constituyentes' of Spanish national character, as in his recommendations for the nation's future, Ganivet clearly reveals fundamental aspects of his own inner crisis.

The basic malady of Spain, says Ganivet, is aboulia, 'extinción o debilitación grave de la voluntad' (286). In a less chronic form, he believes, the malady is known to all of us:

> Hay una forma vulgar de la abulia que todos conocemos y a veces padecemos. ¿A quién no le habrá invadido en alguna ocasión esa perplejidad del espíritu, nacida del quebranto de fuerzas o del aplanamiento consiguiente a una inacción prolongada, en que la voluntad, falta de idea dominante que la mueva, vacilante entre motivos opuestos que se contrabalancean, o dominada por una idea abstracta, irrealizable, permanece irresoluta, sin saber qué hacer y sin determinarse a hacer nada? Cuando tal situación de pasajera se convierte en crónica, constituye la abulia, la cual se muestra al exterior en la repugnancia de la voluntad a ejecutar actos libres (*IE*, 286–7).

To Ganivet, certainly, 'esa perplejidad del espíritu' was well known and he probed it frequently in letters to his friends. 'Cada día,' he writes in the first letter of his *Epistolario* (18 February 1893), 'me va siendo más difícil concretar mis ideas y fijar mi pensamiento sobre un objeto determinado' (II, 811). Lacking the 'instrucción compacta' of either seminary or Institución Libre (II, 813; cf. above, 'la voluntad, falta de una idea dominante que la mueva'), Ganivet finds the world around him aimless and repugnant, and is unable to assimilate its data. 'En tal estado,' he says, 'el espíritu se va [. . . pero . . .] el espíritu que abandonó la realidad por demasiado baja no puede elevarse a la infinitud por demasiado alta' (II, 811–12; cf. above, 'la voluntad . . ., dominada por una idea abstracta, irrealizable'). The outcome is inaction: 'la vida retrograda, no pudiendo vencer la pereza, que le impide con-tinuar asimilándose elementos nuevos para renovar la vida al compás del tiempo' (II, 812; cf. 'el entendimiento parece como que se petrifica y se incapacita para la asimilación de ideas nuevas', 287). As in the *Idearium* so also in this letter, Ganivet diagnoses the malady as 'la *abulia* o debilitación de la voluntad' (II, 812). Spain's alleged illness, then, is clearly Ganivet's own.

Similarly, the alleged basic 'fuerzas constituyentes' of Spanish national character correspond closely to characteristic aspects of the writer's own inner being and it is a relatively easy task to establish parallels between what Ganivet reveals of himself in letters to friends and what he finds in Spanish character in *Idearium español*. Thus, the stoicism that he believes to constitute 'el elemento moral y en cierto modo religioso más profundo' of Spain's ideal constitution (151) reminds one of his own insistent concern, amidst life's misfortunes, to live 'lo más decente y filosóficamente posible' (II, 926), and in his emphasis on independence one is reminded of his own repeated affirmations of personal independence, whether it be from organization and administrative restraints (II, 1010; NML, 44), from the 'mecanismo judicial' of the legal system (*IE*, 202) or from the social obligations imposed on him by his consular appointment (II, 817). Even the fervour that Ganivet claims to have evolved from stoicism under the influence of the Moorish occupation has clear parallels with the author's own intoxicated flights into an ideal realm free from the impurities of base matter, 'un castillo imaginario que llegue hasta donde se pueda' (II, 971). 'Reality and the ideal, necessity and desire, fatalism and the will, withdrawal and expansion, and, embracing all these dualities, stoicism and fervour —*Idearium español*, like its author, moves incessantly between these extremes' (HR, 144).

Finally, in his recommendations for Spain's future there are clear similarities between what Ganivet finds on a personal plane in the *Epistolario* ('Quizá el placer que se busca en vencer se encontraría retirándose', II, 986) and what he urges on a national plane in *Idearium español* ('la necesidad perentoria de destruir las ilusiones nacionales; y el destruirlas no es obra de desesperados, es obra de noble y legítima ambición', 271). And here, within the basic similarity imposed by the determinist system, Ganivet represents the opposite pole from Unamuno. Unamuno, as we have seen, consistent with his own exuberant, expansive personality, advocates a confident opening of Spain to influences from abroad. Ganivet, more contained, more cautious, more timorous, more obviously concerned to impose a simple logical structure on the complexity and confusion of Spanish history, advocates concentration within and emphasizes the need to adapt foreign influences to what already exists in Spain (267). There must be careful supervision, he believes: 'mano fuerte' (233), 'mano firme' (296), '[la] subordinación absoluta de la actividad a la inteligencia' (294). 'Es indispensable forzar nuestra nación a que se desahogue racionalmente' (280); 'aun a los espíritus más independientes hay medio de someterlos a la obra común, si se les rodea de espíritus que les cerquen y les aprisionen' (219–20). Significantly, whereas Unamuno, with his predominantly biological terminology, is concerned very especially to awaken the slumbering vitality of the young (860–3), Ganivet, with his predominantly logical terminology, is more concerned to keep in check the 'yerros' and the 'trabajos de demolición' commonly associated with the young (298–9). Similarly, whereas Unamuno, with his extrovert belief that the people's experience should be diversified, believes also that language should accommodate that diversification (791, 802), Ganivet, more exclusively insistent on the truth that lies within, emphasizes the need to 'conservar la unidad y pureza del lenguaje' (251). Here as elsewhere Ganivet sets up against Unamuno's own prime emphasis on receptive continuity his own main emphasis on containment and purity.

In Thomas a Kempis and Fray Luis de Granada, Ganivet finds two personalities apparently alike but in reality very different. He concludes: 'Del uno podría decirse que es un alma enfermiza, linfática; del otro, que es un alma robusta, sanguínea' (165). Perhaps one can make a similar distinction between Ganivet and Unamuno. The basis of their manifest similarities, I suggest, lies in their common determinism; the key to their differences lies in their separate personalities. Determinism, with its possibility of free interplay between reality and the ideal, has offered to both an apparently scholarly justification for what are basically personal responses to the problem of Spain.

I have been concerned in this sub-section with the treatment of Spain and have therefore confined my observations to Unamuno and Ganivet. Indeed, given Taine's impressive documentation in his monumental study of the origins of contemporary France, given, too, his own repeated insistence that he had written 'pas une phrase, pas un adjectif, sans une ou plusieurs preuves à l'appui' (VC, IV, 211), one would hardly expect much intervention here of the writer's own personality. Yet Aulard, writing fifteen years after Taine's death, found his illustrious predecessor biased to the point of mental illness: 'Théories préconçues, parti pris, impatience fébrile, ce n'est pas assez dire,' he claimed; 'il faudrait presque parler d'une sorte d'état pathologique.'[49] Thirty years later K. de Schaepdryver explored the question more fully in his book *Hippolyte Taine, essai sur l'unité de sa pensée* (Paris 1938). The title of the book is misleading, for what Schaepdryver shows is not so much the unity of Taine's thought as the persistence throughout his work of certain basic obsessions, traceable back to his earliest writings and backed up by impressive documentation and vivid writing in his final work, the eleven-volume *Origines de la France contemporaine*: his pessimism, his misanthropy, his fascination with violence, his 'psychologie alarmiste', his political and social and religious views. In a characteristic passage Schaepdryver observes:

> Pour ce qui a trait à ses attitudes d'impersonnalité et d'impassibilité, ayons le bon esprit de ne pas le croire quand il nous déclare qu'il a fait abstraction de son goût personnel, de son tempérament, de ses inclinations, de son parti, qu'aversion et dégoût il a 'laissé ses sentiments à la porte de l'histoire' (op. cit., p. 107).

Taine, according to Schaepdryver, is a man haunted by the *mal du siècle* and his whole work is a sort of *Confession d'un enfant du siècle*. The critic continues:

> Que l'on n'objecte pas: que voilà une étrange Confession, sans confidences ni effusions passionnées, sans détails autobiographiques scabreux d'aucune sorte! Qu'une Confession puisse fort bien être écrite, sans que l'auteur s'ingère dans la vie privée, sans fournir aucun renseignement sur ce qui est strictement personnel et intime, l'œuvre de notre philosophe est là pour en fournir la preuve (op. cit., pp. 112–13).[50]

We have come round in full circle to the starting-point of our present sub-section: Romantic emotion and Determinist study.

[49] A. Aulard, *Taine, historien de la Révolution française*, Paris 1907, p. 328.

[50] Cf. 'Back of Taine's assertiveness, we can descry a depth of anguish and despair. Like Baudelaire and Flaubert, he belonged to a generation of wounded romanticists. Science—for he thought of himself as a scientist—was his refuge; his tower, not of ivory, but of grey steel. The fastness turned into a jail: he tried to be a Euclid, a Spinoza, a Darwin, and he was first of all a soul in prison' (Albert Guérard, in the Foreword to S. J. Kahn, *Science and Aesthetic Judgment: A Study in Taine's Critical Method*, London 1953, viii).

Are they as different as they might at first appear? Taine himself suggests the answer:

> Ce mal [awareness of the unattainable] a été nommé la maladie du siècle; il y a quarante ans qu'elle était dans toute sa force, et, sous la froideur apparente ou l'impassibilité morne de l'esprit positif, elle subsiste encore aujourd'hui (*PhA*, I, 97).

Unamuno and Ganivet would doubtless have agreed. Certainly they were similarly aware of the tormenting limitations of human existence. 'El sentimiento primordial del hombre,' says Unamuno, 'es el dolor, la molestia, la sensación de obstáculo y estorbo que experimenta su voluntad al chocar con el mundo' (1892; IV, 294–5). 'Nada hay más doloroso,' adds Ganivet, 'que ambicionar grandezas que están fuera de nuestra acción' (NML, 57), 'Toute ma vie,' lamented René, 'j'ai eu devant les yeux une création à la fois immense et imperceptible, et un abîme ouvert à mes côtés.'[51] It is just such an ideal 'création' that we have seen Taine, Unamuno and Ganivet aspiring to; it is just such an 'abîme' that we have seen them seeking to overleap with their determinist rationalizing.

## 5. UNAMUNO'S REACTION AGAINST TAINE

There can be no doubt, I suggest, about Taine's profound influence on Unamuno and Ganivet during the 1890's. Yet, as we have seen (above, p. 47), by 1900 Unamuno was describing Taine as 'el gran falsificador francés' and, a few years later, as 'un portentoso falsificador y sistemático caricaturista'. Must we assume from this that by 1900 Unamuno's thought had undergone such a profound change that our findings so far—all indicative of a Taine-like application of the new determinism—cease to be relevant? Unamuno's repeated insistence on his own consistency of thought does not support such an assumption (above, pp. 4–6). Nor does the evidence of his later writings, as we shall see in Part III. 'Los hechos que expone Taine son un revestimiento de conceptos previos,' wrote Unamuno in 1907; 'no salen las ideas de los hechos, sino que vienen éstos, hábilmente seleccionados, a corroborar aquéllas' (III, 691). In the light of the previous subsection one might find Unamuno's comment even more accurate

---

[51] Chateaubriand, *OC*, XVI (1826), 153.

if, instead of 'conceptos previos', he had written 'obsesiones personales'. But with or without this re-wording, the same charge can surely be directed equally against Unamuno himself. This, at least, is what I have sought to demonstrate in the preceding pages. Nor shall we find any notable change in his later writings. As Unamuno said of Taine:

> Puede un hombre ser estudioso, sincero y amante de la verdad y ser falsificador y caricaturista. Su genio mismo le impulsaba a ello (1907; III, 593).

The only truly impersonal writers, he claims, are those who lack personality (1914; I, 421). And elsewhere:

> Nuestra filosofía, esto es, nuestro modo de comprender o de no comprender el mundo y la vida brota de nuestro sentimiento respecto a la vida misma. Y ésta, como todo lo afectivo, tiene raíces subconcientes, inconcientes tal vez (1913; VII, 110).

But the fact remains that during the first decade of the twentieth century Unamuno made several attacks on Taine. Did he perhaps, like Ortega y Gasset, wish to dissociate himself from a thinker who was coming increasingly under attack from critics and historians? It is possible, though in 1910 he still felt able to affirm that he found greater enjoyment reading Taine's historical works than he did by reading any French novelist (III, 538). The main reason for his criticism of Taine, I suggest, lies elsewhere. From his early readings of the French writer Unamuno had acquired a method. By 1895 he had made that method his own and, with the flexibility that it allowed, was using it, like Ganivet, to justify his own personal findings on Spain. In our writings on Spain, declared Ganivet in 1898, we shall be taken for 'dos ideólogos' (PE, 653), a description that Unamuno himself accepted (PE, 663). But there is perhaps no one more sensitive to the weaknesses of another thinker's *ideología* than an *ideólogo* working with the same basic premises and arriving at different conclusions. 'Unamuno es buen intencionado,' wrote Ganivet, the supreme *ideólogo*, in 1898, 'pero es demasiado ideólogo a pesar de sus aficiones a la Economía' (AG–LSLP, p. 106). Such a comment, I suggest, is not evidence of a divergent method, only of disagreement on the 'conceptos previous' that the method has been made to serve. It is a sign of maturity, an indication that, despite the common method, one is working out one's own solutions (or working off one's own obsessions)—as indeed I have tried to demonstrate in my comparative study of *En torno al casticismo* and *Idearium español*.[52] I find no justification for attributing greater significance than this to Unamuno's criticisms of Taine. Nowhere, I think, does Unamuno criticize Taine's underlying determinism; only— as with Ganivet—the arguments and findings that Taine's determinism is used to justify.[53]

---

[52] On this point recall also p. 16 n.5.

[53] There is room here for what could be a fascinating enquiry into the possible correlation between Unamuno's change of attitude to Taine and his change of attitude to Europeanization. In his early years of maximum receptivity his emphasis, both on a personal plane and on a national plane, is on 'immersion in varied experience' as a means of self-discovery (above, p. 35): 'Cosquilleos de fuera despiertan *lo que duerme en el seno de nuestra conciencia*' (*ETC*, 853, my italics). Once awakened by foreign influences to personal and national self-awareness, Unamuno feels able to affirm this awareness in personal and national terms already evident in *En torno al casticismo* (most notably perhaps in his emphasis on 'la fe viva que no consiste en creer lo que no vimos, sino en crear lo que no vemos', 797). It is in this context, I suggest, that one should consider his declared aim to 'españolizar a Europa' (MU–PJI, 9 May 1905). Here as elsewhere I attribute less pivotal significance to the crisis of 1897 than scholars are now wont to do.

# III

TOWARDS THE UNDERSTANDING
OF THE 1898 MOVEMENT

## I. INTRODUCTION

Angel Ganivet y Miguel de Unamuno, esos dos nuncios y arqui-
tectos del futuro (Pedro Salinas, *Ensayos de literatura hispánica*,
Madrid 1958, p. 291).

So far I have tried, firstly, to demonstrate the basic similariites
between *En torno al casticismo* and *Idearium español* and, secondly,
to explain those similarities as the outcome of a characteristically
nineteenth-century view of civilization in which science and
religious crisis both appear to have played a significant part. It
remains for me to consider the influence of the works on others.

But I can give, at best, only a few indications of probable
influence. For as we have seen in an earlier section, evolutionism
and its associated methodology were characteristic of advanced
Spanish thought in the later 1890's and for some thinkers at least
the acceptance or rejection of evolutionism and its consequences
was a basic criterion by which to distinguish *lo nuevo* from *lo viejo*.
Taine's influence, then, did not operate alone. In establishing
parallels between his writings on the one hand and *En torno al
casticismo* and *Idearium español* on the other, it has been a temptation
to indicate also parallels with Spencer and other non-Spanish
writers of the time. No clear dividing-line is possible between the
specific influence of Taine and the more general influence of
contemporary intellectual currents. Similarly, it is impossible, I
find, to distinguish in a whole generation of Spanish writers
between the influence of the two works here studied and that of
the intellectual environment that helped to produce them. Even
Taine's influence, we have seen, did not reach Spain only through
the medium of *En torno al casticismo* and *Idearium español*. From
1893 to 1900 'La España Moderna' published fifteen volumes of
Taine's writings in translation (besides another fifteen by Spencer,
his principal co-evolutionist).[1] 'Toda la generación española que
ahora llega a las preocupaciones intelectuales,' wrote Ortega y

---

[1] Only Tolstoy occupied a comparable position in the publication lists of
'La España Moderna' and his influence, notably on Unamuno, has still to be
studied (There is much of *Del sentimiento trágico* . . ., for example, in the final
part of *War and Peace*). Zola, too, was strongly represented in the same lists,
but principally by his short biographies (in the series 'Biografías de Extran-
jeros Ilustres').

Gasset in 1908, 'ha sido educada, mal educada, por Hipólito Taine' (I, 86). We cannot reasonably assume that this education, or mis-education, reached the Spanish reading public only through *En torno al casticismo* and *Idearium español*.

Nevertheless, Unamuno and Ganivet, it seems, were the first Spanish writers to draw from Taine an integrated, comprehensive system with which to study the long-standing problem of Spain, and in a fairly close perusal of Spanish books and periodicals of the period 1895–98 I have found little outside these two writers corresponding to the material studied above in Part I, Sections 3–4. There is abundant evidence of the study of Spain as a problem (Section 1), even as a psychological problem viewed from a would-be medical standpoint (Section 2). There is even evidence of other writers' insistence on the need for national self-knowledge (Section 3a). But I have found nothing significant corresponding to Unamuno's and Ganivet's progression from complexity to a nucleus (Section 3b), nor to the means by which they seek to explain that nucleus (Section 3c), nor to the means by which they attempt to confirm their findings (Section 3d). Consequently, I have noted nothing, either, corresponding to the application of their findings (Sections 4a–c) or to the further consequences of their method studied in Part II, Sections 3–4.[2]

In fundamental aspects, then—aspects that were to exert a notable influence during the following decades—*En torno al casticismo* and *Idearium español* were apparently forerunners in Spain and can perhaps reasonably be considered to occupy a privileged position. But influences tend to exert themselves only when the ground is well prepared. In a general way, we have seen, the ground had been—and was being—prepared by the growing influence in Spain of Taine, determinism and the natural sciences; in a more specific way it was prepared, quite suddenly, by the national crisis of 1898. It is this latter point I aim to demonstrate in the following section. The fame of *En torno al casticismo* and *Idearium español*, I shall suggest, was to a large extent a product of Spain's 'Disaster year'. Thereafter, without wishing to distinguish between the specific influence of those two works

---

[2] I make all these statements with misgivings, conscious that I have been able to cover only a small part of the available background material. I offer them, then—in Sir Karl Popper's terms—as 'conjectures', eager that others should bring forward their own 'refutations'.

and the general influence of evolutionary currents of thought, I shall consider some of the consequences.

## 2. *En torno al casticismo* AND *Idearium español*: THEIR RISE TO FAME

### (a) *The initial impact of the works*

Initially *En torno al casticismo* and *Idearium español* attracted only limited attention. 'El *Idearium*,' wrote Ganivet's friend Nicolás María López in July 1898, 'a pesar de su importancia, pasó desapercibido: nadie (que yo sepa) dijo una palabra de él; fuera de Granada, la prensa de Madrid [. . .] no se fijó siquiera en este libro de tan jugosa labor intelectual'.[3] In fact, the neglect was rather less than these lines suggest, but when Ganivet died four months later (on 29 November 1898) the Spanish press in general was clearly embarrassed by its lack of knowledge of his writings and, except for *El Globo*, *El Imparcial* and *Madrid Cómico*, which printed substantial and enthusiastic appreciations by personal friends of the deceased writer, newspapers carried only brief obituary notices of almost identical wording. '¡Un desconocido!' exclaimed Enrique Mercader in *Vida Nueva*, '¡Un hombre que ha necesitado morir de una manera extraña para que la gente se entere de que ha existido!' (11 December 1898). Thereafter, acclaim came rapidly. On 3 March 1899 Rubén Darío referred to Ganivet as 'quizás la más adamantina concreción' of the new thought of the country and observed:

> Ganivet no tenía enemigos, y por lo general, si conversáis con cualquiera de los intelectuales españoles, os dirá: 'Era el más brillante y el más sólido de todos los de su generación' (*España contemporánea*, Paris 1901, p. 84).

Later in 1899 a German scholar, Hans Parlow, looked back to Ganivet as the one great promise amidst the general barrenness and stagnation of contemporary Spanish literature. The work for which he was principally known and esteemed was *Idearium español*.[4]

---

[3] Prologue to Angel Ganivet, *Cartas finlandesas*, Granada 1898, p. xxi.
[4] For a fuller treatment of the above see HR, 12–18, 173–85.

Nicolás María López was to attribute the sudden change to Navarro Ledesma's obituary article in *El Imparcial* and this doubtless played an important part, as did López's own obituary tribute. But this hardly explains the fact that amidst all Ganivet's writings special enthusiasm was accorded to the methodologically unsound, factually inaccurate and logically untenable *Idearium español*.

To Unamuno's *En torno al casticismo* fame came more slowly, and the years following its first publication reveal a somewhat pitiful and none too dignified clamour by the author for public recognition. A detail of etymology gave Unamuno the opportunity he had been looking for to enter into correspondence with Clarín, during the publication of *En torno al casticismo* in *La España Moderna* (MU–LA, 28 May 1895), and lest this most influential of critics should have missed the point of his writing, Unamuno declared it openly in his next letter: he wished to know if Clarín had read his works and whether he would care to draw the public's attention to them, 'que sin recomendación es muy difícil salir adelante' (31 May 1895). Clarín complied and praised *En torno al casticismo* in *Heraldo*. He also referred to it in a letter to Unamuno as 'fuerte, nuevo, original' but annoyed Unamuno by later describing it in print merely as 'discreto'.[5] The announcement in the press of the death of Clarín's mother prompted Unamuno to renew their correspondence, expressing his condolences and drawing attention to the forthcoming publication of *Paz en la guerra* (28 September 1896). He sent Clarín a copy three months later, reminded him about the work in two further letters, and finally, incensed by Clarín's review of *Tres ensayos* in which the critic declared openly that he had not yet read *Paz en la guerra* and was insufficiently enthusiastic about *Tres ensayos*, wrote a long, impertinent letter of pique and thwarted ambition, describing himself as 'un espíritu inquieto, sediento de atención, ávido de que se le oiga' who was not receiving the attention he felt he deserved:

> creo firmemente que tendría un público diez, doce o cien veces mayor, con sólo que se decidiesen a leerme, con sólo que acabara esa leyenda de mi sibilítico enrevesamiento y la de mi sabiduría.

[5] There is a retrospective account in Unamuno's letter to Clarín dated 9 May 1900.

Creo más, creo que, con algún esfuerzo, llegaría a ser popular, y lo ansío (9 May 1900).[6]

But despite the continuing insistence of reviewers and personal correspondents on his heavy erudition and lack of clarity in expression Unamuno's merits and authority were in fact well recognized by 1900. As early as 1894 his proclaimed socialism had been celebrated with front-page honours in *La Lucha de Clases* and *El Socialista*, and conservative opponents were quick to single out Unamuno as a notable threat to Spain's social edifice.[7] Moreover, in 1897 *Paz en la guerra* had attracted generally favourable comment and been described by Rodrigo Soriano as an 'obra notabilísima' by 'uno de los más atrevidos y profundos pensadores con que cuenta España'.[8] In October 1898 Unamuno himself felt able to assure the still little known Ganivet, 'sin presunción de mi parte, que un artículo mío puede darle algunos lectores de calidad',[9] and in December of the same year he informed Arzadun that, despite the difficulty of establishing oneself as a writer, he himself was now beginning to 'recoger producto pecuniaro de mis escritos'. In 1899–1900 further letters reveal his delight at his

[6] Clarín's article appeared in *Los Lunes de El Imparcial*, 7 May 1900. A fortnight earlier Unamuno had claimed for himself a right that he repeatedly denied to Clarín:

¿Crearme la obligación de leer lo que en España se produce, aunque sólo sea lo más granado de ello? ¡Dios me libre! ¡No, amigo Orbe, no! Me va muy bien sin leer apenas nuestra producción española contemporánea, ignorándola casi por completo (25 April 1900; VIII, 192).

Moreover, eighteen months earlier, at a time when he was still looking to Clarín for public support, he drew Ganivet's attention to an article of his own, confessing that 'no poco de ello lo digo para zaherir bajo cuerda a Clarín y otros por el estilo' (20 November 1898; in *Insula* 35). Unamuno as a person does not come well out of this affair.

[7] 'Un socialista más' (in *La Lucha de Clases*, 21 October 1894), 'Bienvenido sea' (in *El Socialista*, 2 November 1894). The following will serve as an example of conservative reaction:

Las bases todas del edificio social son rudamente combatidas en la colección de esta revista anárquico-comunista [*La Ciencia Social* of Barcelona] y a veces por hombres que, como don Miguel de Unamuno, están a sueldo del Estado en concepto de catedráticos de Universidades (Damián Isern, *Del desastre nacional y sus causas*, Madrid 1899, p. 41).

[8] In *Los Lunes de El Imparcial*, 26 April 1897.

[9] Letter of 14 October 1898; reproduced in *Insula* 35 (15 November 1948). Unamuno is referring to the article he subsequently published in *La Epoca* (23 October 1898).

growing fame. 'Empieza para mí la época de la siega y la cosecha,' he wrote to Jiménez Ilundain on 24 May 1899, and a few months later: 'Este año es el mejor que se me presenta. Parece ser el de la siega, después de años de siembra' (16 August 1899). 'Veo con gran satisfacción,' his friend wrote on 1 May 1900, 'que su nombre se está haciendo sitio en España. Va Vd. por buen camino.'

Because of its initial appearance in article form and the consequent scarcity of critical comment it is difficult to know what part *En torno al casticismo* played in this growing fame. Eight years after its first appearance, in a review of the first book edition, Gómez de Baquero was to describe it as 'la primera obra importante de Unamuno, por lo menos la primera que se difundió entre el público y dio a su autor la fama, que desde entonces ha ido creciendo, de escritor original y pensador profundo',[10] and R. D. Perés affirmed that its publication in 1895 'atrajo la atención de muchos hacia el nombre del autor', adding, however, 'no le reconocieron todos en seguida, porque el reconocimiento del público suele ser, entre nosotros, lento y difícil, y las cualidades especiales de Unamuno añadían aun dificultades, como las añaden todavía hoy para el gusto de algunos'.[11] Indeed, as his letters reveal, Unamuno in 1899 was still trying unsuccessfully to have his five essays republished in book form. Moreover, as we have seen, the earlier popularity of *Idearium español* appears to have been one of the factors that led a number of writers to concede priority to Ganivet in Spain's 'second Golden Age'. Yet again, neither Rubén Darío in *España contemporánea* nor Hans Parlow in 'Estado de la literatura española' mentioned *En torno al casticismo*, though both were witnesses to Ganivet's remarkable posthumous success. More surprisingly, Rafael Altamira considered *Idearium español* at length in his *Psicología del pueblo español* (Madrid 1902) but made no reference to *En torno al casticismo* and seems to imply in a footnote to the second edition that he had not then known the work (p. 114). Perhaps we must look for an explanation in the fact that the work had appeared only in article form, too early to serve the special public needs of 1898, and that happily there was no reason in the Disaster year to remind the public of it in enthusiastic obituary notices. When the work did finally appear in book form, at the end of 1902 or the

[10] In *La España Moderna*, March 1903, p. 145.
[11] In *La Vanguardia*, 27 March 1903.

beginning of 1903, it was received both inside and outside Spain as a notable work by an established authority, 'l'un des penseurs les plus originaux, l'un des écrivains les plus alertes, et peut-être le littérateur universitaire le plus goûté en Espagne depuis que Clarín n'est plus'.[12] Gómez de Baquero found in it 'el método de Buckle', Maeztu 'los métodos de Taine'.[13] Maeztu was nearer the truth but Gómez de Baquero was not mistaken. Buckle and Taine both belong to the remarkable generation born 1820–34 that pioneered the application to civilization of concepts and methods derived from the natural sciences. With the success of *Idearium español* and *En torno al casticismo* these concepts and methods were finally established in Spain and shown to be relevant to Spanish national problems.

But why were the works so successful? The explanation, I suggest, can scarcely lie in their intrinsic value. And why did they rise to fame only after the Disaster of 1898? I have referred to 'the special public needs of 1898'. I look, then, for an explanation in the historical context of the Spanish reading public. To justify this we must consider the impact of Spain's Disaster year.


## (b) *The Disaster of 1898*

Nunca como en 1898 fue evidente nuestra inferioridad (1904; Miguel S. Oliver, *Entre dos Españas*, Barcelona 1906, p. 74).

The first Cuban war had been brought to an end by the Peace of Zanjón in February 1878. But by the spring of 1895 the island was in revolt again and, under the leadership, first of Martí, then of Gómez and Maceo, the revolt spread rapidly through the rural areas. General Weyler's hard-line policy of concentration camps contained the situation during 1896 but conciliatory administrative reforms approved in March 1897 proved inadequate and Sagasta's introduction of autonomy in November 1897 satisfied neither revolutionaries nor unionists. Amidst the ensuing riots the American cruiser 'Maine' anchored in Havana harbour for the proclaimed purpose of protecting American lives and property. Three weeks later, on 15 February 1898, the ship was blown

[12] G. C[irot], in *Bulletin Hispanique* V, 1903, 198.
[13] E. Gómez de Baquero, in *La España Moderna*, March 1903, 145–51; Ramiro de Maeztu, in *La Lectura* III (1903), 1, 282–6.

up, allegedly by a Spanish mine. Under pressure from public opinion the American government issued an ultimatum to Spain to withdraw from Cuba immediately (approved by President MacKinley on 20 April) and five days later declared war. Raymond Carr has summarized the main events of the following months:

> The first blow fell on the Philippines where the army had been successful against a separatist revolt. The Spanish Pacific squadron was a fighting force on paper only; in May 1898, Admiral Dewey, in a battle which lasted an hour, blew the Spanish ships out of the sea from the safe range of two thousand yards, as if they had been practice targets. In the Atlantic, Admiral Cervera knew he must be defeated should his squadron be ordered to the Antilles. His advice was rejected by the government and a board of admirals who could not face up to a confession of impotence and an immediate peace; Cervera's commanders later maintained 'in honour and conscience their conviction that the government in Madrid was determined that the fleet should be destroyed as soon as possible in order to find a means of arriving rapidly at peace'— an accusation which cannot be entirely dismissed. Once in the Antilles, Cervera, without coal to operate, shut himself in Santiago Bay, only to be ordered out of harbour and to certain destruction by the blockading American fleet. On 3 July 1898 the whole Spanish squadron was destroyed outside Santiago at the cost of one casualty to the Americans. Cervera had to swim from his flagship and the one modern ship with speed enough to escape ran out of coal. The two most complete naval disasters of modern times meant that Spain had to sign away, in the Treaty of Paris, Cuba, Puerto Rico and the Philippines (*Spain, 1808–1939*, Oxford 1966, p. 387).

A three-year drain on men and resources had ended finally in swift and decisive defeat. Cánovas's resolve to answer war with war if the United States intervened, Admiral Beránger's assurance of victory, General Weyler's offer to invade the United States, the patriotic clamours of the Spanish press, the revival of enthusiasm in the Spanish people themselves when it seemed that their forces were at last to be in conflict with a recognizable enemy instead of with disease—all had come to nothing. In bringing the war to an official close the Paris Peace Treaty proclaimed aloud Spain's defeat as a colonial power. The following lines from an editorial leader in *El Liberal* ('el periódico de mayor circulación de España') give some indication of the reaction in the Spanish press:

Hoy se firmará en París el Tratado por el cual renuncia España a la posesión de Cuba, de Puerto Rico y de Filipinas.

Hoy se cerrará para siempre la leyenda de oro, abierta por Cristóbal Colón en 1492, y por Fernando de Magallanes en 1521.

Los tres meses y medio invertidos en estériles negociaciones diplomáticas habían embotado la sensibilidad del pueblo español, y héchole perder en parte la noción de su inmensa desdicha.

Hoy, ante el despojo material, despertará de su sopor, sentirá el desgarrón en la carne viva, y recobrará, para maldecir y abominar de los que a tal abismo le han empujado, el uso de la propia conciencia.

No somos ya potencia colonial, ni tenemos nada de lo que todavía constituye el orgullo y el provecho de las de segundo y tercer orden.

Holanda, Dinamarca, Portugal, conservan y explotan vastos territorios en Asia, Africa y Oceanía.

Nosotros lo hemos perdido todo. Apenas si nos quedan en el golfo de Guinea algunos islotes inhospitalarios y en el Norte de Marruecos unos palmos de costa y media docena de peñascos bautizados con el siniestro nombre de presidios.

Al cabo de cuatrocientos años volvemos de las Indias Occidentales, por nosotros descubiertas, y del extremo Oriente, por nosotros civilizado, como inquilinos a quienes se desahucia, como intrusos a quienes se echa, como pródigos a quienes se incapacita, como perturbadores a quienes se recluye.

Desde hoy no será el símbolo nacional un león colocado como señor entre dos hemisferios.

Lo será uno de esos infelices repatriados que, sin armas, sin sangre, y casi sin vida, regresan de las que fueron nuestras colonias.

En ellos está representada España, consumida por la anemia, rendida por la inanición, más que por la derrota, y tan privada de energías como de recursos ('Día nefasto', in *El Liberal*, 28 November 1898).

Such lamentation did not come totally unheralded. The Spanish press during the years 1896–98 bears witness to a growing awareness of national adversity and to a consequently widening breach in the pompous self-satisfaction of the Restoration. On 1 January 1897 the Madrid periodical *Apuntes* published a long and depressing review of the year just ended:

En Cuba guerra con los negros, con los malos españoles, con el clima y con los Estados Unidos, únicos que sostienen, moral y materialmente, la rebelión. En Filipinas guerra con los malayos, con los masones y quizá con otros enemigos que no pasan por tales [. . .].

De todo lo anterior [it concluded] se deduce que nos haría un señalado servicio la divina Providencia si nos diera un año 97 un poquito mejor que el 96.

But 1897 was not better than 1896, and 1898 was worse. In September 1897 Joaquín Dicenta noted 'las dudas, los recelos, las desconfianzas, los ecepticismos (pasajeros) de la generación presente'.[14] '¿Por qué tanto desastre, tanta confusión y tanta incertidumbre?', asked Enrique Lluria a few months later, when the brief upsurge of national fervour during April 1898 had been stemmed by the defeat at Cavite.[15] The Treaty of Paris was the final indignity. 'El buque, desarbolado, sin máquina y sin timón, se va a pique';[16] 'todos nuestros históricos lauros no nos sirven para maldita la cosa'.[17] Two years later, in what is probably the best contemporary study of the period, Luis Morote summed up the general impact of the defeat: 'Si ha habido quiebra, no es sólo la de la energía militar, sino la quiebra y ruina de un concepto total y orgánico de nuestros destinos en el mundo y también de nuestras fuerzas.'[18] It was an age of lamentation and indignation, wrote Azorín a few years later; an age of negations, declared Maeztu; an age of shattered historical ideals, said Unamuno; an age of shame and rejection of the past, added Pío Baroja.

Perhaps inevitably the lamentation was accompanied by anger: 'el maldecir y abominar de los que a tal abismo le han empujado' (above, p. 106). The pre-1898 trickle of protest, represented notably by Francisco Pi y Margall among the older generation and, since 1896, by Ramiro de Maeztu among the younger writers, grew to a flood during 1898 under the impact of successive defeats in Cuba and the Philippines. *Vida Nueva*, which first appeared on 12 June 1898, was notably in the forefront, partly no doubt because it was not constrained as other papers and periodicals were by earlier editorial positions. In the first number Vicente Blasco Ibáñez lamented the 'sublime estupidez del hombre' in giving himself up to violence, bloodshed and death, Jacinto

---

[14] In *Germinal* 19, 10 September 1897.
[15] In *Vida Nueva* 2, 19 June 1898.
[16] In *El Liberal*, 28 November 1898.
[17] In *La Vanguardia*, 30 November 1898.
[18] *La moral de la derrota*, Madrid 1900, p. vii.

Octavio Picón found the underlying stagnation and lack of direction even worse than the war, Zeda declared that the people had been deceived by lies, and the Socialist leader Pablo Iglesias, in an article that was to have considerable repercussions, castigated both government and press for supporting the war and called for immediate peace whatever the terms imposed by the Americans. Similarly, in the second number blame was cast by Eusebio Blasco on 'el sentimentalismo y el honor nacional' and by Zeda (Francisco Fernández Villegas) on the political system of *turnos* which prevented the existence of a responsible opposition party. In the third number Zeda implied criticism of the armed forces, and unsigned editorials criticized General Polavieja ('¡¡El general de los jesuitas!!'), the religious orders, and the state's monopoly of power. Also in the third number Unamuno returned to his earlier condemnation of the '*damnosa hereditas* de nuestras glorias castizas' (*ETC*, 805) in his well-known article '¡Muera Don Quijote!'[19]

Other papers and periodicals gradually joined the clamour, notably *El Liberal* with an impressive series of declarations by leading politicians, intellectuals and industrialists.[20] Conservatives blamed Liberals, Liberals blamed Conservatives, Republicans blamed both, and Pablo Iglesias, reminding readers that Spain had no Socialist member of Parliament, blamed all three: 'Cánovas y Sagasta han pecado por acción, los republicanos por omisión, olvidando que se gobierna tanto desde la oposición como desde el poder' (4 October 1898). Nor is it merely a question of this

[19] The immediate historical context of this article has been strangely overlooked. Juan Villegas, for example, in 'El "¡Muera Don Quijote!" de Miguel de Unamuno' (in *BHS* 44, 1967, 49–53), makes the obviously valid equations, Don Quixote = historic Spain (the nation and its glories)/ Alonso Quijano = intra-historic Spain (the people and their peaceful, unchanging lives), but makes no reference to the *Vida Nueva* anti-war campaign of which the article forms part—and which presumably explains the especially condemnatory tone of the article.

[20] Published under the collective titles 'Cerradas las Cortes' (16 September–10 October 1898), 'Habla el país' (18 October–24 November 1898) and 'Firmada la paz' (2–10 December 1898). These have now been collected and republished in volume form by Hélène Tzitsikas under the title *El pensamiento español (1898–1899)* (Mexico 1967), together with a series of replies by distinguished personalities to the *Heraldo de Aragón*'s question, '¿Qué piensa usted, qué teme, qué espera del año 1899?' (First published 1–4 January 1899).

party or that party, he continued; 'fracasaron todos, políticos, militares, administradores'. Similar opinions appeared frequently, especially in commentators not content to argue within a *turno pacífico* context of Liberals and Conservatives. 'Ha fracasado todo,' declared the former Republican Minister, José Fernando González: 'el ejército, la marina, la administración activa, la justicia, la Universidad, la Iglesia' (1 October 1898). Moreover, these views were apparently shared by a large part of the Spanish population. 'Acabo de recorrer media España,' claimed Dr Esquerdo, 'y no he oído más que una sola voz, la voz del pueblo, que pide se vayan de una vez, para no volver más, los que nos han desgobernado, empobrecido y conducido a la derrota. Esa es la opinión unánime en todas las provincias' (26 September 1898). Santiago Ramón y Cajal made a similar point: Spain's present decadence, he declared, is attributed by many to 'la impericia política, guerrera y administrativa de nuestras clases directoras' (26 October 1898).

Newspapers and periodicals were backed up soon by books and pamphlets written by ex-soldiers, sailors, journalists, politicians, educationalists . . .: Luis Pérez de Vargas's *La opinión y la marina* (El Ferrol 1898), Carlos Saavedra y Magdalena's *Algunas obser-vaciones sobre los desastres de la marina española* . . . (El Ferrol 1898), Manuel Corral's *¡El desastre! Memorias de un voluntario en la campaña de Cuba* (Barcelona 1899), Vicente de Cortijo's *Apuntes para la historia de la pérdida de nuestras colonias por un testigo presencial* (Madrid 1899), Vital Fité's *Las desdichas de la patria: Políticos y frailes* (Madrid 1899), J. Rodríguez Martínez's *Los desastres y la regeneración de España: Relatos e impresiones* (La Coruña 1899), Rafael María de Labra's *El pesimismo de última hora* (Madrid 1899), Damián Isern's *Del desastre nacional y sus causas* (Madrid 1899), the anonymous *¿Hispania fuit? Reflexiones dolorosas y provechosas* (Madrid 1899) . . . Charges and counter-charges: against army and naval officers for their professional incompetence; against colonial administrators for their corruption; against religious orders for their corrupt and oppressive feudal rule, notably in the Philip-pines; against the government for its ignorance or disregard of basic economic and psychological realities, for its lack of an ade-quate colonial policy, for its surrender of national interests to private and sectarian pressures, for its failure to supply the armed forces with the necessary weapons and equipment; against the press, too, for aiding and abetting the government in its deception of the Spanish people, and against educationalists for encouraging the acceptance of historical illusions rather than the recognition of historical truths. These were the topics of the age. No doubt, as Unamuno himself was to suggest a few years later, this flood of criticism, 'aquel nuestro movimiento espiritual del 98, aquella refriega de pluma, que halló su principal tribuna en *Vida Nueva*', was in part at least a means of washing one's own hands of responsibility: 'Fue un "¡sálvese quien pueda!" En el derrumbamiento moral de la patria nosotros, los jóvenes de entonces, nos lavábamos, nuevos Pilatos, las manos y acusábamos. Acusábamos a todos y a todo; pero atentos a salvar nuestra irresponsabilidad, nuestra personalidad' (1916; III, 1173).

But as the names so far mentioned indicate, the young were not alone in their hand-washing. Nor can their criticisms be considered merely as a form of personal self-defence. What they amount to, in fact, is a national crisis of confidence: a loss of faith in the nation's ruling minorities, a loss of faith in the nation's traditional ideals and a *threatening* loss of faith in the nation itself. But my reservation on the final point is important. If the nation's rulers can be shown to have been incompetent or if traditional ideals are found to have been mistaken, if it can be believed that the real Spain lies elsewhere than in its leaders and historical traditions, one can perhaps still retain one's faith in the nation. During the years 1898–99 attacks on leading figures and traditional policies abound in the Spanish press; so do expressions of despair and clamours for new ideals; so also, increasingly, do declarations of faith in the hidden qualities of the hitherto neglected Spanish people.

*Vida Nueva* is again an invaluable guide. In the first number Eusebio Blasco finds millions of Spaniards clamouring for new life, for a way out of the stagnation of the last fifty years: '*Todo* es antiguo entre nosotros,' he declares; 'lo *nuevo* se impone, se ansía por todos una solución a tantas desdichas, a tantas miserias, a tantos desalientos, a tantas indiferencias, a tanto tiempo perdido.' But what is the solution? He does not say but in the second number makes it clear that peace is the necessary preliminary and that this outweighs 'el sentimentalismo y la pasión del honor nacional'. Meanwhile, also in the first number, Zeda declares: 'Se siente la necesidad de fe, de nuevos ideales, de sinceridad y de entusiasmos;

hay impaciencia porque desaparezcan mentiras en que nadie cree',
and Jacinto Octavio Picón comments:

> No hay nación de Europa que no tenga aspiración definida:
> Inglaterra, valerse de las discordias ajenas convirtiendo el mundo
> en mostrador de sus mercaderías; Rusia [...]; Austria [...];
> Alemania [...]; Italia [...]; Francia [...]. ¿Cuál es nuestro ideal?
> Ni la influencia en el Mediterráneo, ni la posesión del Norte de
> Africa, ni la Unión Ibérica, ni la reivindicación de Gibraltar. ...
> Nada.

There is dissatisfaction, then, with the misfortunes inherited
from the past and with traditionally accepted values. Writers feel
a need for faith and enthusiasm. But the old ideals will no longer
serve. One must look elsewhere.

Two further articles by Zeda press the point and carry us a
stage further in our argument. In the third number of *Vida Nueva*
(26 June 1898) he writes bitterly of 'la vergüenza nacional'. Fear
drove the government (N.B.) into war and fear now brings it out
of war. But yes, let us have peace:

> ¡Y el honor nacional! ... Hemos convenido ya en que el honor
> nacional es una cursería, propia de pueblos atrasados y semi-
> salvajes. A la luz de esta filosofía novísima, lo mejor que hay que
> hacer es quemar el libro de nuestra historia [...]. Ahora somos
> prácticos. ¿El honor? ... Valiente tontería. Pidamos la paz con las
> manos bien repletas; hagamos salir a nuestros soldados de tierras
> que conquistaron nuestros antepasados y regaron con sangre las
> generaciones de cuatro siglos.

Despite the declared scorn of honour, the tone of the article suggests that the writer would have preferred victory ('al ver perdidos
los restos gloriosos de nuestra grandeza, contentémonos en llorar
como hembras ya que no hemos sabido defenderlos como hombres'). He has adopted a defensive sour-grapes attitude characteristic of the age. In his next article, however, Zeda turns from
national policy to a consideration of the Spanish people and in
doing so finds pointers to a solution that will become increasingly
common. Now, as in the days of Figaro, he declares, people are
saying that Spain is exhausted and that the Spanish race has lost
its former virtues. 'Aquí ya no hay entusiasmo, ni energía, ni
patriotismo, ni nada.' But the real Spain is not to be found on the
surface but underneath, in the ordinary people:

El país no hay que buscarlo en la corteza de España, sino en el *subsuelo*. Para conocerlo es menester penetrar en los talleres, recorrer los campos, bajar a las minas, estudiar sus cualidades, sus aptitudes, sus creencias, penetrar, en fin, en lo más íntimo de su ser (*Vida Nueva* 4, 3 July 1898).

In the ordinary people, he finds, Spanish energies are undiminished. The masses are not to be blamed for the country's present misfortunes; the fault lies with those who should lead, with the state of education, with the economy, with the lack of investment, with landlord absenteeism, with the system based on favouritism. Spain is not 'un pueblo muerto o moribundo, sino un pueblo atado de pies y manos'.

In short, Spain has been betrayed by its traditional leaders and misled by them into the acceptance of false ideals and mistaken policies. Gradually, during the months following the defeat at Cavite, anger and despair yield increasingly to emphasis on the hidden and hitherto neglected merits of the ill-used Spanish people. It is to them that one must look for a new and better future:

Bajo la costra helada del presente dormitan, esperando una voz redentora, gérmenes vivos de entusiasmo y de fe. Romper la costra, sacudir la pereza, hacer que actúen las fuerzas que en potencia están sedimentadas en nuestro genio nacional, será bastante para que España resucite, una vez más, a nueva vida (April 1899; César Silió y Cortés, *Problemas del día*, Madrid 1900, p. 60).[21]

[21] I am concerned above with emphasis on the psychological potential of the Spanish people, urged by Unamuno under the name *renovación* (1898; III, 686–8), and leave aside the other principal positive response to the Disaster, about which Unamuno was less enthusiastic: that of economic, technological and educational *regeneración* (1898; III, 698–701). Under the latter heading Joaquín Costa was the key figure. Since his visit as a young man to the Paris Exhibition of 1867 he had worked tirelessly to probe and bridge the abyss between what he had observed in France and what he found in Spain. 'No había en 1898 ningún español que hubiese estudiado más aspectos diversos del problema español,' wrote Maeztu in 1911 (*Debemos a Costa*, p. 53). But it needed the Disaster to oust him from his scholarly retreat and open men's hearts—if not their understanding—to his message of national regeneration. Like Pi y Margall with his federal-autonomist doctrines, like Pablo Iglesias with his socialist beliefs, so also Costa with his ideal of *escuela, despensa* and *europeización* found unprecedented attention amidst the general foundering of traditional reputations and ideals that accompanied Spain's colonial misfortunes. As a Spaniard, said Costa, I detest the English

## (c) *The appeal of* En torno al casticismo *and* Idearium español

Y, sobre todo, procuremos, ya que es indispensable comenzar toda obra por los cimientos, restaurar los ideales en nuestra pobre España, contribuir, en la forma y en la medida que permita el esfuerzo de cada uno, a que renazcan la confianza y la fe en el porvenir, a que huya de nosotros el frío de muerte que ha seguido al desastre (César Silió y Cortés, *Problemas del día*, Madrid 1900, p. 6).

race, but as a man I revere it as 'la que más cantidad de labor sólida ha traído hasta ahora a la Historia, la educadora más sabia entre cuantas ha tenido la Humanidad' (cit. Maeztu, p. 34). Others applied a similar notion more obviously related to the defeat of 1898. The United States, it was said, had defeated Spain because the Americans had better schools, more factories and a sounder economy. Spaniards must learn from their victors.

'Los periódicos abrieron sus columnas a la palabra nueva' (Maeztu, p. 63). 'En este momento tenemos todos la boca llena de una palabra: "Regeneración"' (*La Vanguardia*, 30 November 1898). Three months later, in a published reply to a would-be contributor to *Vida Nueva*, the editors commented: '"Regeneración"—¡Siempre esta palabra! ¿Nos creerá usted si le decimos que los cincuenta y tantos artículos recibidos en poco tiempo sobre este o *esta* tema dicen todos poco más o menos lo que el suyo?' (26 February 1899). Two months later still, César Silió y Cortés wrote of 'el martilleo continuo con que hiere [los] oídos la palabra "Regeneración", repetida en las hojas impresas de los periódicos, en revistas, en discursos y libros' ('Después del desastre', 1899; in *Problemas del día*, Madrid 1900, p. 4). Also in 1899 Ricardo Macías Picavea published *El problema nacional (Hechos, causas, remedios)*, and the following year Luis Morote published *La moral de la derrota*. The way seemed set for new national prosperity. But the movement was short-lived. By 1905 one writer at least was lamenting its demise:

Después de la rendición de Santiago, hubo un momento solemne, de verdadera y consoladora esperanza; un instante de contrición magnánima en que cuando menos las clases directoras en masa parecían inclinadas a algo grande y eficaz, a un movimiento de conversión de las fuerzas e impulsos nacionales hacia derroteros de trabajo restaurador y orientaciones de nueva y fecunda vida. No faltaba más que el empujón decisivo para que la masa vacilante cayera, toda y de golpe, alrededor de un nuevo centro dinámico, de un nuevo principio de vitalidad nacional, en forma y con energía comparables a los ejemplos de Alemania y el Japón [. . .]. Ahora parece que las multitudes vacilantes vuelven poco a poco la cabeza, recobran su primitiva posición, invaden el antiguo cauce, reinciden en la habitual confianza e indiferentismo, vuelven a las panaceas exclusivamente políticas: anticlericalismo, reacción, república, dictadura . . . [. . .]. Los partidarios del *statu quo* y del sistema de calmas engañosas han sofocado hábilmente el movimiento de emulación que

In studying the impact of the Disaster of 1898 we have touched, I suggest, at the very heart of the rise to fame of *En torno al casticismo* and *Idearium español*. For in both works, under the influence of determinism and more specifically of Taine whose own major work had been a response to national disaster,[22] the two authors had anticipated the characteristic defensive attitudes that defeat was to force upon their fellow-countrymen during 1898: Spain had been misled by its ruling minorities; its national ideals and policies were mistaken; the key to a more successful future lay with the anonymous mass of the people.

Thus, according to Unamuno in *En torno al casticismo* the nation's leaders, both on the Right and on the Left, 'se salen de la verdadera realidad de la cosas, de la eterna y honda realidad' (786); the newspapers, too, neglect the 'vida silenciosa de los millones de hombres sin historia' (793); 'el camino de [la] regeneración [de España]' lies in Don Quixote's end and Alonso el Bueno's rebirth (791–2, 797–8); 'la tradición eterna es lo que deben buscar los

---

estuvo a punto de invadirnos y transformarnos, convirtiendo una derrota en occasión de posibles y grandes encumbramientos. Unas veces contrariando esa corriente, otras veces apoderándose de ella con pretexto de dirigirla y monopolizarla, le han hecho perder toda su fuerza y caudal (Miguel S. Oliver, 'Sobre *Terapéutica social*', 1905; in *Entre dos Españas*, Barcelona 1906, pp. 166–9).

Costa himself turned in vain from producers to intellectuals, to different political parties and finally, in ultimate despair, to the army. He died in 1911, an embittered recluse. With him, it seems, died also—at least until the coming of Primo de Rivera's dictatorship—the ideal of material *regeneración* as a significant factor in Spanish national life.

It is a fascinating subject that cries out for study. In the context of this work, however, I must regretfully leave it aside—as I leave socialism aside —as of only limited relevance to the long-term characteristics and influence of the writers with whom I am here principally concerned. I must also leave aside the question of a possibly significant relationship between the above mentioned national crisis of faith and the upsurge of regionalism. 'La fiebre catalana,' observed Miguel S. Oliver, 'nace del supuesto de considerar incorregibles a los políticos y al mecanismo director del Estado' (op. cit., p. 247).

[22] I refer, of course, to France's defeat in the Franco-Prussian War of 1870 and to the Commune of 1871. Together they caused Taine to revise his research plans and, 'en présence des ruines amoncelées par la guerre et la Commune, et du désarroi des esprits devant l'œuvre de reconstitution nationale' (*VC*, III, 155–6), to begin work on his monumental *Origines de la France contemporaine*.

videntes de todo pueblo, para elevarse a la luz, haciendo conciente
en ellos lo que en el pueblo es inconciente, para guiarle así mejor'
(794). Ganivet had been even more outspoken in *Idearium
español*: in his emphasis on the 'refinada estupidez de que dieron
repetidas muestras los hombres colocados al frente de los negocios
públicos en España' (231), in his allegation that there was not a
single one of them 'que vea y juzgue la política nacional desde un
punto elevado o por lo menos céntrico' (231), and in his own
attempt to show that the true future of Spain must be based not
on traditional policies but on a 'fuerza hoy desconocida, que vive
en estado latente en nuestra nación' (300). Unamuno's 'tradición
eterna' and Ganivet's 'espíritu territorial', then, are clearly an
anticipation of Zeda's 'subsuelo'.[23] Unamuno's desire that 'una
verdadera juventud, animosa y libre, rompiendo la malla que nos
ahoga y la monotonía uniforme en que estamos alineados, se
vuelva con amor a estudiar el pueblo que nos sustenta a todos'
(869) is equally clearly a foretaste of Zeda's own 1898 emphasis
on the necessity '[de] penetrar en los talleres, recorrer los campos,
bajar a las minas, estudiar sus cualidades, sus aptitudes, sus
creencias, [de] penetrar, en fin, en lo más íntimo de su ser'.

There were other probable reasons, too, for the appeal of the
two works. Not only did Unamuno and Ganivet anticipate the
characteristic responses of 1898–1899; they incorporated them
into a new and apparently scientifically based approach to the
long-standing problem of Spain. 'Al cabo,' says Maeztu, 'España
no se nos aparece como una afirmación ni como una negación,
sino como un problema' (in *Nuevo Mundo*, 13 March 1913). But
Spain is not an abstraction; Spain is a land and a people and a
civilization, and no one, reading these two works with this in
mind, can overlook the very considerable amount of affirmation
and negation that they both contain (for example, in *ETC*,
859–60, and *IE*, 157–60). Indeed, in the opening pages of *En torno*

[23] 'Lo que yo llamo espíritu territorial no es sólo tierra, es también
humanidad, es sentimiento de los trabajadores silenciosos de que usted
[Unamuno] habla' (AG, *PE*, 671). One may recall, too, a slightly later
statement by Unamuno: 'Repítese hoy aquí mucho que no en el suelo, sino
en el subsuelo de España está su mayor riqueza. Y así sucede con la raza; no
en el suelo de su alma, único casi que hasta hoy se ha cultivado, y con arado
romano, sino en su subsuelo, en sus entrañas espirituales, está su mayor
riqueza. Lo he dicho más de una vez; hay que buscar a Alonso el Bueno
debajo de Don Quijote' (1900; VII, 419).

*al casticismo* Unamuno even felt it necessary to forewarn his readers 'respecto a las afirmaciones cortantes y secas que aquí leerá' (784), and Ganivet, in a letter to Rafael Gago y Palomo, acknowledged 'el tono dogmático que he empleado [in *Idearium español*]' (LSLP, 120).

But Maeztu was making an important point. In earlier works on the problem of Spain affirmation and negation tend to stand out as the expression of a personal or political or religious *parti pris* and thereby draw attention to themselves as manifestations of prejudice. In *En torno al casticismo* and *Idearium español*, on the other hand, affirmation and negation appear as the necessary consequence of an apparently scientifically founded and rationally argued interpretation of Spanish civilization. Indeed, as we noted earlier, the most important areas of affirmation and negation are to a large extent imposed by the method itself, for if it is true that a given civilization can be likened to a living organism, adapted by millennia of contact to a given physical environment, it follows almost inevitably that that civilization should continue to develop in harmony with its environment, that there should be no rupture of the 'hidden bonds of connection' between the different stages of its evolution, past, present and future, and that those European-izers who press for a break with tradition are therefore in error. Similarly, if it is true that a civilization, like a living organism, is dependent also on present environment and must adapt to that environment ('Con el aire de fuera regenero mi sangre, no respirando el que exhalo', *ETC*, 302), it follows, too, that with easier communications and a consequently expanding environment one must develop also in harmony with that wider environment and that those traditionalists who wish to close Spanish frontiers to influences from outside are likewise in error. As Azorín was later to point out, '*comprender* es el camino del desin-terés y de la verdad' (1911; III, 148). The determinist method underlying *En torno al casticismo* and *Idearium español*, so apparently in harmony with the scientific aspirations of the age, gave readers confidence that the authors *had* understood the problem; the accompanying affirmation and negation appeared, in consequence, not as opposition-prompting statements of belief, but as justified and relatively inoffensive expressions of disinterest and truth.

Doubtless readers would have been more critical of the method if the findings had been less appealing. But after a century of

conflict between Right and Left, it was perhaps difficult to resist
the appeal of works that appeared to prove the need for a conciliatory middle course of national action. And at a period of such
manifest misfortune, when writer after writer was calling for an
end to deceptions and political manœuvrings and for a rebirth of
faith, enthusiasm and energy, how could one resist the reasoned
and apparently scientifically justified faith of Unamuno and
Ganivet in Spain's national potential: faith that, despite national
decline and stagnation (both realistically accepted), one could
awaken that 'espíritu colectivo intracastizo que duerme esperando
un redentor' (*ETC*, 869), faith, even, that 'al renacer hallaremos
una inmensidad de pueblos hermanos a quienes marcar con el
sello de nuestro espíritu' (*IE*, 305)? In this respect the following
extract from an early review of *Idearium español* is surely significant:

> y francamente, en los momentos de adversidad y de flaqueza, de
> decaimiento del espíritu que vivió en la gloria, consuela el recuerdo
> del pasado; y pensando en que llegamos en la evolución a vivir
> para nosotros, embriagados por la propia vida, dan los efluvios
> de la patria alientos a la juventud que, con generosas aspiraciones,
> contempla el ideal y se apresta a la reforma (Leopoldo Palacios, in
> *Revista Crítica de Historia y Literatura* III, 1898, 280).

Chronology prevents us from explaining *En torno al casticismo* and
*Idearium español* as products of the national Disaster of 1898, but it
does not prevent us from explaining their success as being, at
least in part, a product of that Disaster. Indeed, it invites us to do
so. And if *Idearium español*, despite its more naïve historicism and
more defective logic, enjoyed greater success than *En torno al
casticismo*, its more profuse offer of hope and crusade ('una
inmensidad de pueblos hermanos a quienes marcar con el sello
de nuestro espíritu') was doubtless a relevant factor. Nationalistic
messianism can rarely have been given such a lamentably successful disguise of science and realism.

In *En torno al casticismo* and *Idearium español*, then, readers—and
in particular that 'nueva generación en busca de una realidad en
que afirmar los pies' (AG, *PE*, 671)—found an apparently scientific approach to the long-standing problem of Spain, saw it based
on a realistic assessment of Spain's current position and infused
with faith in the nation's potential, while tending to a conciliatory
middle path between Europeanizers and Traditionalists. It may

well be that they found also something of the more intimate, personal appeal of determinist systematization that I have suggested was experienced by Taine, Unamuno and Ganivet. But this, one may suspect, comes not so much from being at the reader's receiving end of determinism as from exploring determinist methods oneself and using them to order the confusing complexity of life and civilization. It is doubtful whether the average reader would see these implications.

But in considering the impact of the two works on Spanish thought and writing in the twentieth century we are of course little concerned with the average reader. We are concerned primarily with that minority of readers by whom the impact of the works was to be perpetuated in successive generations of writers: the Maeztus and Azoríns and Barojas and Ortegas. And here one is forced back to a point that was made earlier: that with readers such as these, fully awake to the intellectual currents of their age, it is impossible to distinguish between the specific influence of *En torno al casticismo* and *Idearium español* and the more general influence of the evolutionary approach to civilization that they exemplify. I repeat, then, that I make no claim that *En torno al casticismo* and *Idearium español* were directly responsible for the characteristics noted in the sections that follow, only that they represent the first notable Spanish expression of those characteristics as integrated and mutually dependent elements in a comprehensive system.

### 3. 'EL PUEBLO QUE NOS SUSTENTA A TODOS'

#### (a) 'Historia de lo humilde, de lo anónimo'

¿Cómo no iban a reaccionar los escritores de 1898 contra el énfasis, el superlativo elogioso y la hipérbole desmandada [in their approach to history]? Y ese era, desde luego, un motivo de pugna. Pero había otra causa de discrepancia. En este punto entramos en lo verdaderamente esencial. De la historia pasamos a la estética en general. No se trata ya nuevamente de escribir la historia, sino de ver la vida, que es materia historiable. La divergencia con lo que se venía predicando es, en punto de materia historiable, fundamental. ¿Qué es lo historiable para Baroja? ¿Cómo entiende Unamuno la historia? ¿De qué modo Baroja ha trazado el cuadro de la España contemporánea? Los grandes hechos son una cosa y los menudos

hechos son otra. Se historian los primeros. Se desdeñan los segundos. Y los segundos forman la sutil trama de la vida cotidiana.
'Primores de lo vulgar', ha dicho elegantemente Ortega y Gasset.
En esto estriba todo. Ahí radica la diferencia estética del 98 con
relación a lo anterior. Diferencia en la historia y diferencia en
la literatura imaginativa [...]. Lo que no se historiaba, ni novelaba,
ni se cantaba en la poesía, es lo que la generación del 98 quiere
historiar, novelar y cantar (1941; Azorín, VI, 232).

The humble, anonymous people of Spain are at the centre of
Unamuno's and Ganivet's determinist system. They also play an
important part in a host of Spanish writings published during the
years following the Disaster. Hitherto, it is claimed, there has
been too much emphasis on the great figures and great events of
history and not enough on the lives of the common people.

'No olvido nunca,' wrote Unamuno in 1893, 'que Napoleón se
levanta en la historia más que por su tamaño por presentársenos
en la cúspide de una inmensa pirámide de olvidados granaderos
y soldados' (MU–PM, 6 March 1893). He made similar points
in *En torno al casticismo* and returned to them in the following
year:

Es una de las concepciones más erróneas la de estimar como los
más legítimos productos históricos las grandes nacionalidades,
bajo un rey y una bandera. Debajo de esa historia de sucesos fugaces,
historia bullanguera, hay otra profunda historia de hechos permanentes, historia silenciosa, la de los pobres labriegos que un día y
otro, sin descanso, se levantan antes que el sol a labrar sus tierras y
un día y otro son víctimas de las exacciones autoritarias. Se les saquea
el fruto de su trabajo y se les lleva los hijos a matar a quienes
ningún daño les han hecho, ni en nada les dificultan su perfeccio-
namiento. Los cuatro bulliciosos que meten ruido en la historia de
los sucesos no dejan oír el silencio de la historia de los hechos. Es
seguro que si pudiésemos volver a la época de las grandes batallas
de los pueblos y vivir en el campo de las conquistas se nos apare-
cerían éstas muy otras de como nos las muestran los libros. Hay en
el Océano islas asentadas sobre una inmensa vegetación de madréporas, que hunden sus raíces en lo profundo de los abismos in-
visibles. Una tormenta puede devastar la isla, hasta hacerla
desaparecer, pero volverá a surgir gracias a su basamento. Así en
la vida social se asienta la historia sobre la labor silenciosa y lenta
de las oscuras madréporas sociales enterradas en los abismos
(1896; I, 981).

A year later Zeda observed the same characteristic in *Paz en la guerra* and suggested it stemmed from Scott and Thierry:

> historia de lo humilde, de lo anónimo, en la cual tiene más importancia la cabaña que el castillo, que mira con mayor interés al mesnadero que al señor feudal, que se fija más en los útiles del trabajo que en las armas de la guerra, en el pensar, en el sentir y en el hablar de las muchedumbres que en las arengas de los generales o en las retóricas oraciones de los tribunos. A esta especie de historia pertenece el libro de Unamuno (In *La Epoca*, 1 February 1897).

Beyond the year of his personal crisis Unamuno continued to make the same points. 'La historia, la condenada historia [. . .] nos ha celado la roca viva de la constitución patria [. . .]. Hemos atendido más a los *sucesos* históricos que pasan y se pierden, que a los *hechos* sub-históricos, que permanecen y van estratificándose en profundas capas' (1898; III, 661–2). It is the ordinary person, especially the countryman, who is the ultimately effective element in history: 'Es una gota de agua; de ellas se compone el río, lento y obstinado, que abre hoces y hace polvo los peñascos' (1902; I, 81). Too much attention has been paid to the noises of history; not enough to the underlying silence. 'Todo eso de las invasiones de cartagineses, griegos, romanos, suevos, visigodos, moros, etc., es una ilusión histórica. Eran cuatro gatos los que venían respecto al fondo anterior de población. Una hueste unida conquista pronto a rebaños de hombres sin unión, y cuatro caballos al galope meten más ruido que cuatro mil bueyes que trillan la mies. Y en nuestra historia apenas se oye al pueblo' (1911; VIII, 983).

Baroja's view of history is similar. He exalts individual adventurers—*alter egos* who enable him to work off his own sense of adventure and remain peaceably at his writing-table—but they are skirmishers rather than generals, Ganivetian *guerrilleros* rather than *militares*, and they are immersed in a world of ordinary people, people with commonplace occupations, ambitions and sufferings. 'Pío Baroja, el enamorado de las *vidas humildes*,' is how Camilo Bargiela epitomized him in 1900.[24] Another contemporary developed the point:

> El muletero, el viandante, el artesano, el simple vagabundo, son para él sujetos de estimación posible; pero a medida que asciende por la escala jerárquica, Baroja se siente demoledor e inflexible. Los

[24] *Luciérnagas*, Madrid 1900, pp. xxii–xxiii.

funcionarios oficiales, las autoridades y las dignidades, los podero-
sos, suelen ser odiados y ridiculizados por el escritor descontento
(José M.ª Salaverría, *Retratos*, Madrid 1926, pp. 90–1).

Finally, in a review of the second volume of Baroja's *Memorias de
un hombre de acción*, Azorín wrote:

> La guerra no es lo artificioso e hiperbólico que hemos visto y
> vemos en los cuadros y en los ingenuos relatos de los libros esco-
> lares. Es una cosa dispersa, lenta, difusa, en que podrá haber
> instantes de emoción, pero en que lo corriente es un estado de
> cosas oscuro, opaco, sin relieve; estado de cosas formado con
> trabajos silenciosos, sufrimientos, angustias y anhelos que no se
> ven ni tienen relieve y color (1914; VIII, 201).

'La guerra de la Independencia la hizo el pueblo,' he comments a
few paragraphs later; 'se ve en esa guerra una afirmación rotunda,
formidable, de lo castizo y lo tradicional de la raza, del pueblo de
España'.

Similarly, Azorín himself. He is 'un observador que se desentiende de los grandes fenómenos y se aplica a los pormenores
triviales' (1909; II, 460). P. Crespo pointed to the characteristic as
early as 1899, in a review of *Los hidalgos* (*La vida en el siglo xvii*),
and described it in terms that recall Unamuno's own distinction
between the *hecho vivo* and the *hechos en bruto* (as well as his *tejido
conjuntivo*, *ETC*, 814):

> La historia interna, la crítica sagaz y viva, lo que impresiona es
> el *hecho-tipo* (que se transparenta a través del bloque de los hechos
> en bruto), el tejido conjuntivo de la existencia moral que en cada
> uno de sus nexos parece despertar impresiones propias; todo ello
> en resumen y en lenguaje conciso y plástico lo expone M. Ruiz al
> producir cuadros de la vida del siglo xvii (In *Revista Nueva*,
> August–December 1899).

A few years later Martínez Ruiz pressed his own view through his
autobiographical Azorín:

> Yo no he ambicionado nunca, como otros muchachos, ser general
> u obispo; mi tormento ha sido —y es— no tener un alma multi-
> forme y ubicua para poder vivir muchas vidas vulgares e ignora-
> das; es decir, no poder meterme en el espíritu de este pequeño
> regatón que está en su tiendecilla oscura; de este oficinista que
> copia todo el día expedientes y por la noche van él y su mujer a
> casa de un compañero, y allí hablan de cosas insignificantes; de este

saltimbanqui que corre por los pueblos; de este hombre anodino que no sabemos lo que es ni de qué vive y que nos ha hablado una vez en una estación o en un café . . . (1904; II, 83).

We are touching, of course, on one of the most notable characteristics of his writing:

> Yo siempre he mirado con una viva emoción estos oficios de los pueblos: los curtidores, los tundidores, los correcheros, los fragüeros, los aperadores, los tejedores que en los viejos telares arcan la lana y hacen andar las premideras (1904; II, 66).

Nine years before, Unamuno had criticized Julián de San Pelayo, the editor of Guevara's *Arte de marear*, for showing 'cierta desafección, heredada acaso de Guevara, a los cerrajeros, tundidores, perailes y pellejeros de Valladolid, Medina, Avila, Burgos, Salamanca, Soria' (III, 956). Azorín could well have made the same criticism—in almost the same words.

But we must return to the year of the Disaster. Unamuno had found 'la sustancia del progreso, la verdadera tradición, la tradición eterna' not in 'libros, y papeles, y monumentos, y piedras' but in the 'vida intrahistórica, silenciosa y continua' of the common people, 'el pueblo que nos sustenta a todos' (*ETC*, 793, 869), and Ganivet had found in the 'clases proletarias' 'el archivo y el depósito de los sentimientos inexplicables, profundos, de un país' (*IE*, 203). By 1898 the notion was becoming commonplace. One must search for Spain not in the outer crust, wrote Zeda, but in the subsoil: in the workshops, the countryside, the mines, 'en fin, en lo más íntimo de su ser'.[25] Spain has lost her colonies, declared Maeztu, 'pero, rascando un poco en la agrietada superficie social, se encuentra siempre el pueblo sano y fuerte, fecundo y vigoroso' (1898; II, 126). The youth of Spain is weary, said Enrique Lluria; a national 'examen de conciencia' is necessary to discover and cultivate the latent 'condiciones de raza'.[26] But where is the *raza* to be found? Enrique Madrazo epitomizes the response of his age: 'la raza está abajo, en la masa, no arriba en la cabeza'.[27] 'Lo mejor que puede hacer el Gobierno,' adds Antonio Royo Villanova a few months later, 'es no estorbar'.[28] Further illustration

[25] In *Vida Nueva* 4, 3 July 1898.

[26] In *Vida Nueva* 10, 14 August 1898.

[27] *¿El pueblo español ha muerto?* (*Impresiones sobre el estado actual de la sociedad española*), Santander 1903, p. 201.

[28] In *Alma Española* 16, 21 February 1904.

would be superfluous. We have touched on a fundamental characteristic of Spanish writing around 1900: the turning away from the nation's traditional leaders and from big-drum history with its 'glorias castizas' and 'venerandas tradiciones'—and its notable colonial defeat—in order to find the allegedly real Spain in the everyday lives of ordinary people.

Such an attitude was not entirely new in Europe. The Romantics and their immediate forerunners had prepared the way with their anti-Enlightenment sympathy for primitive and unsophisticated states of culture. Amidst nascent industrialization, trade unions, co-operatives and friendly societies added their own impetus. Men of conservative disposition, initially in Germany amidst the search for national identity that followed upon the Prussian defeat at Jena (1806), looked for the general will in Herder's folk-spirit and, in the belief that traditional forms, being the expression of the life of the people, were also vital forms, emphasized the need for law, government and economic structures to be firmly rooted in customary practice. Radical thinkers, on the other hand, less concerned with traditions than with the needs and rights of men, pressed for the emancipation of the working class. On the one hand, then, Wilhelm von Humboldt, Eichhorn, Savigny, Jacob Grimm, Freytag, with their emphasis on popular traditions; on the other hand, the champions of the French Revolutionary Constitution of 1793, Saint-Simon, Robert Owen, Engels, Marx, with their emphasis on popular rights. Basically both sides were alike in their homage to the Rousseauesque ideal of the sovereignty of the people. And lest surprise be felt that such different thinkers should find support in a common ideal, one may recall that men as far apart as Taine and Marx found support for their own views in the doctrine of evolution. The inroads of new thought do not easily sway a determined thinker. During the second half of the century traditional political historiography came increasingly under attack as greater emphasis was placed on conditions, culture and collective psychology. In W. H. Riehl's *Die Naturgeschichte des Volkes als Grundlage einer deutschen Social-Politik* (1851–64)—a title that would surely have appealed to Unamuno in his search for 'buenas historias del pueblo alemán (y no digo de Alemania)' (MU–PM, p. 205)—in Gustav Freytag's *Bilder aus der deutschen Vergangenheit* (1859–67) and in J. R. Green's *Short History of the English People* (1874) it is the people, not kings, politicians and generals, who are seen as the real protagonists of history.[29]

Even within Spain the turning away from conventional history did not come totally unprepared. Pi y Margall had long opposed the nation's continuing colonial involvement, Pablo Iglesias had emphasized the importance of the working classes, and Joaquín Costa, much influenced by the German Historical School, had concerned himself with customary social, political and legal structures. But what we find in the Spanish press in the closing years of the nineteenth century, the widespread aversion to great figures and events and historical illusions, and the accompanying emphasis on the importance of the common people, this was new in Spain and seemed to upholders of *lo nuevo* as one of the characteristics that most distinguished them from the nation's established writers. Thus, when in 1899 Emilia Pardo Bazán launched her celebrated attack in Paris on Spain's 'golden legend' she prompted the following angry and revealing response from the editors of *Vida Nueva*:

> La leyenda *áurea*, la de los 'pechos de granito', la del general 'No importa', la del heroísmo sobrehumano y único, la que tanto nos ha costado, la culpable de nuestra incultura, la que nos incapacita para la administración de la cosa pública y para el trabajo, ha muerto definitivamente.
>
> Así, cuando menos, lo proclama en París una escritora ilustre: doña Emilia Pardo Bazán.
>
> De hoy en adelante comienza para España la existencia práctica, del engrandecimiento individual, del sentido positivo de la realidad.
>
> Así nos lo dice la afamada novelista.
>
> ¡Lástima que los golpes asestados a nuestra *áurea* leyenda por la señora Pardo Bazán, lleguen un poco tarde!
>
> Cuando en tiempo oportuno combatían esa leyenda un político verdaderamente ilustre, don Francisco Pi y Margall y un obrero de fibra, Pablo Iglesias, no hubo un solo escritor de nombradía que se atreviera a secundarlos. Era más cómodo encerrarse en Sanhedrines literarios que arrojar el guante a la impostura de nuestro heroísmo cerveriano y nuestra hidalguía a lo general Tejeiro y a lo coronel Zamora (*Vida Nueva* 46, 23 April 1899).

[29] For a fuller treatment of the above, see especially G. P. Gooch, *History and Historians in the Nineteenth Century*, 2nd ed., London 1952.

Zola showed the way in France with his *J'accuse* (prompted by the Dreyfus affair), the writer continues, but there was no one similar in Spain. Spain's established writers are out of touch with ordinary people and have been misled by minority factions clamouring for war. They have tried to preserve Spain's '*áurea* leyenda' and can hardly boast now at its death. Pardo Bazán herself refuses to study the 'leyenda *negra*' impartially and continues to write nice moral tales, 'cuentecillos muy morales, muy decentitos, que no rompan el encanto de la *áurea* leyenda, que no molesten la soberbia hegemonía de la realidad negra'. In a recent book the most she asks of writers is that they should not obstruct the coming of a new Spain. '¡Que no estorben!' Indeed, recent changes have left them untouched: 'nuestros intelectuales (?) han seguido aferrándose a lo viejo, sordos y ciegos al caminar del tiempo. Ninguno de ellos ha cantado la patria nueva [. . .]. La vida nacional ha pasado por delante de sus narices y no la han visto.' Galdós, it is true, has written 'fragmentarios poemas de la epopeya del trabajo' ('En *Marianela* está la mina, en alguna otra novela el campo; en las otras la guerra, la guerra estúpida, o la política, la baja intriga'), but despite his incomparable merits, when he comes face to face with the fever of money it is usually to condemn it, 'como si ella no hubiera engendrado los pocos síntomas de vida que en el letargo nacional se observan'. 'Si algo grande ha de hacerse con España, será abandonando la ciudad, para destripar terrones, buscando el oro entre sus intersticios.' Campoamor, too, has done much to ridicule the values inherited from the 'maldito siglo de oro', 'burlándose dolorosamente de ideales librescos que nadie sentía'. But Campoamor has always been pessimistic and old. 'Derrumbando los ideales que nacen del ensueño, no acertó a comprender los de la voluntad, los de la potencia del trabajo. Se recreó en oponer la muralla de la muerte a los impulsos individuales. El fue grande, pero fatal su influjo.' The content and tone of the editorial is summed up in the final sentence: 'Lo menos que puede exigírsenos es la confesión de que hoy por hoy es en España el escritor un animal inferior al hombre'.

Spain the land of the noisy few, or Spain the land of the silent many. Azorín, too, saw this as a basis for distinguishing—and not only among writers—between the previous generation and his own. The previous generation, he claimed in 1905, lacked knowledge of the peculiar character and language of the country:

> Porque ocurre—y esto es lo peregrino—que esta generación que se extiende desde 1840 hasta fines del siglo XIX ha sido, a pesar de sus protestas de patriotismo, a pesar de sus idas, venidas y afanes múltiples para hacer feliz a España (por medio de motines, conspiraciones, partidos, discursos y manifiestos, claro está); ha sido, repetimos, la que menos idea ha tenido del país en que vivía, de sus tradiciones, de su arte y de su lengua (In *ABC*, 31 October 1905).

He returned to the point thirty-five years later:

> Y lo que los escritores de 1898 querían era, no un patriotismo bullanguero y aparatoso, sino serio, digno, sólido, perdurable. A ese patriotismo se llega por el conocimiento minucioso de España. Hay que conocer, amándola, la historia patria. Y hay que conocer, sintiendo por ella cariño, la tierra española. ¿Y quién será el que nos niegue que en nuestros libros hay un trasunto bellísimo —bellísimo en Baroja y Unamuno—de nuestra amada España? (1940; VI, 254).

But what was the new generation of writers looking for in the country's 'cerrajeros, tundidores, perailes y pellejeros'? What were they hoping to discover in the 'muchas vidas vulgares e ignoradas' of the neglected provinces? What was the underlying basis of the 'patriotismo serio, digno, sólido, perdurable' that young writers sought to affirm against the 'patriotismo bullanguero y aparatoso' of earlier generations? Azorín gives an answer that I find to be strongly supported by the evidence of contemporary writings:

> Un patriotismo meditado y racional se impone a los espíritus cultos; y se ve que no podrá caminar la Humanidad si no fomentamos, si no hacemos florecer, con intenso amor, las cualidades congénitas, según el medio, según la raza, del pueblo en que vivimos (1940; VI, 270).

We have returned then, yet again, to the alleged importance of national character: to Enrique Lluria's call for an 'examen de conciencia' in order to discover the latent 'condiciones de raza', to Maeztu's invitation to find, beneath the 'agrietada superficie social', 'al pueblo sano y fuerte, fecundo y vigoroso', to Zeda's *subsuelo* ('en lo más íntimo de su ser'), to Unamuno's *tradición eterna* ('el sentimiento de los trabajadores silenciosos'), to Ganivet's *espíritu territorial* ('los sentimientos inexplicables, profundos, de un país'). 'Lanzarse dentro de esa gran ola anónima de la muchedumbre,' declared José María Salaverría, 'es lo mismo que sorprender los ecos del alma popular.'[30] The new search for Spain is a search for the hitherto neglected character of its people.

## (b) *The psychological approach*

Después del desastre colonial ha entrado en España a no pocos escritores cierta comezón por el estudio de la psicología de nuestro pueblo o de nuestros pueblos, comezón muy natural y muy de alabar, pues si el 'conócete a ti mismo' es razón de la conducta del individuo, ha de serlo también de la del pueblo (1902; MU, III, 715).

Disillusioned both with the nation's leaders and with its traditional ideals writers looked increasingly during the period immediately following the Disaster to the hidden qualities of the Spanish people. The emphasis was on the collectivity (*raza, pueblo, nacionalidad*), on its geographical roots (*español, castellano, nacional*) and, very especially, on its basic psychology (*psicología, carácter, genio, alma, voluntad*): J. Martínez Ruiz's *El alma castellana* (1899), M. Sales y Ferré's 'Psicología del pueblo español' (1902), Rafael Altamira's *Psicología del pueblo español* (1902), Juan Fernández Amador's *Los orígenes de la nacionalidad española y su cultura* (1903), the periodical *Alma Española* (1903–4),[31] Vicente Gay's *Constitución y vida del pueblo español* (1905), Eloy Luis André's *El histrionismo español: Ensayo de psicología política* (1906), Gustavo de la Iglesia's *El alma española: Ensayo de una psicología nacional* (1908) ... They are titles characteristic of the age—and notably uncharacteristic of Spain prior to the publication of Unamuno's *En torno al casticismo* in 1895.

Not that the psychology of the Spanish people had been entirely neglected by earlier generations. Attempts to determine Spanish character have a long lineage, wrote Altamira in 1902; 'con intento sistemático podemos remontarlas al siglo XVIII siendo su más ilustre y acabado representante, Masdeu'. What is still lacking, however, is the study of the 'notas *constantes* que, en medio de la variedad enorme de los distintos tiempos hasta hoy, presenta

---

[30] *Vieja España: Impresión de Castilla*, Madrid 1907, p. 88.

[31] See also, within this periodical, the series of articles on 'regional souls': Miguel S. Oliver's 'Alma mallorquina', José Nogales's 'Alma andaluza', Francisco Acebal's 'Alma asturiana', Unamuno's 'Alma vasca', Blasco Ibáñez's 'Alma valenciana', Juan Maragall's 'Alma catalana', etc.

nuestro pueblo'.[32] In these few words—akin to Taine's on the need for historians to discover 'les grandes forces agissantes et *permanentes*' (*VC*, IV, 129; my italics)—Altamira touches on the most notable difference between what we can call the 'pre-98' and 'post-98' approach to Spanish national character.

Masdeu himself will serve to illustrate the 'pre-98' approach. His most relevant work, the one referred to by Altamira, is the first volume of his *Historia crítica de España y de la cultura española*, sub-titled *Discurso histórico-filosófico sobre el clima de España, el genio y el ingenio de los españoles para la industria y la literatura, su carácter político y moral* (1783). At first sight it seems likely to undermine my case, for the author not only concerns himself with Spanish psychology; he finds also that Spanish psychology is influenced by climate. Concern with a persistently distinctive climate would suggest concern also with a persistently distinctive national psychology. But the difference between Abbot Masdeu, with his emphasis on free will, and writers around 1900, with their emphasis on causal relationships, is considerable. Basically Masdeu sets out to rebut Montesquieu's emphasis on the advantages of more northern countries where a cooler climate, it is alleged, encourages greater virtue. Spain, says Masdeu, enjoys a 'temperamento dulce' and a 'clima apacible', having a clear sky, pure air, gentle breezes, generally moderate rainfall and a generally temperate climate. Successive section headings illustrate sufficiently his somewhat idealized view: 'Delicias del clima de España', 'Fecundidad del terreno', 'Aguas copiosas en España no comunican su humedad al clima', 'Aguas minerales', 'Metales de todas suertes' . . . Spain, in short, 'siempre madre de gentes belicosas, es rica y fecunda de todo' (45). Masdeu thereupon considers the different areas of possible climatic influence on human character, distinguishing between 'el genio nacional' where climate exerts a clear influence and 'el genio personal' where it does not (57). But even in the former case Masdeu emphasizes no climate-produced distinguishing national characteristic. Instead, he lays stress on the encouragement that Spain's favourable climate gives to the desirable personal qualities of the Spanish people: their industry, their skill, their valour, their 'juicio profundo' and 'agudeza sublime' . . .— all abundantly (even over-abundantly) illustrated with evidence drawn from various fields of commercial, political, social and

[32] Rafael Altamira, *Psicología del pueblo español*, Madrid 1902, p. 60.

literary activity. 'El clima templado de España,' Masdeu concludes, 'con alguna inclinación más al calor que al frío, produce hombres amantísimos de la industria, hombres de sumo ingenio para las ciencias y para las bellas letras, hombres de un carácter excelente para la sociedad, en quienes las virtudes exceden en número a los vicios' (269–70). As Altamira himself observed, Masdeu is much concerned with 'cualidades morales que no son privativas de ninguna nación determinada' (op. cit., p. 66). There is no indication in the book of a clear causal relationship between climate and any distinctive 'notas constantes' of Spanish national character.

A more interesting example of the 'pre-98' approach to Spanish character is offered by Lucas Mallada's *Los males de la patria* (1890), subsequently described by Azorín as 'el libro más representativo del momento' (1941; VI, 255). For Mallada there are two basic weaknesses in Spain and he reviews them in turn in his opening chapters, 'La pobreza de nuestro suelo' and 'Defectos del carácter nacional'. Under the former heading he seeks to combat 'la creencia de que vivimos en un país muy rico y de muchos recursos naturales'. Spain, despite its low density of population, is a country from which approximately 25,000 people emigrate annually. Why? '¡Por la pobreza de nuestro suelo, nada más que por la pobreza de nuestro suelo!' Outside a few limited areas of prosperity the country presents a deplorable aspect: a dry, barren landscape, abandoned, neglected villages, poorly dressed and underfed people. As the principal causes Mallada points to the extremes of climate, the lack of adequate rainfall, the geographical relief, the geological composition of the land and the lack of trees which he believes would help to counteract these disadvantages. In his second chapter he turns to the character of the inhabitants: 'esa raza tan grandiosa, tan noble, no es toda heroísmo, no es toda bondad, no es toda excelencia, y como todo lo humano, tiene que estar fatalmente sometida a grandes defectos, al lado de sus magníficas, de sus brillantes virtudes'. Thereafter, his emphasis is on the alleged defects. Physically inferior to almost all other civilized peoples, the Spaniard is beset also by 'cierta flojedad de espíritu, origen de nuestros defectos morales, unos inveterados, otros sumamente comunes en los tiempos modernos, y casi todos decididamente irremediables.' Mallada finds four basic defects: *fantasía, pereza, falta de patriotismo* and *ignorancia.*

As in Masdeu's more laudatory study there is little attempt to explain the declared psychological characteristics in terms of physical environment (though the author does attribute them in part to 'cierta flojedad de espíritu', which is in turn a product of of under-nourishment and thence of the poverty of the land), and there is no attempt to establish a single, all-pervading, key characteristic to which the rest can be related (his nearest approach, the alleged 'flojedad de espíritu', is a merely negative characteristic). Consequently, Mallada cannot attribute Spain's decline to a deviation from any such key psychological trait, nor offer such a trait as a basis for future regeneration. In all these things Mallada's study of Spanish character is clearly different from Unamuno's and Ganivet's—and from what we have seen in Taine. Perhaps Azorín had this in mind when he noted the absence from Mallada's work of 'el carácter peculiar de las cosas en España', a failure to seize upon the 'definida y fuerte personalidad' of the *desierto* de España' (VI, 256). And one may recall, yet again, Maeztu's observation that until the coming of the 1898 Generation writers had failed to ask the basic question: '¿qué es lo central, qué es lo primero, qué es lo más importante?' Mallada, like Masdeu, concerns himself with national characteristics; like Masdeu he does not offer a basis for a global interpretation of Spanish national character. Of course, he may be wise in his modesty. Writers of the following decades, however, were to be more ambitious.

The way had been prepared, in part at least, by Joaquín Costa and Eduardo Pérez Pujol, both of whom had been emphasizing since the 1870's the role of the people as bearers of the country's political, legal and social institutions. Since these institutions were seen to be moulded by the people it was a short step from the institutions to the alleged character beneath them. The Goths, wrote Pérez Pujol in his monumental four-volume *Historia de las instituciones sociales de la España goda* (1896), 'asentándose en la Península Ibérica, aliándose a la raza hispano-romana, de cuyo espíritu eran congéneres a pesar de aparentes diferencias, consolidaron el carácter comprensivo, el espíritu a la vez individual y social que constantemente representa en la Historia la nacionalidad española' (II, 139). We are already close, here, to Altamira's notion of 'notas *constantes*', close also to Unamuno's 1887 declaration, 'Si hay un espíritu fuerte, señores, es el espíritu de raza, sangre de nuestra sangre, jugo de nuestro jugo' (IV, 155). The racial spirit as the insistent guide to national action. The moment of generational consecration has not yet come, but Ganivet urges the need to study a given society as an integrated whole, with its own characteristic 'modo de ser interno del sujeto colectivo' (1889; II, 582), its own particular 'carácter y genio' (1889; I, 868), and gradually finds in Taine an indication of how to discover the underlying 'idea directiva'. Unamuno, too, is enthusiastic about Taine, asks about 'buenas historias del pueblo alemán (y no digo de Alemania)', continues to write *Paz en la guerra*, 'en la que se hace la psicología de un individuo y de un pueblo y una raza', and is confident that one can find in language 'el reflejo más fiel de la psicología del pueblo'.[33] In the Disaster year he is but one of many to urge on Spain the need for national self-knowledge.

The nineteenth-century drawing together of biology and psychology doubtless encouraged the quest.[34] 'La psicología como ciencia data de este siglo,' wrote Unamuno in 1887; 'las ciencias naturales, absorbiéndola, la han hecho progresar' (IV, 154). As evidence of this absorption one can look to Spanish books and periodicals published during the last years of the nineteenth century and the first of the twentieth. Again and again one is struck by the notion of national inadequacies as symptoms of sickness and the historian's consequent view of himself as a consultant physician ('un médecin consultant', 'un médico espiritual'). Thus, amidst a profusion of medical terminology Pérez Pujol himself, in the 1894 preface to his *magnum opus* just quoted, wrote: 'Las leyes del desarrollo de las epidemias y de las enfermedades infecciosas, tan poco estudiadas todavía, pertenecen a la Medicina social tanto como a la individual' (I, xiv). Similarly, Enrique Lluria, in an article entitled 'La voluntad nacional enferma'. urged the training and strengthening of the national will 'como se fortifican los músculos, y como se agigantan los sentidos';[35] J. Vidal y Jumbert asked '¿Cuál es el elemento enfermo?' and found

---

[33] All references are to MU–PM letters written from 1890 to 1893: pp. 118/141, 205, 122, 100 respectively.

[34] F. E. Beneke and R. H. Lotze are key names: Beneke with his view of 'psychology as natural science' (*Lehrbuch der Psychologie als Naturwissenschaft*, Berlin 1833); Lotze with his insistence on 'medical psychology' (*Medicinische Psychologie oder Physiologie der Seele*, Leipzig 1852).

[35] In *Vida Nueva* 10, 14 August 1898.

it to be the political element;[36] Ricardo Macías Picavea, in one of the most celebrated works of the period, wrote: '¿Son las angustias de un enfermo las que nos solicitan? Luego a la clínica médica debemos pedir nuestro plan. Diagnóstico, patogenia, tratamiento: no hay otra manera de proceder'.[37] Finally, I offer an example from a doctor, one of the many who during the next half century were to devote themselves to the problem of Spain —and, by elective affinity perhaps, to the study of the 98 Generation: 'Estoy convencido de que el padecimiento toca a su fin; porque al examinar el curso de la dolencia, al tomar el pulso al enfermo, le hallo débil, sí, pero tranquilo y sin la irregularidad e inquietud de la próxima muerte; porque al buscar a qué órganos afecta el mal, encuentro que, si bien tiene su asiento en una clase social que está a la cabeza, no compromete el *totius sustanciae*'.[38]

In all these quotations, I suggest, the biological influence is clear. But more important than the influence are the consequences. Formerly, the study of national psychology had consisted principally in the indication of desirable and undesirable characteristics —generally desirable in Masdeu, generally undesirable in Mallada —the *afirmación* and *negación* that Maeztu believed his generation to have superseded. Under the joint influence of the 1898 reaction against the nation's leaders and of the new organic determinism national weaknesses are attributed more and more to deviations from, neglect of, or sickness in basic and therefore inescapable national character. The source of the illness, it is maintained, 'tiene su asiento en una clase social que está a la cabeza'; the people have been misled; regeneration lies in the recognition and adequate cultivation of the *totius sustanciae*: 'le vrai gouvernement est celui qui est approprié à la civilisation du peuple'. But how does one determine what is appropriate to the people? By judging from a basis of psychological understanding. Writers have concerned themselves since the eighteenth century with the psychology of the Spanish people but they have not paid sufficient attention to the 'notas *constantes*'; they have failed to ask those basic questions, '¿qué es lo central, qué es lo primero, qué es lo más importante?' Henceforth such questions are asked and the anonymous people are seen as the guardians of the answers: 'En

[36] In *La Vanguardia*, 18 August 1898.
[37] *El problema nacional*, Madrid 1899, p. 18.
[38] Enrique Madrazo, *¿El pueblo español ha muerto?*, Santander 1903, p. 130.

España, la obra magna sería la de armonizar las ideas de la civilización con el carácter y la manera de ser íntima de nuestra raza, y si
había algo de inadaptable, ver por qué motivo era' (1917; PB, V,
107). For writers at the turn of the century the search for Spanish
character becomes a search for the key to national action.

In this, of course, Spanish writers were in harmony with their
age. But whereas the quest for historical constants rooted ultimately in national character faded in most countries during the
first three decades of the new century, in Spain it continued almost
unabated into the 1950's.[39] We have seen the relevant list for the
period 1898-1908. Forty years later we can take the list up again:
Federico Alcázar, *Espíritu español* (1948), Rafael Altamira, *Los
elementos de la civilización y del carácter españoles* (1950), Luis Sánchez
Agesta, *En torno al concepto de España* (1951), Juan José López Ibor,
*El español y su complejo de inferioridad* (1951). Luis Pericot García,
*Las raíces de España* (1952), Antonio Almagro, *Constantes de lo
español en la historia y en el arte* (1955), Antonio Hernández, *Eternidad
de España* (1958) . . . Between the first works listed earlier and the
latest listed here lie most of the writings of the generally accepted
members of the 1898 Generation. Also within this sixty-year span
are to be found numerous writings by contemporaries and near
contemporaries who place a similar emphasis on allegedly fundamental national character. I refer to writers as different as
Salvador de Madariaga (*The Genius of Spain*, 1923; *Ingleses, fran-
ceses, españoles. Ensayo de psicología colectiva comparada*, 1929) and
Julio Camba (*Alemania*, 1916; *Londres*, 1916; *La rana viajera*, 1920).
I refer also to some of the most notable historians of the period:
Rafael Altamira, Ramón Menéndez Pidal, Américo Castro and
Claudio Sánchez-Albornoz.

Rafael Altamira (1866-1951) appears at the end of the nineteenth century as the self-declared champion of a new 'integral
historiography' that brings together external history (political
events, wars, territorial conquests, etc.) and internal history
(social and political institutions, intellectual development, cus-
toms). Underlying time's changes, he declares, are the 'notas
*constantes*' of national character referred to in his *Psicología del
pueblo español*. A quarter of a century later he makes the point
again:

[39] In fact, among young writers there appears to have been a dropping off
in the 1920's and 1930's and a resurgence around 1940.

Ahora, lo que gustaría saber a los investigadores y lo que nos convendría saber a nosotros mismos (puesto que se refiere a la orientación original de nuestra vida, a las cualidades que hacen a un pueblo apto o no para la acción fecunda, al motor interno de la actividad social, en suma, al carácter y al ideal colectivos), es cuál ha sido exactamente el resultado psicológico de los distintos factores que en nosotros han ido influyendo, y qué es, por tanto, lo propio de nuestro espíritu, sus notas genuinamente fundamentales (*Epítome de historia de España*, Madrid 1927, p. 52).

The historian's studies, then, have 'un valor práctico, es decir, para la conducta de la vida'. By studying history we are able to say, 'Tal pueblo ha sido esto o lo otro en la Historia, y tiene por notas constantes o preferentes tales o cuales' (op. cit., p. 64). The year before his death Altamira returned to the point yet again in *Los elementos de la civilización y del carácter españoles* (1950). Historical interpretations, he declares, are used by men to guide their acts. It is therefore the duty of the historian to arrive at and to expound his interpretations with the utmost critical rigour (10):

> Nada puede haber más emocionante y angustioso para un buen patriota como ignorar la sustancia espiritual de la nación a que pertenece y vivir obsesionado por la dolorosa pregunta que no logra contestación en lo que más le importa saber; no para amar a su patria, porque de todos modos la amaría, sino para conocerla a fondo y, así, poder dirigir con acierto su cooperación individual en el buen cumplimiento de lo que corresponde a ese fondo [. . .]. Muchos hombres cultos y diestros en la observación histórica y psicológica, no saben bien todavía cómo son el alma y la historia de nuestro pueblo (18–19).

His book is an attempt to fill the gap: 'El individualismo español', 'La facultad organizadora', 'La sobriedad de la vida española' . . . Basically it is a study in national psychology, a last, moving reminder of the book—the declaration of faith—that he wrote half a century before, 'entre lágrimas de pena y arrebatos de indignación', 'en aquel terrible verano de 1898, que tan honda huella dejó en el alma de los verdaderos patriotas'.[40]

Ramón Menéndez Pidal (1869–1968) has summarized his own historical credo in an extensive introduction to the Espasa-Calpe *Historia de España* (I, 1947, ix–ciii). His first sentence offers the essential key: 'Los hechos de la Historia no se repiten, pero el

---

[40] *Psicología del pueblo español*, Madrid 1902, p. 11.

hombre que realiza la Historia es siempre el mismo'. Thereafter the author declares his concern to establish the 'permanente identidad' of the Spanish people as it has revealed itself across the ages: 'sin poder renovar estudios especiales que modernamente se han hecho, nos limitaremos a destacar algunos caracteres hispanos que consideramos como raíz de los demás' (ix). 'Para mí,' he continues, 'la sobriedad es la cualidad básica del carácter español' (x), a statement that is thereupon abundantly illustrated by reference to a wide range of historical evidence (x–xxiii). Other allegedly notable qualities are considered in like fashion: 'Idealidad' (xxiii–xxix), 'Individualismo' (xxix–li), 'Unitarismo y regionalismo' (li–lxx). From this last section it is but a short step to the consideration of Spain's lack of national cohesion: 'Las dos Españas' (lxxi–ci). Our future national aim, says Don Ramón, must be to reconcile the opposing bands by encouraging mutual tolerance and a balanced approach to the history of the past and the problems of the present. It is here, he concludes ('Propósito de la historia', ci–ciii), that the historian can help, rectifying by his research the omissions and biases of the past:

> En una estimación integral del modo como la gente hispana supo conducirse frente a las varias y coactivas exigencias de cada tiempo, en una interpretación harmónica de las muy diversas épocas, está la verdad histórica, la única verdad que, trayendo la savia del pasado a nutrir los afanes del presente, puede conferir al pueblo español robusta fe en la plenitud de su desarrollo, en el aunamiento de sus fuerzas para desplegar íntegramente la energía vital de que él es capaz (ciii).

According to Altamira the essential character of the Spanish people was moulded at the time of the Reconquest, 'quizá sobre estratos muy vigorosos y resistentes de tiempos prehistóricos' (*Epítome* . . ., p. 53); according to Menéndez Pidal it was already formed in Roman—even pre-Roman—times. In neither case is much weight given to elements of non-Celtiberian heredity. In a series of books and articles published since 1938 Américo Castro (1885–1972) has presented a very different case. The Celtiberians, he affirms, were not Spaniards, *Hispania romana* was not Spanish, and there was nothing peculiarly Spanish about the Visigothic way of life. Spanishness, that 'dimensión de conciencia colectiva' that characterizes the Spanish people, appeared only during the Reconquest, as a result of the interaction of Christians, Moors and

Jews in a three-dimensional society. Subsequent Spanish history, he believes, stems directly from that fact:

> Cuanto de bueno y de malo ha acontecido a los españoles enlaza, en un último análisis, con el hecho de haber tenido que hacer frente, quienes aún no eran españoles, a las desastrosas circunstancias creadas por la ocupación musulmana de la tierra de Hispania—un país romano-visigótico. Aquel abrumador acontecimiento obligó a adoptar nuevas actitudes colectivas, a la larga estabilizadas como habituales (*La realidad histórica de España*, Mexico 1962, p. 263).

The chronological range of Spain's allegedly unchanging character has clearly been reduced. The approach, however, is still basically psychological and the reader is still invited to accept the notion of significant, time-resistant features ('actitudes colectivas, a la larga estabilizadas como habituales'):

> Concebimos la historia como una biografía [. . .]. La elasticidad de una forma de vida, individual o colectiva, tiene un límite, y si nuestro contacto con la vida biografiada es muy íntimo, podremos predecir qué tipo de acciones le será inaccesible (*España en su historia*, Buenos Aires 1948, p. 10).

Moreover, as the final words suggest, Spain's collective consciousness is still seen as a necessary guide to future action: 'Ningún ensayo de auténtica reforma de la vida española será viable, si no se tienen en cuenta los cómos y los porqués de esta peculiarísima condición humana' (*Realidad* . . ., pp. xii–xiii). 'Mi obra hispánica aspira a ser constructiva y alentadora'; the necessary basis is 'bucear previamente en las honduras del sentir colectivo', 'preguntarse cómo llegaron a adquirir los españoles su identidad y conciencia colectivas' (*Realidad* . . ., pp. xiv, xix):

> *Si el español no se decide a convivir con su propia historia*, ¿cómo se pondrá de acuerdo con sus prójimos españoles? ¿Cómo sabrá eludir la opresión, la anarquía o el caos? O quizá algo todavía peor: la insignificancia (*Realidad* . . ., p. xxiv).

Claudio Sánchez-Albornoz (b. 1893) composed his most ambitious work, his two-volume *España, un enigma histórico* (Buenos Aires 1956), with his soul afire for Spain's 'inquietante destino', believing that students of history have a duty to contribute to the formation of the 'conciencia nacional' (I, 19). 'Todos y cada uno de los pueblos del mundo muestran características más o menos disímiles,' he affirms in the opening sentence of the work. 'Son incuestionables las singularidades de la contextura vital hispánica,' he continues a few lines later. His aim is to record the forging of 'nuestra peculiar herencia temperamental' (I, 9–10) and to show the relevance of his findings to Spain's future. Castro, he believes, is mistaken in looking for the beginnings of Spanishness in a medieval fusion of Christians, Moors and Jews. The *homo hispanus* was already a reality in pre-Roman times, being formed, in part at least, by the Castilian climate and landscape, 'llanos de soleada desnudez, en que el ojo humano se dispara hacia la lejanía sin tropezar con velos de humedad ni con fronteras arbóreas' (I, 92). During the Reconquest he developed in opposition to Moor and Jew rather than by fusion with them and his temperament imposed itself on the Moor as it had previously imposed itself on the Roman and the Visigoth. Thus, there are clear psychological constants across the whole recorded span of peninsular history: for example, 'una constante histórica perdurable que aproxima y enlaza en la exaltación de los valores de la persona humana y en los desbordamientos de su yo irrefrenable—pluma en mano y lanza en ristre y desde Séneca a Unamuno—a las más señeras personalidades de todas las Españas que ha conocido el pasado [. . .] a través de sus engarces distintos en culturas muy diversas y aunque hayan vivido bajo cúpulas religiosas diferentes' (II, 627). The key to Spanish civilization, according to Sánchez-Albornoz, is to be found through an adequate understanding of the collective national psyche and its response to historical circumstances: to the 'tres desembarcos', for example—of Tariq in Gibraltar (711), of Columbus in San Salvador (1492) and of Charles of Ghent in Villaviciosa (1517). Given the character of the *homo hispanus*, these 'tres desembarcos' together caused the nation to persist in a heroic and theocentric medievalism at a time when other nations were evolving towards a secular bourgeois culture. This, says Sánchez-Albornoz, hindered Spain's progression to modernity and led eventually to the 'dos Españas' conflict that has dogged Spain since the eighteenth century. But the nations of Europe will one day come together in a higher historical unity, perhaps an *universitas christiana*. It is for present-day Spaniards, temperamentally suited for the task by their own peculiar 'contextura vital', to hasten the day and to ensure Spain's own active and dynamic participation.

From the above brief surveys certain common characteristics stand out, and stand out rather strangely in the context of modern historiography: the continuing priority afforded to the 'notas constantes' of Spanish history; the search for these 'notas constantes' in the allegedly unchanging basic character of the Spanish people—unchanging at least since the sixteenth century; the notion that the psychology of the Spanish people, besides being unchanging, is also significantly different from that of other peoples, and that in this difference lies the key to a proper understanding of Spanish history and civilization; the emphasis on Spain's past, even its distant past, as a storehouse of evidence by which to judge the present and from which to make recommendations for the future. Despite their immeasurably greater range of historical erudition, one has an uneasy feeling that all four writers, like Unamuno and Ganivet, still invoke the past to confirm an intuition rooted in the present rather than to test a hypothesis derived from the study of the past. Moreover, all would doubtless subscribe to Américo Castro's view: 'El conocimiento del mundo antaño español no es apéndice o complemento de cultura, sino materia de nutrición primordial' (*Realidad* . . ., p. xxvi). As with Unamuno and Ganivet, 'the prober of national destinies is no longer a mere observer; the subject and object of study are fused; knowledge henceforth is involvement, necessity, anguish' (above, p. 82). The historian is still a somewhat over-involved 'médico espiritual'.

I am not the first to make such observations. In its Spanish context, A. A. Parker remarked in 1953, Menéndez Pidal's Introduction to the *Historia de España* naturally and inevitably takes the form of an extensive analysis of the national character as exemplified throughout history and concludes with a political appeal; 'the equivalent would not, I suppose, be natural in any other country'. Moreover, Américo Castro 'takes the present as the norm of the past, or more exactly, makes his reactions as a historian to the events of the past identical with his own personal reactions to the present'.[41] P. E. Russell has made similar observations on Sánchez-Albornoz's study: 'This postulate of a psychological substratum exercising a continuing influence on the Spanish

[41] A. A. Parker, in *The Cambridge Journal* VI (1952–53), 466, 467. Compare R. B. Tate: '[These prologues to *Historia de España*] teach us a great deal more about certain strands of political thought during the first half of this century than about the mediaeval past' (In *BHS* 48, 1971, 260).

temperament throughout the ages is one which is likely to be received with scepticism by Professor Sánchez-Albornoz's foreign readers'; Sánchez-Albornoz 'attempts to mould the Spanish past to fit his own subjective needs'.[42] 'Modern Spanish historians,' wrote H. G. Koenigsberger in 1960, 'have had a tendency to look for some special, distinguishing characteristic in the history of their country [. . .]. This preoccupation has led many historians to emphasize, and perhaps to overemphasize, the permanent characteristics of Spanish history.'[43] In the same year Vicens Vives was making similar criticisms—in the new Prologue to his *Aproximación a la historia de España*—urging the abandonment of 'los tópicos y las frases hechas' and emphasizing the proper concerns of the historian, 'los factores básicos de la historia peninsular':

> hombres, miseria y hambre, epidemia y muerte, propiedad territorial, relaciones de señor a vasallo, de funcionario a administrado, de patrono a obrero, de monarca a súbdito, de sacerdote a creyente, de municipio a municipio, de pueblo a pueblo, de capital a provincia, de producción individual a renta nacional, del alma con Dios. Factores que no están tan alejados de los que han experimentado los países mediterráneos vecinos, por lo que es muy dudoso que España sea un enigma histórico, como opina Sánchez Albornoz, o un vivir desviviéndose, como afirma su antagonista. Demasiada angustia unamuniana para una comunidad mediterránea, con problemas muy concretos, reducidos y 'epocales': los de procurar un modesto pero digno pasar a sus treinta millones de habitantes (*RTV*, 1970, pp. 30–1).

Partly under the impact of the Vicens Vives revolution, partly no doubt under the influence of Spain's rapid industrial and urban development (cosmopolitan and therefore not obviously related to the allegedly distinctive characteristics of the primitive Iberian peasant), Spanish writers themselves have in recent years come to the forefront in condemning 'el mito de los caracteres nacionales',[44] 'el tópico del carácter nacional',[45] 'la gran trampa enaje-

[42] P. E. Russell, in *BHS* 36, 1959, 222, 224.

[43] H. G. Koenigsberger, in *BHS* 37, 1960, 245.

[44] José Antonio Maravall, 'Sobre el mito de los caracteres nacionales', in *Revista de Occidente*, Second Series, I (1963), 257–76. See also Julio Caro Baroja, *El mito del carácter nacional*, Madrid 1970, pp. 69–135.

[45] Julio Busquets, *Introducción a la sociología de las nacionalidades*, Madrid 1971, pp. 136–9.

nadora del carácter nacional'.[46] Tourist posters may continue to proclaim that 'Spain is different'; there is increasing evidence that the new Spain at least is not.

But we must return to the older concept of Spain. In an article published in February 1972 Richard Herr surveyed five notable interpretations of Spanish history—by Menéndez Pelayo, Unamuno, Ortega, Castro and Sánchez-Albornoz—and observed a number of common features. He questioned the emphasis on national character and commented:

> Todos estos cinco autores parecen creer (Menéndez Pelayo es una posible excepción) que por causa de unos sucesos que ocurrieron antes de que comenzase la historia, o en cierto momento de la Edad Media, o a más tardar en el siglo XVI, los españoles a partir de 1700 han sido condenados a perder el paso del resto de Europa. Es como si la España moderna sufriera de un tipo de pecado original del cual no tuviera escape. Resulta irónico que los dirigentes intelectuales de un país que Menéndez Pelayo llama católico por esencia, nieguen a sus compatriotas el beneficio del libre albedrío. ¿Se ha infiltrado la predestinación protestante donde el racionalismo es incompatible? (*Revista de Occidente* 107, pp. 294–5).

The observation, I find, is justified and could have been applied also to Altamira and Menéndez Pidal. But does the explanation really lie in 'la predestinación protestante'? Is it not to be found rather in the continuing impact of the 98 Generation's basic determinism? The admitted 'posible excepción' of Menéndez Pelayo is surely significant.

Outstanding success at one stage of civilization, it seems, commonly causes excessive entrenchment in the tenets of the time and thereby exerts a retarding influence on later generations. So it was with the 1898 Generation in its impact on Spanish historiography. At a time when thinkers in England, France and Germany were coming to recognize the importance of social and economic factors in the historical process, writers in Spain were encouraged by the example of the 98 Generation to concentrate

---

[46] Antonio Alvarez-Solís, 'El carácter nacional', in *Destino*, 8 January 1972. The supplement to *Triunfo* 532 ('Los españoles', 9 December 1972) offers valuable evidence on the critical attitude of modern Spanish writers to the notion of an unchanging national character. As José Luis L. Aranguren comments in his introductory survey, 'Todos o casi todos [los autores] se dedican a debelar el estereotipo del carácter nacional.'

instead on allegedly permanent traits of national character. Of course, several members of the Generation were themselves involved initially with socialism or anarchism—and with currents of *regeneración*—but Spain was still basically a rural community and Marx's revolutionary economics-based urban determinism yielded soon to Taine's conservative, psychology-based rural determinism. The emphasis on eternal tradition, I have suggested, precludes the notion of social revolution. The 98 Generation's search for Spain is basically a search for the unchanging character of the Spanish country people:

> En esa familia agrícola es donde reside el alma de la raza, que la naturaleza crea y que espontáneamente crece, es donde se encontrarán nuestras virtudes intrínsecas, ese es el verdadero ambiente de la patria, eso es eterno (Enrique Madrazo, *¿El pueblo español ha muerto?*, Santander 1903, p. 302).

### 4. THE QUEST FOR SPAIN

#### (a) *The quest for Spain through travel*

Me asomé a la ventanilla [del tren] y vi la profundidad de la noche, la extensión desolada de la llanura. ¡Cuán grave y expresiva era aquella planicie castellana, vieja patria del Cid, cuna del españolismo! Iba yo a conocer el secreto de una tierra de dominadores; iba a sentir el aliento de un país antiguo que imprimió en el mundo tan honda y duradera huella; quería desentrañar el misterio de aquella tierra esquilmada, rasa y humilde, que había sabido sujetar a su feudo otras tierras más ricas, más ágiles y mejor dotadas por la naturaleza (José Mª Salaverría, *Vieja España: Impresión de Castilla*, Madrid 1907, p. 5).

The 98 Generation's emphasis on the unchanging character of the Spanish rural population apparently exerted a retarding influence on Spanish historiography. It also brought in its wake a notable broadening of Spanish experience: a new sensitivity to the landscape that was believed to have formed that character, and a new delight in the various aspects of provincial life in which that character was believed to reveal itself. The 98 Generation, perhaps inevitably, stands out as a generation of *excursionistas*.

'Tres días de vacaciones,' comments Unamuno; 'el último de octubre y los dos primeros de noviembre . . . La cosa está clara; a huir de la ciudad y de sus cuidados, a respirar aire de campo libre, a correr tierras, villas y lugares' (1909; I, 329). 'Estas excursiones no son sólo un consuelo, un descanso y una enseñanza; son además, y acaso sobre todo, uno de los mejores medios de cobrar amor y apego a la patria [. . .]. Cóbrase en tales ejercicios y visiones ternura para con la tierra; siéntese la hermandad con los árboles, con las rocas, con los ríos; se siente que son de nuestra raza también, que son españoles. Las cosas hacen la patria tanto o más que los hombres [. . .]. No, no ha sido en libros, no ha sido en literatos donde he aprendido a querer a mi Patria: ha sido recorriéndola, ha sido visitando devotamente sus rincones' (1909; I, 281-5). 'Recorriendo estos viejos pueblos castellanos, tan abiertos, tan espaciosos, tan llenos de un cielo lleno de luz, sobre esa tierra, serena y reposada, junto a estos pequeños ríos sobrios, es como el espíritu se siente atraído por sus raíces a lo eterno de la casta' (1912; I, 370).

We recognize here, in brief synthesis, some of the most notable characteristics of the new generation. Disillusioned with the country's ruling minorities and traditional ideals, seeking to replace the 'patriotismo bullanguero y aparatoso' of their elders with a '[patriotismo] serio, digno, sólido, perdurable' (1940; Azorín, VI, 254), young writers of around 1900 set out in search of the allegedly unknown and hitherto neglected Spain. 'Si algo grande ha de hacerse con España, será abandonando la ciudad, para destripar terrones, buscando el oro entre sus intersticios.'[47] 'La base del patriotismo es la geografía. No amaremos nuestro país, no le amaremos bien, si no lo conocemos' (1916; Azorín, III, 561). For men of the Restoration, says Baroja, 'la ciudad lo resumía todo, el campo no era nada'; his own generation, on the other hand, 'siente afición al campo, a las excursiones y a los viajes pequeños' (1926; V, 571, 575). Not that they scorn cities in all their aspects, but they do look for something different in them: 'En las ciudades, los hombres de esta generación no buscarán las plazas elegantes, de aire parisiense o madrileño; preferirán visitar los barrios antiguos, los arrabales, y estarán siempre ansiosos de encontrar lo típico y lo característico' (1926; V, 575). In cities as elsewhere, then, their emphasis is on traditional aspects that link past and present. 'Hacíamos excursiones en el tiempo y en el espacio,' comments Azorín; 'visitábamos las vetustas ciudades castellanas.

[47] An unsigned editorial, in *Vida Nueva* 46, 16 April 1899.

Descubríamos y corroborábamos en esas ciudades la continuidad nacional' (1941; VI, 229) '¿No está en estas iglesias, en estos calvarios, en estas ermitas, en estos conventos, en este cielo seco, en este campo duro y raso, toda nuestra alma, todo el espíritu intenso y enérgico de nuestra raza?' (1909; Azorín, II, 529).

The evidence is overwhelming. Like Taine (*Voyage aux Pyrénées, Notes sur Paris, Carnets de voyage, Voyage en Italie, Notes sur l'Angleterre*) the men of 98 are notable travellers. 'Fue Baroja quien viajó más. Y fue Maeztu quien, saliendo de España, viviendo en el extranjero, quiso contrastar la realidad histórica nacional con la de otros países. Contentábame yo con emprender cortos viajes, y siempre a solas' (1940; Azorín, VI, 229). Their underlying quest is for 'lo eterno de la casta' (Unamuno), for 'lo típico y lo característico' (Baroja), for 'la continuidad nacional' (Azorín); in short, for a basic, time-resistant national identity. But their enthusiastic contact with the physical realities of Spain prevents the acceptance of an abstracted, over-simplist 'peninsular' vision such as we found in *Idearium español*. As in *En torno al casticismo* their emphasis is on the physical realities of Castile: Castile, the area of Spain's most distinctive landscapes (and therefore likely to hold the key to the nation's distinctive character); Castile, the forger of Spanish unity and the traditional guide to its destinies (and therefore likely to be the area most relevant to an understanding of the nation's history).[48] 'Lo castellano es, en fin de cuenta, lo castizo' (*ETC*, 805):

En el aspecto íntimo del arte, para el que busca sensaciones profundas, para el que tiene el espíritu preparado a recibir la más

[48] Traditionally the main (and even exclusive) emphasis is placed on the latter point. I suspect myself that the former was more important. 'Cosa triste es un pueblo que deja de ser *uno*, distinto de los demás' (1888; MU, IV, 184). To a geographical determinist the meseta landscape especially gives an assurance of Spain's unique character. Besides, writers of the 98 Generation (Baroja and Azorín, for example, in their descriptions of Yecla) are often concerned with meseta landscape that is not Castilian. Finally, there is evidence in the closing years of the century of a newly awakened interest in Castile in its geographical aspects:

Ahora le ha tocado estar de moda a las mesetas castellanas; antes nadie se acordaba de que en España hubiese tales mesetas; sencillamente se decía: la Tierra de Campos o la Mancha; pero alguien ha sacado de los libros de geología o de geografía este nombre tan sugestivo y tan bonito, y rápidamente se ha puesto en circulación (E. H.-Pacheco, 'Las mesetas de moda', in *Revista Nueva*, 5 May 1899).

honda revelación de la historia eterna, os digo que lo mejor de España es Castilla, y en Castilla pocas ciudades, si es que hay alguna, superior a Avila. Váyase a Sevilla, váyase a Valencia el que quiera divertirse o distraerse el ánimo, el que quiera matar unos días viviendo con la sobrehaz del alma; pero el que quiera columbrar lo que pudo antaño haber sido, vivir con el fondo del alma, ése que vaya a Avila; que venga también a Salamanca (1909; MU, I, 275).

But the writers of 98 want to know Spain in its variety, too. 'En nuestra comprensión y en nuestro amor entraban todas las regiones de España,' says Azorín (1941; VI, 303). 'De Castilla, el deseo de describir ha ido hasta Levante, hasta Andalucía y hasta Vasconia. España se ha visto a sí misma en su verdadera faz y por primera vez' (ibid., 218). The combination of determinism and travel obliges the men of 98 to be regionalists ('[el] regionalismo que pide que se deje a cada pueblo desarrollarse según él es', 1896; MU, I, 982); the determinist quest for an underlying national identity prevents them from being separatists ('Cosa triste es un pueblo que deja de ser *uno*, distinto de los demás', 1888; MU, I, 184).

They set out, then, in search of a basic, time-resistant national identity. They look for it in the character and lives of ordinary people:

Repítese hoy aquí mucho que no en el suelo, sino en el subsuelo de España está su mayor riqueza. Y así sucede con la raza; no en el suelo de su alma, único casi que hasta hoy se ha cultivado, y con arado romano, sino en su subsuelo, en sus entrañas espirituales, está su mayor riqueza. Lo he dicho más de una vez; hay que buscar a Alonso el Bueno debajo de Don Quijote (1900; MU, VII, 419);

in the physical environment that has formed the people:

Decidme, ¿no es este el medio en que florecen las voluntades solitarias, libres, llenas de ideal—como la de Alonso Quijano el Bueno—; pero ensimismadas, soñadoras, incapaces, en definitiva, de concertarse en los prosaicos, vulgares, pacientes pactos que la marcha de los pueblos exige? (1905; Azorín, II, 262–3);[49]

and in the culture (cities, towns and villages; way of life; arts and literature) in which, across the centuries, the unchanging character of the people has come to reveal itself:

[49] I give the *OC* reference but, because of an error in that text, quote from the first edition.

El espíritu de la antigua España—y esto es el todo—se respira en estas callejas, en estos zaguanes sórdidos, en estas tiendecillas de abaceros y regatones, en estos obradores de alfayates y boneteros, en este ir y venir durante toda la mañana de nobles y varoniles rostros castellanos, llenos, serenos, y de caras femeninas pálidas, con anchos y luminosos ojos que traducen ensueños (1909; Azorín, II, 459).

My view assumes, then, a basic harmony between landscape, character and culture: 'la unión suprema e inexpresable de este paisaje [de España] con la raza, con la historia, con el arte, con la literatura de nuestra tierra [. . .]; un paisaje concordado íntima y espiritualmente con una raza y una literatura' (1913; Azorín, II, 1155–7). We have noted it in *En torno al casticismo* and *Idearium español*; it is also, I suggest, an important characteristic of other writings by alleged members of the 1898 Generation.

Pedro Laín Entralgo's view, however, is very different. Guided perhaps by his belief that the 98 Generation represents a reaction against evolutionism,[50] he claims that the men of 98 are alike in seeing the Spanish countryman, 'campesino o pastor', as a disturbing, disruptive element amidst the purity of the landscape: 'para los escritores del 98, el habitante de los campos ibéricos es, ante todo, un perturbador del paisaje' (op. cit., 41). This view, I believe, is mistaken; the countryman is seen at one with the landscape that formed him. 'Nunca como ahora, la flor de los ingenios castellanos se ha empeñado en descubrir esta conexión entre el alma y el paisaje.'[51] We must look critically at Laín Entralgo's contrary evidence (op. cit., 33–45).[52]

The first two pieces of evidence offered on Unamuno are irrelevant to my case (and to Laín Entralgo's): they are not concerned with man and the landscape amidst which he lives; they are concerned with free, unfettered landscape and fettered, socialized—in one case, even urbanized—man. It is the well-known Unamuno conflict between countryside and city, between Cain and Abel: '¡Pueblos pastores que pasan sobre la tierra! ¡Pueblos labradores que se agrupan en torno a las ciudades!' (1900; I, 66–7). The next

[50] *La generación del noventa y ocho*, 2nd ed., Madrid 1948, p. 69.

[51] Miguel S. Oliver, *Entre dos Españas*, Barcelona 1906, p. 191. The context makes it clear that 'castellanos' here refers to all those writing in Spanish.

[52] On all the points to be discussed Laín Entralgo's case remains unchanged in *El problema de España*, Madrid 1956, II, 68–83.

piece of evidence is from *En torno al casticismo* where 'tras haberse exaltado con el paisaje "monoteístico" de Castilla, [Unamuno] habla así de los hombres que habitan ese paisaje: "A esa seca rigidez, dura, recortada, lenta y tenaz, llaman naturalidad; todo lo demás tiénenlo por artificio pegadizo o poco menos. Apenas les cabe en la cabeza más naturalidad que la bravía y tosca de un estado primitivo de rudeza"'. Laín Entralgo comments: 'El habitante del paisaje español empieza por ser un perturbador de la *natural* pureza de ese paisaje, como Adán pecador en un Paraíso todavía inmaculado'. This reveals a grave misunderstanding of Unamuno's basic case, for the lines here quoted are simply a gathering together of elements that have run like a *leitmotiv* through the whole preceding description of Castile. *Recortado*, for example, has been applied to 'el paisaje', to 'colinas', to the clear outline of the village 'recortadamente demarcado', to the Castilian's impressions 'tan recortadas como las tintas del paisaje de su tierra', to the highly spiced food 'impresiones recortadas para el paladar' and to the clear-cut presentation of objects in the paintings of Ribera and Zurbarán. Unamuno's whole aim is to show that the Castilians are at one with their environment, 'hechos a la inclemencia del cielo y a la pobreza de la vida'. Amidst this determinist panorama there is no question of man's being an 'elemento perturbador'; he is simply a product, 'producto de una larga selección'.[53]

We can pass over Laín Entralgo's remaining evidence on Unamuno, for it supports my own view entirely, and come to his treatment of Azorín. Most of his evidence illustrates the young Martínez Ruiz's affection for the landscape of Castile and Levante. Where I differ from Laín Entralgo is again in his interpretation of man as 'una nota agria y discordante [que] perturba y contamina la mansa o tremenda candidez de la naturaleza de los seres cósmicos o biológicos'. My best argument is to invite the reader to examine for himself the relevant pages from *La voluntad*, to note Azorín's description of the plain of El Pulpillo, 'adusta, desolada, sombría', to note the 'amarguras pasadas' that El Abuelo recounts —'los pedriscos asoladores, las hambres, las sequías, las epidemias, las muertes remotas de remotos amigos'—to observe El Abuelo himself, 'sencillo como un niño [. . .], sanguinario exas-

[53] Cf. '¿No se refleja acaso en el paisanaje el paisaje? Como en su retina, vive en el alma del hombre el paisaje que le rodea' (1901; MU, VIII, 910).

perado', slow in speech and movements: 'Impasible, inexpresivo, silencioso, camina tras el arado tardo en los llanos inacabables; o permanece, si los días son crudos, inmóvil junto al fuego, mientras sus manos secas tejen automáticamente el fino esparto'. Laín Entralgo's evidence, over-selective and with the addition of a misleading comma between 'sanguinario' and 'exasperado' that changes the meaning considerably, conceals too crudely Azorín's manifest compassion for the Manchegan peasant.[54] As for the denied harmony of landscape and people one might recall, in this same novel, Azorín's own statement: 'Yo soy un determinista convencido [. . .]. El Universo es un infinito encadenamiento de causas y concausas: todo es necesario y fatal; nada es primero y espontáneo. Un hombre que compone un maravilloso poema o pinta un soberbio lienzo, es tan autómata como el labriego que alza y deja caer la azada sobre la tierra, o el obrero que da vueltas a la manivela de una máquina . . . ¡Los átomos son inexorables!' (I, 932–3).[55] The following lines, also from the novel on which Laín Entralgo chooses to base his case, are conclusive:

'Se habla—piensa Azorín—de la alegría española, y nada hay más desolador y melancólico que esta española tierra. Es triste el paisaje y es triste el arte. Paisaje de contrastes violentos, de bruscos cambios de luz y sombra, de colores llamativos y reverberaciones saltantes, de tonos cegadores y hórridos grises, conforma los espíritus en modalidades rígidas y los forja con aptitudes rectilíneas, austeras, inflexibles, propias a las decididas afirmaciones de la tradición o del progreso. En los países septentrionales, las perpetuas brumas difuminan el horizonte, crean un ambiente de vaguedad estética, suavizan los contornos, velan las rigideces; en el Mediodía, en cambio, el pleno sol hace resaltar las líneas, acusa reciamente los perfiles de las montañas, ilumina los dilatados horizontes, marca definidas las sombras. La mentalidad, como el paisaje, es clara, rígida, uniforme, de un aspecto único, de un solo tono. Ver el adusto y duro panorama de los cigarrales de Toledo es ver y comprender los retorcidos y angustiados personajes del Greco, como ver los maciegales de Avila es comprender el ardoroso desfogue lírico de la gran santa, y ver Castilla entera, con sus llanuras inacabables y sus rapadas lomas, es percibir la inspiración que informara nuestra literatura y nuestro arte' (I, 925–6).

The 'aptitudes rectilíneas, austeras, inflexibles' that Azorín finds

[54] All the above references are to La voluntad; I, 907–10.
[55] Cf. 'El medio hace al hombre' (1903; Azorín, I, 1135).

in Spanish character are clearly akin to the 'seca rigidez, dura, recortada, lenta y tenaz' observed by Unamuno. Behind both lies a physical environment characterized principally by its contrasts and clear lines.

In the writings of Antonio Machado, as in those of Unamuno and Azorín, man is marked by the land around him. Again Laín Entralgo's view is very different. To illustrate his case he quotes one of the poet's harshest descriptions of the Castilian peasant (from 'Por tierras de España'), overlooks the accompanying— and similarly harsh—description of the Castilian landscape and quotes instead one of the poet's most idyllic landscape descriptions (from 'Orillas del Duero'). Man, then, is again seen as a disruptive element. But this frivolous use of evidence will not do. I invite the reader to examine 'Por tierras de España' for himself. The 'hombre malo del campo y de la aldea, / capaz de insanos vicios y crímenes bestiales' clearly bears the imprint of his environment:

> El numen de estos campos es sanguinario y fiero [. . .].
>
> Veréis llanuras bélicas y páramos de asceta
> —no fue por estos campos el bíblico jardín—;
> son tierras para el águila, un trozo de planeta
> por donde cruza errante la sombra de Caín.

It is because of man's presence, says Laín Entralgo, that Machado describes this land as accursed ('páramo maldito'). I suggest, on the contrary, that man is emphasized as the sufferer from the curse, not as its cause. 'Por tierras de España' itself offers evidence that Laín Entralgo regretfully overlooks: 'en páramos malditos trabaja, sufre y yerra'.

Laín Entralgo proceeds in similar fashion in his treatment of Baroja. 'La tierra castellana y la tierra vasca,' he maintains, are objects of love for Baroja, 'una realidad consistente, pura, incontaminada', amidst which man is 'ante todo, un perturbador del paisaje'. In support of this view he adduces three pieces of evidence on Castile from *Camino de perfección* and claims that the case is similar in Baroja's Basque novels. Since no specific evidence is offered on the latter point I confine myself to refuting the evidence offered from *Camino de perfección*.[56] It is contained completely in the following lines:

[56] On Baroja's Basque peasant I merely recall Granjel's finding: that he is shown to be 'en plena compenetración con la tierra que le sustenta', 'tan

Topa Fernando Ossorio con unos campesinos de Manzanares:
'Eran tipos clásicos . . .—comenta Baroja—. Las caras terrosas, las
miradas de través, hoscas y pérfidas'. Más duras son todavía las
expresiones del novelista frente a los habitantes de otro pueblo
serrano: 'aquella gentuza innoble y miserable, sólo capaz de fecho-
rías cobardes'. No salen mejor librados los moradores de Yécora:
'gente de vicios sórdidos y de hipocresías miserables'. La abierta y
sincera crudeza del lenguaje barojiano no deja lugar a dudas
respecto a la verdad de la conclusión que más arriba adelanté:
para los escritores del 98, el habitante de los campos ibéricos es,
ante todo, un perturbador del paisaje (op. cit., pp. 40-1).

The first quotation is misleadingly introduced, for the 'campesinos' (sic) are in fact women coming out of church; their
'miradas de través, hoscas y pérfidas' can more appropriately be
related to Baroja's view of clerical influence ('en aquella ciudad
levítica [. . .] me hice vicioso, canalla, mal intencionado', VI, 11)
than to Laín's view of man as a disruptive element in nature. In
the second quotation Baroja's description has been prompted by
an unpleasant meeting in a *posada*; as in the previous case there is
no accompanying landscape description. Finally, in the third
quotation, as in the first, Baroja is concerned with the impact of
'una religión áspera, formalista, seca'; the 'gente de vicios sórdidos
y de hipocresías miserables' are the 'pequeños caciques, leguleyos,
prestamistas, curas'. The immediately succeeding words are:

> Los escolapios tienen allí un colegio y contribuyen con su educa-
> ción a embrutecer lentamente el pueblo. La vida en Yécora es
> sombría, tétrica, repulsiva; no se siente la alegría de vivir; en
> cambio pesan sobre las almas las sordideces de la vida (VI, 87).[57]

Again, then, the emphasis is not on man in close contact with
nature, 'el hombre habitante de esa tierra—campesino o pastor—'
(Laín, p. 33); it is on unnatural, deformed, corrupted man, akin
to urban man, to whom we shall return in a later section. He,

---

identificado con la naturaleza, que se funde con ella' (*Retrato de Pío Baroja*,
Barcelona 1953, pp. 240-1).

[57] The words 'y contribuyen con su educación a embrutecer lentamente el
pueblo' have been omitted from the *OC* edition. Similarly, also on the
repressive and corrupting influence of the *colegio* in Yécora, four characteristic paragraphs have been omitted from the end of Chapter 37. A collected
volume of such omissions (from Baroja and from other writers) would be
an interesting document on Spain during the years following the Civil War.

certainly, is an 'elemento perturbador'. But, I repeat, 'el hombre habitante de esa tierra—campesino o pastor—' is not. At the end of *Camino de perfección* Ossorio finds himself gradually won over from his own 'ideas perturbadoras, tétricas, de arte y de religión' by 'la costumbre adquirida de vivir en el campo, el amor a la tierra, la aparición enérgica del deseo de poseer y poco a poco la reintegración vigorosa de todos los instintos, naturales, salvajes', and resolves to bring up his son in Rousseauesque fashion 'en el seno de la Naturaleza', away from the 'pedante pedagogo aniquilador de los buenos instintos' and from 'la masa triste, de la masa de eunucos de nuestros miserables días' (VI, 128). Not, of course, that nature is always or everywhere beneficent in Baroja's writings. In *Camino de perfección* itself, for example, we find harsh nature, too:

> Corría un viento frío. Veíase enfrente un cerro crestado lleno de picos que se destacaba en un cielo de ópalo. Allá, a lo lejos, sobre la negrura de un pinar que escalaba un monte, corría una pincelada violeta y la tarde pasaba silenciosa mientras el cielo heroico se enrojecía con rojos resplandores. Unos cuantos miserables, hombres y mujeres, volvían del trabajo con las azadas al hombro; cantaban una especie de guajira triste, tristísima; en aquella canción debían concretarse en queja inconsciente las miserias de una vida animal de bestia de carga. ¡Tan desolador, tan amargo era el aire de la canción! Oscureció; del cielo plomizo parecían llegar rebaños de sombras; el horizonte se hizo amenazador . . . (VI, 96).

But here too, it will be noted, man is the receiver of nature's influence rather than a disruptive element. Unfortunately, Laín Entralgo overlooks such evidence, overlooks Baroja's determinist reference to this poor planet of ours as 'regido por leyes inmutables' (VI, 103)[58] and, as in his comments on Machado, overlooks Baroja's compassion for the suffering Spanish people.

Laín Entralgo's final reference is to Valle-Inclán. Since I do not seek to associate Valle-Inclán with the basically determinist thought of the 1898 Generation I make no comment on Laín's view that here, too, man is presented as a disruptive element in nature.

The case, I suggest, is indisputable. In the writers we have considered there is a basic harmony between landscape, people and culture, and it is determinism—the determinism that we found in

[58] Cf. 'El hombre es producto del medio' (1904; PB, V, 49).

Taine, in *En torno al casticismo* and in *Idearium español*—that offers the underlying intellectual justification. But the word 'underlying' is important and becomes increasingly so in works published after 1900. Indeed, the scant critical attention that has been paid to the Generation's determinist, psychological approach to Spain is itself a tribute to the literary success of the Generation. For in the most notable writings of the period Spain does not appear merely as an abstract collective psychology at the centre of a cultural network of causality—as it does in Ganivet's *Idearium español* and, to a large extent, in Unamuno's *En torno al casticismo*. The writers of 98 are concerned with national, regional and period character, but, at their literary best—and it is their literary magic, not their determinist thought, that keeps them alive for us today —they make it live for us through individuals, through 'don Cándido, don Luis, don Francisco, don Juan Alfonso y don Carlos', men immersed in an acutely observed and vividly evoked physical context of home, village and landscape. In the context of this study I am unable to do justice to the available evidence. Azorín's *La ruta de Don Quijote* (1905; II, 241–323) must serve merely as an illustration.

For Azorín, the Manchegan—and, beyond him, the Spaniard— oscillates between moments of exaltation and long periods of stagnation (the characteristic diagnosis of the time: *voluntad* and *abulia*). But except for sundry Quixotic enthusiasms the exaltation belongs to the past; in the present Azorín finds almost only faded energies. Don Rafael is a superb example (II, 271–3):

> No he nombrado antes a don Rafael porque, en realidad, don Rafael vive en un mundo aparte.
> —Don Rafael, ¿cómo está usted?—le digo yo.
> Don Rafael medita un momento en silencio, baja la cabeza, se mira las puntas de los pies, sube los hombros, contrae los labios y me dice, por fin:
> —Señor Azorín, ¿como quiere usted que esté yo? Yo estoy un poco echado a perder.
> Don Rafael, pues, está un poco echado a perder. El habita en un caserón vetusto; él vive solo; él se acuesta temprano; él se levanta tarde. ¿Qué hace don Rafael? ¿En qué se ocupa? ¿Qué piensa? No me lo preguntéis; yo no lo sé. Detrás de su vieja mansión se extiende una huerta; esta huerta está algo abandonada; todas las huertas de Argamasilla están algo abandonadas. Hay en ellas altos y blancos álamos, membrilleros achaparrados, parrales largos,

retorcidos. Y el río, por un extremo, pasa callado y transparente entre arbustos que arañan sus cristales. Por esta huerta pasea un momento, cuando se levanta, en las mañanas claras, don Rafael. Luego marcha al Casino, tosiendo, alzándose el ancho cuello de su pelliza (II, 271).

One would like to quote the whole three pages. Don Rafael lives for us as an individual—his gestures, his speech, his daily round—and yet, as we read, we become conscious that he is also the very incarnation of the Manchegan (and Spanish) broken will. Moreover, his faded energies are significantly in harmony with the state of his garden, with the state of all the gardens of Argamasilla, with the delays, across the centuries, in the building of the church, of a canal, of a railway.

The presentation of Don Silverio is similar: he is an individual with his own individual characteristics, but he is also an incarnation of collective character—and again he is significantly in harmony with his environment (II, 309). Similarly, too, La Pacheca ('esta dama, tan española, tan castiza') and Juana María ('Esta es la mujer española') and Doña María ('estas señoras de pueblo') and Doña Pilar ('esta dama tan manchega, tan española, discretísima, afable'). Nor is it merely in people that Azorín finds individual pointers to the general; it is also in buildings and towns and landscapes:

Y hay en toda la casa—en las puertas, en los techos, en los rincones —este aire de vetustez, de inmovilidad, de reposo profundo, de resignación secular—tan castizos, tan españoles—que se percibe en todas las casas manchegas [. . .].

Y luego, cuando salimos a la calle, vemos que las anchas y luminosas vías están en perfecta concordancia con los interiores. No son éstos los pueblecillos moriscos de Levante, todo recogidos, todo íntimos; son los poblados anchurosos, libres, espaciados, de la vieja gente castellana (II, 259).

¿Habrá otro pueblo, aparte de éste [Alcázar de San Juan], más castizo, más manchego, más típico, donde más íntimamente se comprenda y se sienta la alucinación de estas campiñas rasas, el vivir doloroso y resignado de estos buenos labriegos, la monotonía y la desesperación de las horas que pasan y pasan lentas, eternas, en un ambiente de tristeza, de soledad y de inacción? (II, 314).

Azorín, then, is much concerned with collective character, but it is character that lives for us in the form of vividly portrayed individuals and physical realities. Perhaps no one has taken greater delight in Spain's provincial heritage. At moments even character is forgotten:

> Cuatro balcones dejan entrar raudales de sol tibio, esplendente, confortador; en las paredes cuelgan copias de cuadros de Veláz-quez y soberbios platos antiguos; un fornido aparador de roble destaca en un testero; enfrente aparece una chimenea de mármol negro, en que las llamas se mueven rojas; encima de ella se ve un claro espejo encuadrado en rico marco de patinosa talla; ante el espejo, esbelta, primorosa, se yergue una estatuilla de la Virgen. Y en el suelo, extendida por todo el pavimento, se muestra una antigua y maravillosa alfombra gualda, de un gualdo intenso, con intensas flores bermejas, con intensos ramajes verdes (II, 263–4).

> Cuando he cenado, he salido un rato por las calles; una luna suave bañaba las fachadas blancas y ponía sombras dentelleadas de los aleros en medio del arroyo; destacaban confusos, misteriosos, los anchos balcones viejos, los escudos, las rejas coronadas de ramajes y filigranas, las recias puertas con clavos y llamadores formidables. Hay un placer íntimo, profundo, en ir recorriendo un pueblo desconocido entre las sombras; las puertas, los balcones, los esqui-nazos, los ábsides de las iglesias, las torres, las ventanas iluminadas, los ruidos de los pasos lejanos, los ladridos plañideros de los perros, las lamparillas de los retablos . . ., todo nos va sugestio-nando poco a poco, enervándonos, desatando nuestra fantasía, haciéndonos correr por las regiones del ensueño . . . (II, 296).

But collective character is never far away when writers of the 98 Generation set out to describe aspects of Spain's neglected heritage: towns and villages with their traditional trades and institutions; the streets, some narrow and winding, some broad and straight, with escutcheons over doorways and *rejas* at win-dows and glimpses of half-hidden patios; and the houses them-selves, with their dark staircases and narrow passages, their stout furniture, their family heirlooms.

> Miraba yo las casas viejas, que tenían sobre sus portales grabados sus escudos nobiliarios, y ante aquellos blasones rotos, polvorien-tos y abandonados, una ola de ideas sentimentales acudía a mi cerebro. Blasones viejos, escudos polvorientos y abandonados, ante ellos me he detenido yo siempre con respeto y curiosidad, porque ellos representan, con la cruz, el alma entera del pasado (Salaverría, *Vieja España*, p. 15).

Salaverría's emphasis here is on escutcheons. But the Cross, he suggests, is similarly important for understanding the collective soul of the past. It is a revealing observation, coming as it does at the height of the writer's anti-Catholicism and even anti-Christianity.[59] The writers of the 98 Generation are in general unorthodox in their attitude to religion, yet they accept both religion and its manifestations as important aspects of Spain's eternal tradition. If Spain should become involved in a Mediterranean policy, declared Ganivet, who was emphatically not a Catholic, it should be 'con su carácter de nación católica' (*IE*, 260). 'A mí, actualmente,' says Baroja, an agnostic, 'España se me representa como algunas de las iglesias de nuestras viejas ciudades [. . .]. Los que esperamos y deseamos la redención de España, no la queremos ver como un país próspero sin unión con el pasado; la queremos ver próspera, pero siendo substancialmente la España de siempre. Si se nos dice que a esa vieja iglesia estropeada, en vez de restaurarla se la va a derribar, y que en su sitio se levantará otra iglesia nueva, o una fábrica de gas, o un almacén de yeso, no nos entusiasmará la idea [. . .]. Hay que sondear en el espíritu de la patria y en el espíritu de la religión' (1904; V, 30–1). Unamuno's view is scarcely different:

> Y si en algún espíritu individual se nos manifiesta y revela típica y representativamente el alma colectiva de un pueblo, es sin duda en el de alguno de sus santos. La santidad, que es lo más divino en el hombre, es también lo más humano en él; la santidad es el supremo triunfo de la humanidad en el espíritu humano.
>
> Y, en general, es en el aspecto religioso donde hay que ir a buscar lo más típico y más radical de un pueblo. Importa poco lo que cada uno de sus habitantes, tomado en singular, piense o diga sobre religión; hay algo como un sentimiento religioso, más o menos vago, y revestido de una aparente irreligiosidad a las veces de la colectividad, y es el que mejor recoge ese sentimiento, el que mejor también representa a su pueblo. Y ni la política, ni la literatura, ni el arte, tendrán eficacia y durabilidad mientras no vivan de ese sentimiento, que no hay que confundir con dogmas concretos y formulables intelectualmente (1909; I, 272).

[59] '*El perro negro* [1906], *Vieja España* [1907] y *Las sombras de Loyola* [1911] hacen patente la opinión desfavorable que el ensayista tenía del cristianismo, especialmente el catolicismo romano, durante la primera década del siglo veinte' (Beatrice Petriz Ramos, *Introducción crítico-biográfica a José María Salaverría, 1873–1940*, Madrid 1960, pp. 239–40).

I pass over a dangerous corollary to all this that was not always avoided as certain members of the Generation came to place increasing emphasis on traditional values.[60] and take my final illustration from Azorín. Besides demonstrating further the 98's concern with Spain's religious tradition it refers to a significant generational event. It also shows admirably how the Generation's sensitivity to physical aspects of Spanish provincial life is prompted by an underlying determinist quest for eternal tradition. Finally, it is by the writer who, in my own view, succeeded better than any other essayist of the Generation in transmuting intellectual theory into poetic reality:

> La visita que en 1900 hicimos a Toledo fue capital en el desenvolvimiento de la escuela. Fuimos a Toledo, no como frívolos curiosos, sino cual apasionados. Nos atraían los monumentos religiosos. En ellos se encarna la nacionalidad española. Interesábannos las iglesias visigóticas y las herrerianas, las iglesitas de pueblo y las grandes y suntuosas catedrales. En las catedrales, verdaderos mundos del arte, íbamos desde la estofa de una casulla antigua a la tabla de un retablo. Y acaso lo que más nos apasionaba era un arte eminentemente español, que en las catedrales, sobre todo en las grandes catedrales, como las de Toledo y Cuenca, alcanza manifestación espléndida: el arte del hierro forjado. Rejas, cruces, atriles, púlpitos, los hay primorosos labrados en hierro. Sobre todo, las rejas. El rejero español ha sido un maestro incomparable. Nos deteníamos ante las inmensas rejas, rejas que separan el coro del resto de la nave; rejas algunas sobredoradas en parte, e íbamos pasando nuestras manos, voluptuosamente por los barrotes (1941; VI, 305–6).

#### (b) *The quest for Spain through literature*

Todos [estos ensayos] se refieren a España; casi todos atañen a los clásicos. Es este libro como la segunda parte de *Lecturas españolas*. Los mismos sentimientos dominan en él: preocupación por el 'problema' de nuestra patria; deseo de buscar nuestro espíritu a través de los clásicos (Azorín, in the Prologue to *Clásicos y modernos*, 1913; II, 741).

[60] I refer to the sort of religious intolerance exemplified in Maeztu's 'En España no se concibe un patriotismo integral que no nazca de un pecho católico' (cit. Antonio Hernández, *Eternidad de España*, Madrid 1958, p.12). It is an attitude regretfully consistent both with the 98 Generation's determinism and with its anti-democratic standpoint in politics.

'He pensado,' says Unamuno, '[. . .] de cuánto mejor nos revelan un siglo sus obras de ficción que sus historias' (*ETC*, 796). 'En lo eterno son más verdaderas las leyendas y ficciones que no la historia' (1905; III, 132). Similar notions appear frequently in his writings. The artist, immersed in a given temporal, geographical and national context, bears inevitably the stamp of his context, communicates it in his writings and thereby offers his readers guidance to an understanding of that context. Moreover, whereas historians and journalists tend to concentrate on superficial aspects of the human context ('ecos y retintines de sonidos muertos', *ETC*, 795) the great creative writer, probing deeper, gives expression to underlying forces rooted in the character of the people themselves. 'El genio,' claims Unamuno, 'es una muchedumbre; es la muchedumbre individualizada, es un pueblo hecho persona' (1905; I, 1263); 'En el genio se verifica el consorcio íntimo entre lo popular y lo artístico, entre el fondo y la forma, es donde las ideas más *sociales* hallan expresión más *individual*, por ser el genio quien tiene más *individualidad social*, quien en la más acusada personalidad recoje mejor el espíritu colectivo, quien regula las palpitaciones de su corazón por las del gran corazón de las muchedumbres' (1894; IV, 717). Ganivet made similar points in *Idearium español*: an artistic masterpiece is inevitably in harmony with the spirit of the nation in which it originated, 'y cuanto más estrecha sea la concordancia, el mérito de la obra será mayor, porque el artista saca sus fuerzas invisiblemente de la confusión de sus ideas con las ideas de su territorio, obrando como un reflector en el que estas ideas se cruzan y se mezclan y adquieren, al cruzarse y mezclarse, la luz de que separadas carecían' (278). 'Sí,' added Azorín three decades later; 'para nosotros, el "genio" es la condensación de la muchedumbre [. . .]. "Yo no creo en el genio—nos decía hace poco Baroja—; el genio no es más que el punto de confluencia, en un cerebro, de las grandes corrientes creadas por las muchedumbres inconscientemente." Y eso es lo exacto. Y la crítica, la verdadera, necesaria, creadora crítica, sanciona lo hecho ya, corrobora lo hecho ya por la conciencia colectiva, pone sobre la obra la estampilla que la hará circular a lo largo de los siglos venideros' (1929; V, 164). A work of art, then, is a potential psychological document. 'Quand ce document est riche et qu'on sait l'interpréter, on y trouve la psychologie d'une âme, souvent celle d'un siècle, et parfois celle d'une race' (*HLA*, I, 54–5). Artistic merit and faithfulness to the spirit of an age or people tend to be equated. Literary classics are seen as keys to collective self-knowledge.

We are touching on another notable characteristic of the new generation: in their reading of literature as in their travels their emphasis is on 'lo eterno de la casta', 'lo típico y lo característico', 'la continuidad nacional'. 'De cada país,' writes Unamuno, 'me interesan los [escritores] que más del país son, los más castizos, los más propios (1910; III, 544). The great writer, like the exceptional historian, holds up, as it were, a mirror to the collective consciousness:

> Hay hombres que representan una raza: la germánica, que construye mundos con ideas, Hegel y Goethe; el genio francés, metódico y positivo, Descartes y Condillac; el espíritu inglés, mezcla del germano y el latino, Shakespeare y Carlyle, Spencer y Stuart Mill (1887; MU, IV, 155).

> La Fontaine pertenece al grupo, castizamente francés, de espíritus claros, sutiles, irónicos, elegantes, despreocupados. Montaigne, Molière, La Bruyère, Fontenelle, Vauvenargues, Chamfort, Voltaire . . . Toda la médula de Francia está en ellos: todo el genio latino, preciso y conciso, se aposenta en sus plumas ([J. Martínez Ruiz], in *Alma Española* 13, 21 January 1904).

> No hay duda de que los héroes de Turguénef y Dostoyevsky están concebidos para representar a Rusia, ni de que Tartarín es símbolo de Francia, ni de que Fausto es Alemania, ni de que Don Quijote de la Mancha es, en la mente de Cervantes, la encarnación del siglo XVI (1935; Maeztu, I, 110).

Applied to Spanish literature—and indeed to the arts in general—the notion reveals itself in the same three immediately recognizable areas of emphasis that were referred to in the previous section: period character, regional character and national character. I offer a single example of each and, in order to emphasize that it is a movement rather than a closely identifiable group of *noventayochistas* with which I am here concerned, I take my examples intentionally from writers not included in Granjel's *noventayochista* quadriga:

> El *Myo Cid* es un balbuceo heroico, en toscas medidas de paso de andar, donde llega a expresarse plenamente el alma castellana del siglo XII, un alma elemental, de gigante mozalbete, entre gótica y

celtíbera, exenta de reflexión, compuesta de ímpetus sobrios, pícaros o nobles (1911; Ortega, II, 42).

Cómplices del tal inopia y pasividad [of Mallorca], son este clima espléndido, esta naturaleza virgiliana y exquisita. 'La verde Helvecia, bajo el cielo de la Calabria, con la solemnidad y el silencio del Oriente', que Aurora Dupin descubrió en Mallorca, infunde como una placidez y ensueño regalado, un 'otium divos' a que es muy difícil sustraerse. Así se engendra un pueblo de artistas: artistas de la vida, artistas de la palabra, de la idea y del color. Por encima de las ruinas y disgregaciones de que he hablado, flota el alma tradicional y poética de Mallorca, llena de fantasía piadosa, de tranquila resignación y contentamiento. Palpita en sus consejas o 'rondalles', en sus canciones populares y sus melodías, impregnadas de misteriosa somnolencia oriental [. . .]. Los dos Aguiló, Roselló, Peña, Costa, son altas encarnaciones de la inspiración genuinamente insular (Miguel S. Oliver, 'Alma mallorquina', in *Alma Española* 4, 29 November 1903).

Para conocer el alma de un pueblo, para sondear en sus sentimientos, prejuicios y estados de ánimo tradicionales, pocos medios existirán tan directos y eficaces como el refranero, ese centón de filosofía anónima en que la conciencia popular deja lo más íntimo de su ser (José Mª Salaverría, *Vieja España*, Madrid 1907, p. 87).

Period character, regional character and national character. But it is often difficult to separate them. As a given hero or work or writer may be seen as the epitome of a particular period or region, so also, within Spain, a given period (notably the Golden Age) or a given region (notably Castile) may be seen as the epitome of the whole nation throughout its history. Esteem is again strangely allied to the notion of 'lo característico' and 'lo fundamental'. An outstanding hero or work or writer may be seized upon as the incarnation of a period or region and, beyond period and region, of the collective, time-resistant national spirit.[61]

*Don Quixote*—book, character and author—is the most notable

[61] One may, of course, go even further than this and Unamuno especially, with his tendency to equate eternal tradition and universality, frequently does:

He de repetir una vez más lo que ya he escrito varias veces, y es que cuanto más de su tiempo y de su país es uno, más es de los tiempos y de los países todos (1910; III, 538–9).

But we are concerned in this section with the quest for Spain. I therefore leave such examples aside.

example. The tercentenary celebrations of 1905 gave an incentive for reinterpretations in the light of contemporary beliefs and national needs:

El año 1905 se señaló, en la historia espiritual de los pueblos de lengua castellana, por las fiestas con que conmemoró España el tercer centenario de la publicación de la primera parte del *Quijote* [. . .]. Con estas fiestas se trató de proclamar solemnemente la obra de Cervantes como lazo espiritual, norma de conducta, fuente de doctrina y manantial común de vida para todas las nacionalidades donde se habla español (Maeztu, *DQ*, 19).

By a tacit determinist equation of greatness and typicality, *Don Quixote*, as the supreme literary masterpiece of Spain, was seen also as the supreme literary incarnation of Spain's collective being and thence also, frequently—by a further determinist assumption that in faithfulness to the collective being lay the path to success —as a guide to national destinies. The notion has underlain a host of subsequent studies. I confine myself here to a few representative examples.

In his *Meditaciones del Quijote* (1914) Ortega y Gasset wrote of Cervantes as follows:

He aquí una plenitud española. He aquí una palabra que en toda ocasión podemos blandir como si fuera una lanza. ¡Ah! Si supiéramos con evidencia en qué consiste el estilo de Cervantes, la manera cervantina de acercarse a las cosas, lo tendríamos todo logrado. Porque en estas cimas espirituales reina inquebrantable solidaridad y un estilo poético lleva consigo una filosofía y una moral, una ciencia y una política. Si algún día viniera alguien y nos descubriera el perfil del estilo de Cervantes, bastaría con que prolongáramos sus líneas sobre los demás problemas colectivos para que despertáramos a nueva vida. Entonces, si hay entre nosotros coraje y genio, cabría hacer con toda pureza el nuevo ensayo español (I, 363).

Maeztu, in *Don Quijote, Don Juan y la Celestina* (1926), stands out from his generation by his reservations, reservations that he had already expressed at the time of the tercentenary celebrations. Certainly *Don Quixote* is 'el libro nacional por antonomasia' (59) and it gives expression to a 'filosofía moral' that has since become the 'máxima universal de nuestra alma española' (59). But Maeztu's emphasis is on the work's purely historical context, a context of exhaustion and disenchantment. 'En el momento actual el problema de España consiste precisamente en recobrar la iniciativa' (64). *Don Quixote*, the supreme representative of its age and indeed of the Spanish soul since then, can no longer be accepted as a guide to national destinies. Here as elsewhere Maeztu, lacking—or, according to one's viewpoint, happily free from—the notion of a 'roca viva' of physical environment, is only partially representative of the main current of thought with which we are concerned in this book.

Salvador de Madariaga, on the other hand, though younger—and therefore not generally considered to be a member of the 98 Generation—is a more faithful representative of what I take to be the classic 98 approach to Spanish civilization. His *Semblanzas literarias contemporáneas* (first Spanish edition, 1924) offer the strongest evidence, but his *Englishmen, Frenchmen, Spaniards: An Essay in Comparative Psychology* (1928), too, is an important document. In it he seeks to establish a basic psychological distinction between the Englishman, the man of action, the Frenchman, the man of thought, and the Spaniard, the man of passion. We must confine ourselves here to his chapter on 'Art and Letters' and, more specifically, to his view of *Don Quixote* as an expression of Spain's basic 'aesthetic attitude' which, consistent with his view of Spanish character, he finds to be 'natural, spontaneous, innate, and general' (204):

> No country has ever worked with greater disregard for rules in literature; yet in no country have men of letters believed in rules with greater faith; while the critical intellect of Spain asserts the rules of the literary game, its creative spirit breaks through them, and this opposition appears even in one and the same person. A score of names might be quoted, but all may be represented by Cervantes himself. *Don Quixote* contains in one and the same work the masterpiece of freedom from rules and the precepts which Cervantes respected in theory, and which in practice he fortunately forgot.
>
> Cervantes may serve also as an example of another feature of Spanish literature and art in general—its concentration on man. This is, as we know, consonant with our views on the Spanish character in general (209).

Madariaga does not specifically hold up *Don Quixote* as a guide to national action, but nor does he, like Maeztu, find it in a threat to Spain's future. The Spanish character that underlies *Don Quixote*, like the English character and the French character, must persist and make its own special contribution to the world. Men should respect 'the admirable variety of national characters' as a manifestation of the wealth of Creation and 'enjoy it as a spectacle and a gift' (249).

But we must return to the key year of 1905 and to the two most notably Quixotic publications of that year: Azorín's *La ruta de Don Quijote* and Unamuno's *La vida de Don Quijote y Sancho*. They epitomize better than any other works known to me the new generation's approach to Cervantes's masterpiece and, thence also, to literature in general. Both authors emphasize Don Quixote as a product of real-life circumstances, both are concerned primarily with the character of the hero, both find in his character pointers to important aspects of Spanish national psychology, both accept that character as basic to Spain's future. And yet, beyond these underlying similarities, the two works could scarcely be more different.

*La ruta de Don Quijote* (II, 241–323) is the account of a literary pilgrimage through Don Quixote's La Mancha: in search of Don Quixote, in search of La Mancha and, beyond these, in search of Spain. The quest for Spain through travel and the quest for Spain through literature are intimately interwoven. La Mancha throws light on Don Quixote; less explicitly but not less forcibly Azorín's reading of the *Quixote* guides him in his findings on La Mancha. We begin, Taine-like, with the alleged influence of race (Chapter III: 'Psicología de Argamasilla') and environment (Chapter IV: 'El ambiente de Argamasilla'):

Todas las cosas son fatales, lógicas, necesarias; todas las cosas tienen su razón poderosa y profunda. Don Quijote de la Mancha había de ser forzosamente de Argamasilla de Alba. Oídlo bien; no lo olvidéis jamás: el pueblo entero de Argamasilla es lo que se llama un pueblo andante (254).

Yo salgo a la calle; las estrellas parpadean en lo alto misteriosas; se oye el aullido largo de un perro; un mozo canta una canción que semeja un alarido y una súplica ... Decidme, ¿no es este el medio en que florecen las voluntades solitarias, libres, llenas de ideal —como la de Alonso Quijano el Bueno—; pero ensimismadas, soñadoras, incapaces, en definitiva, de concertarse en los prosaicos, vulgares, pacientes pactos que la marcha de los pueblos exige? (262–3).[62]

The former quotation is from a chapter that was probably written before Azorín set out on his travels, for it is based on an imaginative, Don Quixote orientated reading of the unpublished *Relaciones topográficas* of 1575–76, which Azorín presumably consulted in the Academy of History in Madrid. The latter quotation, on the other hand, is from a chapter that was clearly written in Argamasilla itself. In other words, the progression in the former case is from Don Quixote (literature) to La Mancha (travel); in the latter case it is from La Mancha to Don Quixote. But the distinction is artificial. The two interact constantly in Azorín's quest for the essence of La Mancha. Nor is it only a quest for the essence of La Mancha; it is a quest also for the essence of Spain. Despite the emphasis on specifically Manchegan formative influences, there is a repeated transition between *manchego, castizo* and *español*. For Azorín, La Mancha and Don Quixote are the epitome of Spain:

> ¿No es esta la patria del gran ensoñador don Alonso Quijano? ¿No está en este pueblo compendiada la historia eterna de la tierra española? ¿No es esto la fantasía loca, irrazonada e impetuosa que rompe de pronto la inacción para caer otra vez estérilmente en el marasmo? (317).

In the immediately following lines—the final lines of the work as it originally appeared in *El Imparcial*—the author weighs the good and the bad in the collective character that he has been probing and, implicitly at least, holds up the *Quixote* as a guide to Spain's future:

> Y esta es—y con esto termino—la exaltación loca y baldía que Cervantes condenó en el *Quijote*; no aquel amor al ideal, no aquella ilusión, no aquella ingenuidad, no aquella audacia, no aquella confianza en nosotros mismos, no aquella vena ensoñadora que tanto admira el pueblo inglés en nuestro Hidalgo, que tan indispensables son para la realización de todas las grandes y generosas empresas humanas, y sin las cuales los pueblos y los individuos fatalmente van a la decadencia . . . (317).

[62] My reference is to the *Obras completas* but because of an error in that text I quote from the 1905 edition.

Unamuno's *Vida de Don Quijote y Sancho* (III, 49–256) is not a travel book and, in comparison with *La ruta de Don Quijote*, Manchegan race and environment play little part. We know nothing of Don Quixote's lineage, says Unamuno in the first paragraph of the work, 'ni de cómo hubieran ido asentándosele en el espíritu las visiones de la asentada llanura manchega en que solía cazar' (65). But his life, like that of his people, was clearly influenced by his immediate physical context:

> La tierra que alimentaba a Don Quijote es una tierra pobre, tan desollada por seculares chaparrones, que por dondequiera afloran a ras de ella sus entrañas berroqueñas. Basta ver cómo van por los inviernos sus ríos apretados a largos trechos entre tajos, hoces y congostos y llevándose al mar en sus aguas fangosas el rico mantillo que habría de dar a la tierra su verdura. Y esta pobreza del suelo hizo a sus moradores andariegos, pues o tenían que ir a buscarse el pan a luengas tierras, o bien tenían que ir guiando a las ovejas de que vivían, de pasto en pasto. Nuestro hidalgo hubo de ver, año tras año, pasar a los pastores pastoreando sus merinas, sin hogar asentado, a la de Dios nos valga, y acaso viéndolos así soñó alguna vez con ver tierras nuevas y correr mundo (66).

'Vino a perder el juicio,' said Cervantes. 'Por nuestro bien lo perdió,' comments Unamuno. 'Hizo en aras de su pueblo el más grande sacrificio: el de su juicio. Llenósele la fantasía de hermosos desatinos, y creyó ser verdad lo que es sólo hermosura. Y lo creyó con fe tan viva, con fe engendradora de obras, que acordó poner en hecho lo que su desatino le mostraba, y en puro creerlo hízolo verdad' (68). Don Quixote epitomizes what is best in his people (87–8, 115–16) and is joined in spiritual brotherhood with the mystics of his own Castilian land, 'con aquellas almas llenas de sed de los secos parameros sobre que moraban y de la serena limpieza del terso cielo bajo el cual penaban' (206). The Spanish people have been called a 'pueblo moribundo', but fortunes change:

> Hay que aspirar, de todos modos, a hacerse eternos y famosos, no sólo en los presentes, sino en los venideros siglos; no puede subsistir como pueblo aquel pueblo cuyos pastores, su conciencia no se lo representen con una misión histórica, con un ideal propio que realizar en la tierra [. . .]. ¿Es que no hay un alma de España tan inmortal como el alma de cada uno de sus hijos? (231).

Don Quixote is there to show the way:

> ¿Hay una filosofía española, mi Don Quijote? Sí, la tuya, la filosofía de Dulcinea, la de no morir, la de creer, la de crear la verdad. Y esta filosofía ni se aprende en cátedras ni se expone por lógica inductiva ni deductiva, ni surge de silogismos, ni de laboratorios, sino surge del corazón (233).

Despite their emphasis on the formative influence of Don Quixote's immediate physical environment, Unamuno and Azorín both generalize outwards from region and period to Spain as a whole. It is characteristic of the age. Moreover, not only do we find, in writings of the time, a frequent overlapping of period, regional and national character. Often—and perhaps most typically—the quest for Spain through literature is inextricably bound up, as in Azorín's *La ruta de Don Quijote*, with the quest for Spain through travel. The juxtaposition of the following lines by Azorín is especially revealing:

> ¿En qué nos hace pensar este florecimiento de la lírica que hay ahora en Castilla? Yo pienso en el paisaje castellano y en las viejas ciudades. La poesía lírica es la esencia de las cosas. La lírica de ahora—bajo someras influencias extrañas—nos da la esencia de este viejo pueblo de Castilla (1909; II, 485).

> Cuando en estas llanuras, por las noches, se contemplen las estrellas, con su parpadear infinito, ¿no estará aquí el alma ardorosa y dúctil de nuestros místicos? (ibid.).

In the former quotation the author's reflections on literature prompt visions of the Spanish countryside; in the latter—only a few lines later—his visions of the Spanish countryside prompt reflections on literature. It is characteristic of the approach with which we are here concerned. A few further examples must suffice:

> Cervantes recuerda a Don Quijote, y Don Quijote a los ardientes, escuetos y dilatados campos de Castilla, tan ardientes, escuetos y dilatados como el espíritu quijotesco. Vamos al campo (1889; MU, I, 125).

> Yo amo esa gran figura dolorosa [Alonso Quijano el Bueno] que es nuestro símbolo y nuestro espejo. Yo voy—con mi maleta de cartón y mi capa—a recorrer brevemente los lugares que él recorriera (1905; Azorín, II, 248).

La palabra del ganadero le recordaba el espíritu ascético de los místicos y de los artistas castellanos; espíritu anárquico cristiano, lleno de soberbias y de humildades, de austeridad y de libertinaje de espíritu (1902; PB, VI, 53).

Y mientras caminaba [The author is climbing up to the castle in Burgos] iba recordando las figuras más salientes de la historia castellana, el Cid, Torquemada, Pizarro, Don Quijote (Salaverría, *Vieja España*, p. 22).

Por tierras de Sigüenza y Berlanga de Duero, en días de agosto alanceados por el sol, he hecho yo—Rubín de Cendoya, místico español—un viaje sentimental sobre una mula torda de altas orejas inquietas. Son las tierras que el Cid cabalgó. Son, además, las tierras donde se suscitó el primer poeta castellano, el autor del poema llamado *Myo Cid* (1911; Ortega, II, 41).

A este ambiente adusto, sin transiciones lánguidas, corresponde la complexión mental del castellano: leñosa, con anteojeras, formalista, dogmática, sin repliegues, imperiosa; la que ergotiza en los dramas de Calderón y Lope, la que dictó la novela picaresca, la que forjó la escolástica, la que destruyó la civilización precolombina, la que enterró y quemó vivos a los protestantes de Holanda, la que atizó las leñeras del Santo Oficio en la Península ... (Emilio Bobadilla—*Fray Candil*—, *Viajando por España*, Madrid 1912, pp. 116–17).

In our study so far we have found little emphasis on purely literary values. The main emphasis has been on literature as document and thence as guide. Not that literary values are therefore irrelevant. Literary greatness and psychological documentary value, we have seen, tend to be equated. At times, as with the *Quixote*, the recognition of greatness appears to have encouraged the use of the work as a source-book for probings into Spanish collective psychology; at other times, as with anonymous, traditional poetry, potential as psychological document appears to have enhanced critical esteem. The same criterion of judgement was applied also to foreign books on Spain. 'La atracción profunda del *Viaje* de Gautier,' wrote Azorín, 'y más que de la prosa, de las poesías *España*, consiste en que este gran poeta, instintivamente, con intuición maravillosa, ha sabido recoger y expresar una partícula de esta esencia española' (1912; II, 608). Similarly, for Unamuno, Borrow's *Bible in Spain* was 'uno de los más preciosos tesoros de la psicología española' (1907; IV, 513), and in Larreta's *La gloria de don Ramiro* he found 'un generoso y feliz esfuerzo por penetrar en el alma de la España del siglo XVI, y, por tanto, en el alma de la España de todos los tiempos y lugares' (1909; I, 270). Similarly again, Maeztu wrote:

> En la emoción de la España vencida se inspiró Rubén para sus *Cantos de Vida y Esperanza*. ¡Qué título para puesto al contraste de las prosas regeneracionistas que la catástrofe suscitó en España! El primero de esos *Cantos* es la *Salutación del optimista*, único himno hispanoamericano que tenemos. Si un instinto de salvación nos quisiera mover a preparar el espíritu de las nuevas generaciones para la defensa de las tierras hispánicas, no habría ceremonial en que no se recitaran las mágicas estrofas:
>
> > ¡Ínclitas razas ubérrimas, sangre de Hispania fecunda,
> > espíritus fraternos, luminosas almas, salve!
>
> > (*DH*, 138–9).

Finally, to step for a moment outside literature, Azorín's claim that the 1898 Generation 'da aire al fervor por *El Greco*, ya iniciado en Cataluña' (1913; II, 917) is well known. What we perhaps do not yet know is whether the aesthetic appeal of El Greco's work encouraged the Generation's view of him as 'este poderoso revelador de lo más íntimo y más bravío del alma castellana' (1908; MU, VIII, 160) or whether their view of him as a revealer of the Castilian soul served rather to enhance their estimation of his aesthetic appeal. Perhaps the two interacted. The 98 movement and Modernism, despite basic differences, are often strangely linked.

In *El oasis de los clásicos* (1952) Azorín makes a case that appears not to accord with my emphasis on the 98's characteristic concern with literature as document. There are two very different approaches to literature, he claims: 'crítica' and 'erudición'. In the former, one looks at literary works of the past exclusively from one's personal, contemporary standpoint and considers how they act upon one's own modern sensitivity; in the latter case, one emphasizes the context of the works: the history, environment and circumstances that influenced their writing, and their significance in their age. The distinction is obviously justified and insufficiently borne in mind. One is lamentably too familiar with the historically minded reviewer who, when confronted with a declared 'critical study' in which the author questions the value of a given work of the past for readers of the present, proceeds to lecture the author on the 'importance' of the work in the context of its age. But we must return to Azorín's *El oasis de los clásicos* and consider a key paragraph:

¿Qué contestaríamos si un extranjero—o nacional—nos preguntase cuáles son los libros o trabajos que se han escrito en España sobre el *Quijote*? Guardaríamos silencio un momento, mientras reflexionábamos, y luego diríamos que . . . en España, en el dominio de la erudición, se ha hecho bastante respecto al gran libro; pero cuando un aficionado a la literatura—o un artista— interroga sobre las obras referentes a un autor, lo que desea— generalmente—es conocer lo que el libro o los libros de que se trate han parecido a la sensibilidad de un artista o de un pensador. La erudición es cosa secundaria; la erudición ayuda a restablecer un medio, un ambiente en que la obra se ha producido; la erudición nos habla de las circunstancias que concurrieron en el autor de la obra. Pero ¿cómo es *por dentro* esta obra? ¿Cómo ha ido evolucionando a través del tiempo? ¿De qué modo suena o disuena a nuestra mentalidad moderna? ¿Qué emoción se produce entre nuestro espíritu y el espíritu del artista pasado? Todo esto no nos lo dicen los eruditos; rara vez la erudición se alía a un temperamento de artista; el caso de un Taine o unos Goncourt no es frecuente (IX, 967-8).

On the one hand, 'la sensibilidad de un artista o de un pensador' with emphasis on our present-day response to the work; on the other hand, 'la erudición', 'cosa secundaria', with emphasis on 'medio', 'ambiente' and 'circunstancias'. There can be little doubt, I suggest, on the evidence offered so far, about where Azorín's own emphasis lies. It is clearly on erudition. His treatment of Larra's theatre in *Lecturas españolas* (1912) will serve to press the point:

En la obra teatral de Larra es preciso considerar la estética, la crítica social y la concepción del problema de España (II, 619).

To the problem of aesthetics Azorín allows little more than half a page; to Larra's criticism of the age in which he lived—Larra as an eye witness of the problem of Spain—Azorín allows a page; to Larra's conception of the problem of Spain—Larra as an interpreter of the problem—he allows two and a half pages. In all, three and a half pages of documentation on the problem of Spain and half a page on purely literary values. 'Pero ¿cómo es *por dentro* esta obra? [. . .]. Todo esto no los no dicen los eruditos'. Nor does Azorín, at least in the case here referred to. Of course he does consider how Larra's work acts on his own 'mentalidad moderna', but his own particular 'mentalidad moderna' is extremely erudite in the sense that he himself gives to the term. 'Me es imposible ver un clásico español desligado, abstraído, de su cielo, de su tierra, de sus coetáneos, de su ambiente' (1952; IX, 1023). It is characteristic of his age: 'La Historia nos tenía captados [. . .]. La generación de 1898 es una generación historicista' (1941; VI, 229).

In Azorín, then, as in many of his most notable contemporaries, erudition—especially historical erudition—plays an important role. But must we therefore consider it as a 'cosa secundaria'? Azorín's reference to Taine and the Goncourt brothers is significant. As in them, so also in Azorín, erudition is fundamental to the author's vision. From a modern critical standpoint one may regret the fact and wish that more attention were paid to the question '¿cómo es *por dentro* esta obra?' But the main concern of the reader of today is not whether Azorín is a critic or a scholar. It is whether, beyond criticism and scholarship, he brings his findings to life as literature.

There is perhaps no need to illustrate my own enthusiastic response. I should simply be echoing the case I made in the previous section. The range of evidence would be different but my findings would be basically the same, with a similar emphasis on the author's vivid portrayal of individuals and physical realities. Travel, we have seen, prompts reflections on Spanish literature, and Spanish literature prompts recollections of travel:

> La coherencia estriba en una curiosidad por lo que constituye el ambiente español—paisajes, letras, arte, hombres, ciudades, interiores—y en una preocupación por un porvenir de bienestar y de justicia para España (1912; II, 535).

> Si amo los clásicos es porque amo los pueblos y el paisaje de España. Para mí todo esto es una misma cosa. ¡Cuántas páginas de los clásicos—de Quevedo, de Cervantes—he visto vivas en los pueblos! (1917; IX, 1195–6).

> Todo es sincrónico y coherente en la vida española: el teatro, la mística, el paisaje—el paisaje de Castilla—, la idiosincrasia del ciudadano (1924; IV, 523).

There is nevertheless a difference of emphasis. In Azorín's search for Spain through literature imaginative reconstruction plays a greater part. The work of literature serves as a springboard to the author's recollections of his own travel experiences recorded in countless 'íntimos cuadernitos inseparables del escritor' (1941; VI, 216).

*Un pueblecito: Riofrío de Avila* (1916) is an extreme example. In the *feria de libros* Azorín has discovered an unknown work published in 1791 by a local parish priest, 'un pequeño Montaigne de Riofrío de Avila' (III, 537). His own book is simply a series of reflections and evocations prompted by his reading. But what of the reality underlying Bejarano Galavis's book? What will the village be like today? One recalls the opening chapter of *La ruta de Don Quijote*. But now Azorín asks these questions at the end of his work. Imaginative reconstruction has taken over from the immediate experience of travel. I quote the final lines of the work:

En distintas ocasiones, mientras redactábamos estas páginas, hemos estado a punto de hacer el viaje a Riofrío de Avila. No quedará ya en aquel pueblecito ni rastro de Bejarano Galavis . . . ¿ Bejarano Galavis? ¿ Quién era este hombre? ¿ Qué realidad evocan estos apellidos? El viaje se ha quedado sin hacer. Pero con la imaginación hemos corrido de Madrid a Avila y de Avila a Riofrío. Con la imaginación hemos entrado en la vieja ciudad; luego nos hemos aposentado en la fondita que está delante de la catedral; a la mañana siguiente, un coche destartalado nos ha conducido, dando tumbos, por un caminejo torcido hasta Riofrío. Y en Riofrío hemos estado unas horas y hemos visto las callejas del pueblo y echado una mirada por la campiña. ¿ Para qué hacer el viaje? Hay un momento en la vida en que descubrimos que la imagen de la realidad es mejor que la realidad misma. No acertamos a decir si este descubrimiento que hacemos en el fondo de nuestra conciencia, nos causa alegría o tristeza. (Alegría; pero ¿ y la disminución de nuestra curiosidad intelectual? Tristeza; pero ¿ y los nuevos aspectos que nuestro desinterés nos hace ver en las cosas y que antes no veíamos?) La imagen del pueblecito de la sierra de Avila era mejor que el mismo pueblecito. Allí no quedará ya nada de aquel hombre que habitó en una de sus casas hace ya más de un siglo. Riofrío no nos diría nada; su imagen nos sugiere algo. Pasan los hombres, las cosas . . . y los lugares. 'Los lugares—dice Joubert en uno de sus *Pensamientos*—, los lugares mueren como los hombres, aunque parezcan subsistir.' Los lugares son nuestra sensibilidad; un lugar que ha atraído y polarizado la sensibilidad humana no dice nada cuando el tiempo ha apagado sus motivos de excitación espiritual. *Los lugares mueren como los hombres.* Riofrío de Avila, siendo una realidad, ya no existe. Sólo nos queda, en lo íntimo del espíritu, su imagen. Una imagen fugaz, como la de un sueño: una imagen de algo que queremos recordar y no recordamos . . . (III, 594–5).

'¿Para qué hacer el viaje? Hay un momento en la vida en que descubrimos que la imagen de la realidad es mejor que la realidad misma.' We are on the verge of our next section: 'The Quest for Self'. But before we finally make the transition I wish to return to the previous sub-section with its emphasis on the quest for Spain through travel. Is travel mere observation? May not the writer, there also, employ imaginative reconstruction?[63] I take my single illustration from the writer who, together with Azorín, is the very epitome of the characteristics I most associate with the movement of 1898. Unamuno and a friend arrive late one night at the village of Brianzuelo de la Sierra, are given beds in the local inn and immediately go to sleep. In the following lines Unamuno describes his awakening:

Desperté temprano, pero con gran pereza de levantarme. Oía rebullicio de gente y de caballería en la calleja. Y pensaba: '¿Qué gente será? ¿Qué harán? ¿Qué dirán? ¿Cuántos serán? ¿En qué pasarán el tiempo en este lugarejo agazapado entre castañares, aquí, en este bravío repliegue de la sierra? ¿Qué idea tendrán del mundo? ¿Cómo será el lugar?' Y me puse a imaginar cómo sería el lugar, sobre la pobre base de mi rapidísima inspección nocturna de la víspera. Todo menos levantarme e ir a verlo.
Vino mi compañero:
—¡Ea, perezoso, arriba! Vamos a ver el pueblo . . .
—¿A ver el pueblo?—le contesté—. ¿Y para qué?
—¿Para qué? ¡Tú estás malo! . . . ¿Pues a qué hemos venido?
—¡A soñarlo! Déjame que me le figure a mi antojo . . .
—Lo mismo podías habértele figurado en la ciudad . . .
—No, lo mismo no. Aquí estoy en él, y la conciencia de estar en él vivifica mi imaginación; aquí respiro con su aire de efluvios espirituales; aquí oigo el rumor de sus gentes . . . ¿Quieres que no salgamos de este cuarto, y que esta noche, a oscuras, prosigamos nuestra excursión? (1900; I, 68).

[63] Cf. 'Todo pintor pinta de memoria, hasta lo que está viendo; pinta un recuerdo. Lo que hay que ver no es la visión presente; lo que hay que ver es su recuerdo, su imagen' (1922; MU, I, 497).

Thirty-six years later, in one of his final articles, Unamuno drew attention to the same characteristic in his most important travel book of the intervening period:

> 'Andar y ver'—se dice—. Y el que esto os dice ha publicado una colección de relatos de excursiones con el título de *Andanzas y visiones españolas*. Pero es más lo que ha soñado que lo que ha visto. Y sobre todo lo que ha soñado ver (1936; I, 712).

If the evidence of these last pages is representative, we cannot accept without reservations the scientific pretensions of the men of 98 or their proclaimed desire to 'acercarse a la realidad' and to attain a 'conocimiento minucioso de España' (Azorín, II, 918; VI, 254).

> The scientific process consists of or makes use of a rapid alternation, a rapid interaction between an imaginative episode of thought and a critical episode of thought. In the imaginative process we form an opinion, we take a view, we frame a hypothesis, we make an informed guess, about what the truth might be. We invent a possible world or possible fragment of the world. We tell a story that might be a story about real life—and of course all this lies outside logic. But then we subject these imaginative conjectures to ruthless criticism to see if our imagined world corresponds to a first approximation to the real world (P. B. Medawar, 'Scientific Method', in *The Listener*, 12 October 1967).[64]

In the writers of 98 the imaginative conjectures are evident. What is lacking, perhaps, is the ruthless criticism. In *En torno al casticismo* and *Idearium español*, we have seen—as in Taine—evidence was apparently used to confirm rather than to test hypotheses, and the underlying determinism, by its very laxity, allowed free interplay between 'la realidad' and 'la imagen de la realidad', between 'lo que [se] ha visto' and 'lo que [se] ha soñado ver'. Moreover, the hypotheses—'la imagen de la realidad', 'lo que [se] ha soñado ver'—were significantly related to each writer's own personal concerns. To what extent is this true of the 1898 movement as a whole?

It would be foolish to attempt an answer within the narrow limits of this study. In the first place, we are not yet sure which

---

[64] I here accept a definition in line with the current Popper-like emphasis on the scientific process as hypothetico-deductive rather than inductive. A definition in line with the latter, orthodox view might suggest that the writers of 98 were unscientific at all stages of their thought.

are the writers of 98; an internal, textual approach to a movement is necessarily a process of *tanteos* aimed at establishing a significant pattern of characteristics by which membership may eventually be judged. In the second place, each author, each work even, requires its own monograph, with an appropriate consideration in each case of the relationship between reality, image of reality and personal concerns. My aim in the rest of this study, then, is merely to show that the type of subjectivity observed in *En torno al casticismo* and *Idearium español* finds significant expression elsewhere in acknowledged members of the 'Generation'. In their travels as in their reading, I shall suggest, the men of 98 were not only looking for Spain; they were also looking for themselves.

## 5. THE QUEST FOR SELF

### (a) *The quest for self through travel*

Ahora, en los días que corren, datos incontrovertibles, procedentes de campos distintos obligan a inferir que el cerebro, órgano de superfetación, necesita un soporte fisiológico, cuyo desarrollo requiere comunión de vida con la naturaleza. Más que exigencia de la moda es necesidad imperiosa (*nolentem trahunt*) la de *ruralizar* los organismos anémicos de los grandes centros de población (Urbano González Serrano, 'El culto de la naturaleza', in *Germinal* 4, 24 May 1897).

We have seen how, in the wake of Unamuno, certain young writers of around 1900 set out on a determinism-guided quest for a new understanding of Spain based on their contact with ordinary people, with the physical environment that formed the people, and with the culture in which it was believed the people's spirit revealed itself. But why, one wonders, at a time of increasing industrialization, after half a century during which the population of Madrid had doubled, did writers look for a key to Spain's future in country people and historical cities rather than in the growing urban masses and industrial development?

The determinist desire to find a 'roca viva' of national being was clearly a powerful influence. Rural existence and historical cities offer an image of permanence that a more rapidly evolving urban society denies. 'Está aquello como estaba hace un siglo, hace dos, hace cuatro, hace veinte. Es la imagen viva de lo inalterable' (1911; MU, I, 357). 'Por estas felices gentes no pasa el tiempo' (1909; MU, I, 295). 'Esa ciudad de Avila, tan callada, tan silenciosa, tan recogida, parece una ciudad musical y sonora. En ella canta nuestra historia, pero nuestra historia eterna; en ella canta nuestra nunca satisfecha hambre de eternidad' (1909; MU, I, 276).

Moreover, as the juxtaposition in the final quotation suggests, the search for national permanence was intimately associated with personal emotional needs. Unamuno's quest for Spain, we have seen—like Ganivet's—was also a quest for personal roots. The prober of national destinies, I have suggested, was no longer a mere observer; the subject and object of study were fused. The quest for Spain's 'roca viva' was also a search for one's own 'roca viva'. 'Recorriendo estos viejos pueblos castellanos, tan abiertos, tan espaciosos, tan llenos de un cielo lleno de luz, sobre esa tierra, serena y reposada, junto a estos pequeños ríos sobrios, es como el espíritu se siente atraído por sus raíces a lo eterno de la casta' (1912; MU, I, 370). Urban society denies the looked for evidence of national permanence; consequently it denies also the 'raíces' of the individual spirit. 'Estamos en un periodo de tran- sición de la vida sencilla a la vida complicada del progreso,' wrote Baroja in an article significantly entitled 'El culto del "yo"'. 'De aquí nace nuestro malestar' (1904; V, 27). There has been a regret- table neglect of 'los mandatos de la Naturaleza'; men should return to 'la ley natural' and reaffirm their 'yo' (ibid.). Claudio Frollo, a friend of Maeztu, probed the 'malestar' further under the title 'Fiebres actuales':

Son ahora enormes los medios de comunicación, de traslación, de fabricación, de producción en todo orden, de publicidad en todas las esferas; de lo cual nace el progreso general, pero, individual- mente, la fiebre, la inquietud, la competencia, la inseguridad de las posiciones, las locuras para asegurarlas ... [. . .]. Todo esto ha producido una crisis, y de ella viene el esfuerzo redoblado, la desesperanza, la impaciencia, la inquietud, el vértigo [. . .]. Se vive tan agitadamente porque sobre nosotros pesa algo a que aún *no nos hacemos* (In *Alma Española* 9, 3 January 1904).

Frollo himself believed that Spaniards would eventually adapt themselves to the new rhythm of life, 'la nueva y poderosa alma del mundo', but others were less optimistic. Enrique Madrazo, for example, clearly looked to the countryside for salvation, 'donde [la familia] viva sin tabernas, sin murmuraciones, sin envidias, sin rozamientos, sin pasiones',[65] and Martínez Sierra was appalled by the *madrileño*'s lack of love for nature:

> ¿No da miedo pensar que la generación que nace se está criando en el amor a las salas infectas, llenas de humo y de malas palabras, de las cuales huyeron por siempre el aire puro y la santa belleza? ¿No da miedo pensar que en las tardes de tantos domingos del año se están envenenando cuerpo y alma dentro de un café centenares de niños? [. . .] Que en nuestras escuelas se olvide un poco para qué son los modos del verbo y se aprenda para qué son los árboles, y qué dicen los pájaros, y qué virtud está dormida en las matas fragantes del tomillo y la menta ('El amor a la naturaleza', in *Alma Española* 21, 16 April 1904).

Nature—in a host of different forms—was looked to as the new panacea. 'El hombre debe regirse por leyes naturales, y no por las leyes falsas y artificiales que hoy tiene.'[66] 'Pide la naturaleza ser vencida con sus propias armas, no luchando contra ella; la dominamos en cuanto seguimos sus leyes.'[67] One is reminded of Unamuno's 'doctrina del pacto'. On a personal plane as on the national plane nature was widely seen, around the turn of the century, as a means by which urbanized man could rediscover firm roots and lost harmony.[68]

On a purely personal plane the Romantics had undertaken a similar quest a century earlier. But not the Spanish Romantics, who in general stand apart from English, French and German Romantics by the limited role that nature plays in their writings. 'Si nos acercáramos a nuestros poetas románticos,' wrote Azorín in 1913, 'acaso viéramos que la Naturaleza ha sido por ellos débilmente sentida' (II, 808). And four years later: 'El sentimiento amoroso hacia la Naturaleza es cosa del siglo XIX. Ha nacido con el Romanticismo poco a poco' (1917; III, 1151). But, as Azorín's own evidence shows, in Spain the words 'poco a poco' are extremely relevant, for his earliest examples are taken from a work

[65] *¿El pueblo español ha muerto?*, Santander 1903, p. 302.
[66] Enrique Lluria, in *Vida Nueva* 21, 30 October 1898.
[67] Urbano González Serrano, in *Germinal* 4, 24 May 1897.
[68] Compare Taine, four decades earlier, in *La Fontaine et ses fables*:

Imaginez le paysan qui vit toute la journée en plein air, qui n'est point, comme nous, séparé de la nature par l'artifice des inventions protectrices et par la préoccupation des idées ou des visites (8).

published as late as 1844: Enrique Gil's *El señor de Bembibre*, in the pages of which 'nace, por primera vez en España, el paisaje en el arte literario' (III, 1154–5). Thereafter, Azorín's emphasis in the nineteenth century is on Rosalía de Castro, Pardo Bazán and Clarín. An understanding of the reasons for the Spanish Romantics' relative insensitivity to nature may help us to understand the contrasting sensitivity of the writers of 98. Those reasons, I suggest, are intimately bound up with three other notable characteristics of the Spanish Romantic movement: its lateness, its relatively short life and, as I believe, its limited scope and intensity. We are involved here in a regrettable but necessary detour.

In the general panorama of European literature Romanticism, if I interpret it correctly, is basically a movement of self-affirmation by individuals born into a world of fallen values. The eighteenth century had taught men to distrust the established hierarchy of society and belief,[69] and the Romantic, in the throes of adolescence, nostalgic for a faith that the external world denied him, turned his eyes inwards upon himself, cultivated his own world of dreams and illusions, and sought to project them on to the world around him: sometimes with the illusion of triumph (the so-called *romanticismo de exaltación*, which included also, in certain cases, revolutionary action strangely parallel to the 98 Generation's early socialist involvement); more often with the acceptance and even exaltation of despair at the inevitable failure (commonly referred to as *romanticismo de lamentación*). Unamuno's own favourite Romantic hero expresses what I take to be the basic Romantic torment: 'Le monde réel n'a rien qui remplace ces besoins d'un cœur juste, d'un esprit incertain, premier songe de

[69] 'Quel contraste! quel brusque passage! La hiérarchie, la discipline, l'ordre que l'autorité se charge d'assurer, les dogmes qui règlent fermement la vie: voilà ce qu'aimaient les hommes du dix-septième siècle. Les contraintes, l'autorité, les dogmes, voilà ce que détestent les hommes du dix-huitième siècle, leurs successeurs immédiats. Les premiers sont chrétiens, et les autres anti-chrétiens; les premiers croient au droit divin, et les autres au droit naturel; les premiers vivent à l'aise dans une société qui se divise en classes inégales, les seconds ne rêvent qu'égalité. Certes, les fils chicanent volontiers les pères, s'imaginant qu'ils vont refaire un monde qui n'attendait qu'eux pour devenir meilleur: mais les remous qui agitent les générations successives ne suffisent pas à expliquer un changement si rapide et si décisif. La majorité des Français pensait comme Bossuet; tout d'un coup, les Français pensent comme Voltaire: c'est une révolution' (Paul Hazard, *La Crise de la conscience européenne*, 2 vols., Paris 1935, I, i).

nos premiers printemps.'[70] Romanticism, then, is a protraction and exaltation of adolescent idealism, an unwillingness to take that step that Eduard Spranger, in his *Psychologie des Jugendalters*, has considered to be essential for the passage from youth to maturity: self-adaptation to the world of reality in which one is immersed. For the Romantic, reality must adapt to him, not he to reality. But reality will not adapt. Men are heartless, women are faithless (or obstinately faithful to others), society is artificial, corrupt, impersonal. Growing urbanization presses the point. One must look elsewhere for one's ideal: to bygone ages which, being little known, can feed illusions that the modern world of man denies, or, in the present, to the unadulterated countryside which, being passive, allows free rein to the Romantic desire for self-projection.

But in Spain the more iconoclastic aspects of the eighteenth century had made little impact. There had been no intellectual and psychological crisis comparable to that studied by Hazard in more northern countries. Even among the educated elite, minority clamours had done little to undermine faith in the nation's traditional religious and social hierarchy.[71] Only during the nineteenth century and more especially in its closing decades does one find a notable questioning of values comparable to that of the French eighteenth century. Spain, then, during the great decades of European Romanticism, lacked what I take to be basic to the Romantic *Weltschmerz*: the sense of fallen values, the individual feeling of rootlessness, the notion of a void to be filled by personal self-projection. It lacked also the Enlightenment's own pointer to nature as a possible positive response to so much emptiness: natural law, natural morality, natural religion, natural sciences. . . . Significantly, perhaps, most of the principal members of Spain's Romantic generation evolved their Romanticism

[70] Senancour, *Obermann*, Letter 46.

[71] 'En el campo político, no es el régimen lo que atacan, sino la intromisión de Roma, que ha desposeído de su autoridad a la monarquía, a la cual quieren restablecer en sus derechos. Nadie le es infiel, mientras sus órdenes sean razonables, y a ella piden la ilustración y las reformas sociales que España necesita.

En el campo religioso, distinguen entre la fe y la Iglesia, entre la religión y sus ministros. El derecho de pensar libremente y de no sacar las opiniones sino de la razón, se detiene, para casi todos, en el reino de la fe' (Jean Sarrailh, *La España ilustrada de la segunda mitad del siglo xviii*, Mexico 1957, p. 710).

abroad. There is another probably relevant factor. During the early decades of the nineteenth century Spain lacked the oppressive, impersonal centres of urbanization from which more northern Romantics sought escape. Not until the second half of the century did the population of Madrid rise rapidly: from slightly over a quarter of a million in 1857 to a little over half a million in 1900.[72] 'Eramos una nación agrícola hasta hace poco,' wrote Ganivet in 1898 (*PE*, 675), and the countryman, declared Unamuno, lives too close to nature and is too subservient to it to see it 'con ojos de alma' (1901; I, 58). The 'sentimiento amoroso hacia la Naturaleza', it seems, is largely a creation of urbanized man, a consequence of his desire to rediscover his own self, away from the harassments of urban—and urbane—existence, in intimate communion with nature. But the greater part of the Spanish landscape is, as Unamuno said of the Castilian meseta, monotheistic rather than pantheistic: 'No hay aquí comunión con la naturaleza, ni nos absorbe ésta en sus espléndidas exuberancias' (*ETC*, 809). It is significant, I suggest, that sensitivity to nature in Spain, when it did come, came from the north: Enrique Gil, Rosalía de Castro, Pardo Bazán, Clarín. . . . And in this perhaps, rather than in any regional racial characteristic, lies the explanation of the notable Basque contribution to the literature of 98.

In short, according to my tentative hypothesis, nature played little part in Spanish Romantic literature because, apart from the absence of a profound consciousness of fallen values serving to direct men's eyes towards nature as a realm of harmony and self-discovery, Spain lacked the necessary combination of repellant urbanization and immediately attractive nature. Unamuno himself is a witness to the subsequent change of attitude in the Basque Country. Recalling the Bilbao of his youth, he wrote:

Empezaba a ponerse de moda entre nosotros lo de la aldeanería y el maldecir la villa, invención de hombres corrompidos (1908; VIII, 168),

and again:

Soplaba por entonces, hacia 1880, entre algunos de nosotros, los mocitos de aquel Bilbao recién salido de la guerra, un romántico

[72] Compare London and Paris which already in 1801 had 864,845 and 547,756 inhabitants respectively (A. F. Weber, *The Growth of Cities in the Nineteenth Century*, Cornell U.P., 1963, pp. 46, 73).

soplo de anti-urbanismo y hasta de desprecio a los refinamientos de la civilización ( ! ! ! ). Había un apóstol del rousseaunianismo que predicaba el odio a las ciudades y se subía, calzado de abarcas, por Iturrigorri arriba. Otro pobre amigo mío, muerto después en América, se subía a Archanda a recitar allí la descripción que de los Alpes hizo el mismo Rousseau (1907; VIII, 249).

Perhaps there is similar contemporary evidence from less verdant areas of Spain, but I myself know of none and Azorín's own limited nineteenth-century non-northern evidence, in *El paisaje de España visto por los españoles*, is in general *costumbrista* rather than *paisajista*. In Spain, then, it was apparently the north that showed the way to a new sensitivity to nature. The determinist quest for an environment-formed nucleus of national being, with its emphasis on Castile, widened the area of geographical interest, but it required the spiritual crisis and the rapid urbanization of the later nineteenth century—notably in Madrid[73]—to convince writers that even the Castilian countryside could serve as an emotional refuge and be elevated to a Romantic-type *paysage état d'âme*. The interaction of these various influences calls for closer documentation than I myself can offer. Their importance, however, seems indisputable. Unamuno's own initial dislike of the Castilian countryside and his change of attitude during the 1890's are themselves highly significant. So is Baroja's association of Fernando Ossorio's spiritual desolation with the desolate landscape of Castile, 'en donde los ojos no podían descansar un momento contemplando algo verde, algo jugoso' (1904; VI, 56), and of his *alter ego*'s subsequent attainment of harmony amidst the 'campos de verdura' (VI, 109) of Alicante and Valencia. So also, finally, is Azorín's account of his own development, under the impact of Baroja's descriptions of the Basque landscape, from a purely determinist response to the interrelation of landscape, character and art to an awareness of the importance of 'lo indeterminado' in literature: 'lo indeterminado con el misterio y el profundo sentido de la vida que lo indeterminado impone' (1946; VIII, 143–6).

[73] Laín Entralgo's interpretation of the impact of Madrid on writers of the 98 Generation is somewhat narrower than my own in that he sees the capital simply as the epitome of what they despised in contemporary Spanish history (*La generación del noventa y ocho*, 2nd ed., Madrid 1948, pp. 88–9). I accept completely, however, his basic contention that for all of them the experience of Madrid was decisive (op. cit., p. 72).

In the Unamuno article from which I last quoted, the author viewed with condescension his own youthful 'desprecio a la civilización urbana' (1907; VIII, 250), but in fact it never left him. The conflict between town and country runs through his work like a *leitmotiv*. Zeda observed it in his review of *Paz en la guerra*,[74] and Altamira, writing on the same novel, commented:

> Nótase al punto que el autor—como la mayoría de *los intelectuales*, fatigados o desengañados de la vida ciudadana—lleva sus preferencias del lado de la vida rural. El campo, y sobre todo el monte, el aire libre, las ideas y caracteres campesinos, le seducen, siéntelos vivamente y los describe y refleja con gran emoción y fuerza de colorido (In *Revista Crítica de Historia y Literatura* II, 1897, 208).

On the one hand there is the city, 'herencia de la obra del fratricida', a source of exploitation, dispute, rancour and war; on the other hand, the countryside, 'escuela viva de paz', 'refugio de verdura y de sosiego', 'alma de la paz y madre de sus frutos' (1902; I, 60–7). At one extreme, the 'gran metrópoli millonaria', the 'cementerio del hombre individual' (1908; I, 303–4); at the other extreme, the open countryside and, very especially for Unamuno, the mountain tops: 'El cuerpo se limpia y restaura con el aire sutil de aquellas alturas y aumenta el número de glóbulos rojos, según nos dijo un catedrático de Medicina; pero el alma también se limpia y restaura con el silencio de las cumbres' (1911; I, 351). Between these extremes are Spain's provincial towns and villages towards which Unamuno's attitude changes according to the circumstances of the moment. After immersion in the impersonality of a great urban centre a small city like Salamanca seems a delightful refuge, 'para volver a salir a tierra firme, a sentirse pisando el suelo' (1908; I, 304). But Salamanca, too, has its harassments and vexations: its professional commitments (1908; I, 264), 'esas ominosas tertulias, que son una de nuestras mayores fuentes de perdición' (1908; VIII, 259), 'la ciudad odiable y odiosa del trajín social' (1911; I, 361). Over-oppressive human contact is one of Unamuno's most persistent dreads, even in his travels:

> No hay, creo, como estas viejas ciudades provincianas, perhinchidas de historia y de poesía íntima, para el que sepa no dejarse ganar de las arteras insinuaciones del trato humano en ellas; no

74 In *La Epoca*, 1 February 1897.

hay como estas ciudades para el que acierte a saber aislarse y gozar de la soledad, yendo de tiempo en tiempo a bañarse en campo libre o a buscar el breve comercio de otras gentes. Para el huésped de poco tiempo es halago (1909; I, 279).

The words 'breve comercio' and 'huésped de poco tiempo' are especially significant. Despite his emphasis on the Spanish country people as bearers of eternal tradition, despite his declared interest in individuals, 'tú, Juan, que lees esto, y tú Pedro y tú Ricardo' (1908; I, 304), despite his delight in talking to 'cabreros, mendigos, gañanes y toda laya de gente sencilla y a la buena de Dios' (1911; I, 353), Unamuno is manifestly wary of allowing himself to become too involved, fearful no doubt lest reality confuse his vision. 'La soledad,' he declares, is 'la gran escuela de sociabilidad' (1905; I, 1263). 'Hay que aprender a conocer a los prójimos en el recato del aislamiento, dentro de sí mismo y fuera de ellos' (1915; I, 432). His reaction to provincial towns and villages is similar. He recognizes—and at times describes—the brutalizing stagnation of Spanish provincial life, but in general he prefers to keep it at a distance. 'Déjame que me le figure a mi antojo,' he says of the village of Brianzuelo de la Sierra; 'la conciencia de estar en él vivifica mi imaginación' (1900; I, 68). And elsewhere: 'Lo mejor que se les ocurre a los hombres es lo que se les ocurre a solas, aquello que no se atreven a confesar, no ya al prójimo, ni aun a sí mismos muchas veces, aquello de que huyen, aquello que encierran en sí cuando está en puro pensamiento y antes de que pueda florecer en palabras' (1905; I, 1263).

And what is the best that occurs to Unamuno in his travels? Basically, his awareness of time's passing. But as the juxtaposition in the last quotation suggests, Unamuno seeks both an escape from his obsession and, at the same time, a fuller awareness of it. Thus, he seeks defences against it in the 'vida difusa, lenta, de pura costumbre' of village life (1900; I, 69), in the resistance to change of old provincial cities like Avila ('En ella canta nuestra historia, pero nuestra historia eterna; en ella canta nuestra nunca satisfecha hambre de eternidad', 1909; I, 276), in the contemplation of evergreen holm-oaks ('un árbol férreo', 'perenne', like 'el follaje de piedra de estos viejos monumentos salmantinos', 1911; I, 360), and finally—and very especially—in the permanence and immobility of the Spanish landscape ('la inmovilidad en medio de las mudanzas, la eternidad debajo del tiempo [. . .], el fondo del mar de la vida', 1911; I, 359). But in his very search for permanence he is struggling also with the obsession of impermanence. 'Los paisajes que describe [Unamuno],' writes Jerónimo de la Calzada, 'no son en realidad otra cosa que traslados del paisaje de su alma atormentada, agónica, iluminada por su "yo" personal e individual. Unamuno no sólo vive en sus paisajes, sino que tiene necesidad de verse en ellos.'[75] The abundance of Jerónimo de la Calzada's evidence makes my own superfluous. Unamuno looks to the Spanish countryside not only as a means of understanding Spain. Like more northern Romantics of a century earlier he looks to it also as an escape from the harassments of urban—and urbane—existence and as a means of self-discovery free from oppressive human contacts. Like the Romantics, too, he finds ultimately in his travels what he takes with him: his own basic preoccupations.

Azorín's case is similar. He too is repelled by the harassments and vexations of urban existence; he too is attracted by the prospect of self-discovery amidst ancient cities and open countryside:

> Para el cortesano, para el hombre de las grandes ciudades, nada hay comparable a este silencio reparador, bienhechor, de los viejos y muertos pueblos; él envuelve toda nuestra personalidad y hace que salgan a luz y floten, posesionados de nosotros, dominándonos, los más íntimos estados de conciencia, sentimientos e ideas que creíamos muertos, que causaban angustias el ver cómo poco a poco iban desapareciendo de nosotros (1912; II, 614).

> Desde aquí, tendidos sobre la suave hierba, espaciamos la vista por el paisaje. ¡Dulces horas de grato descanso! Atrás, en la populosa y turbulenta urbe, quedan las concupiscencias, las pasiones, las mezquindades. Aquí está el aire sutil, limpísimo; el aroma no pasado por alquitaras; el silencio no turbado por máquinas ni gritos. ¡Dulce, dulce haronía! (1923; IV, 394).

Beyond the determinist quest for Spain, then, lies, as in Unamuno, a Romantic-type quest for self. Despite his much emphasized notebooks Azorín does not allow reality to impose itself. Like his fictional *alter ego* he is 'un hombre de recogimiento y soledad' (1903; I, 1114). His quest for La Mancha starts amidst conversations in a third-class compartment; a fortnight later we find the author, still on his quest, alone in a first-class compartment (1905; II, 251, 294). There are times, one recalls, when 'la imagen de la

[75] 'Unamuno paisajista', in *CCMU* III (1952), pp. 55–6.

realidad es mejor que la realidad misma' (1916; III, 595). Travel may be accepted as a stimulus; it must not be allowed, through over-involvement, to become a fetter:

> Y es que no se llega a dominar la realidad circundante sino cuando nos hallamos desasidos de esa realidad. Y entonces es cuando el artista es artista. De otro modo, se mezclan al arte elementos que lo desnaturalizan (1946; VIII, 391).

'La Castilla de Azorín,' observed Ramón Pérez de Ayala, 'en nada se parece a la de Galdós, Picavea, Unamuno, Machado, Mesa, etc. Es un estado de alma, una materialización de la personalidad de Azorín. Es, sin duda, una Castilla para todos, pero es de Azorín exclusivamente. A través de ella claro que comprendemos una buena parte del alma y la tierra castellana, pero entendemos mejor el alma y la personalidad de Azorín.'[76] Sharing Unamuno's obsession with time's passing—and lacking his Basque elder's confident projection of his own immortalizing *yo*—Azorín appears, in his travels as elsewhere, characteristically poised between vague regrets and indefinable longings:

> Gana el espíritu en esta ciudad y en esta hora una sensación de serenidad y de olvido. Se escucha el alma de las cosas. Sentimos añoranzas por cosas que no hemos conocido nunca; anhelamos algo que no podemos precisar y cuya falta no llega a producirnos amargura (1909; II, 492).[77]

[76] *Ante Azorín*, Madrid 1964, p. 140.

[77] For a fuller treatment of the above with special reference to *La ruta de Don Quijote*, see HR, *Azorín's 'La ruta de Don Quijote'*, Manchester University Press, 1966. Here a single paragraph will serve as a pointer to my findings:

On a plane of mere logic or intellect, I have suggested, as the expression of a determinist case, *La ruta de Don Quijote* is unsatisfactory. Nor should it be seen, as Mulertt saw it, simply as the work of an 'agudo, crítico observador, el que procura seguir la técnica de los Goncourts y tan sólo pintar lo que sus ojos ven y lo que sus oídos oyen'. The terms 'libro sencillo', 'una especie de diario de viaje', 'trabajo rápido de periodista', 'impresiones manchegas', if true in part, are nevertheless misleading. They suggest that the book is a mere series of notes and observations, of disparate and unintegrated scenes. But as I have tried to show in this chapter and shall show further in the next, this is far from the truth. Apart from one or two possible lapses the book is a coherent, consistent, integrated work of art. And at the centre of it, giving it its essential unity, is not La Mancha—nor Don Quixote—but Azorín himself, a sensitive being obsessed with the passage of time and with his own vain quest for illusion (pp. 174–5).

Like Unamuno and Azorín, Baroja too stands out as a notable *excursionista*, 'un apasionado de la vida errática' (1936; Azorín, VIII, 289). Like them, too, he seeks to escape especially from the enforced social contacts of urban existence:

> Yo siento un profundo desdén por la vida de las ciudades, por las redacciones de los periódicos, por los saloncillos de los teatros, por el público de los estrenos, por la política, por todas esas cosas que constituyen lo que se llama la civilización.[78]

Not that he scorns cities in all their aspects. 'En las ciudades,' he says, 'los hombres de esta generación [the 1898 Generation] no buscarán las plazas elegantes, de aire parisiense o madrileño; preferirán visitar los barrios antiguos, los arrabales, y estarán siempre ansiosos de encontrar lo típico y lo característico' (1926; V, 575). But they do not look only for 'lo típico y lo característico': Baroja's quest for Spain, like Unamuno's and Azorín's, is intimately interwoven with his quest for self. 'No debemos nunca sacrificar nuestra personalidad a nada ni a nadie' (1904; V, 27). In an article significantly entitled 'Oasis' he describes the pleasure of escaping from the 'vileza del ambiente', 'este mundo del chanchullo, del hampa, del baraterismo', and of savouring, in silence and solitude, the delights of one's own soul:

> En medio de las andanzas de la vida del día, se ha experimentado el contacto del sableador sinvergüenza en la calle, del pincho de la casa de juego en el café, del periodista chanchullero en la redacción; se ha cambiado una palabra amable con un idiota a quien se desprecia y que lo desprecia a uno; se ha adulado a un político ilustre que no sabe ni escribir [. . .]; se ha cubierto el alma de lepra, y cuando se llega al silencioso rincón en donde se vive, se respira más libremente ante las cuatro blancas y frías paredes del cuarto (1904; V, 34).

Moreover, like Werther before him—and like several of his most notable contemporaries—Baroja finds his ideal not only within himself but also, by projection, in the unsophisticated lives of humble people:

> Yo he pasado muchas veces por la noche horas enteras mirando desde la calle por la ventana del taller de algún tornero, de algún

---

[78] *El tablado de Arlequín* [1904], Caro Raggio, Madrid n.d., p. 168. 'País vasco', the article from which the quotation is taken, is apparently not included in the *Obras completas*.

encuadernador. Se nota en el interior la placidez y el trabajo. La luz confidencial de una lámpara alumbra el rincón pacífico. La gente trabaja sin apresurarse.

Yo he creído muchas veces—quizá equivocadamente—que ahí dentro, en esos interiores tranquilos, debe refugiarse la dicha. Se me figuran esos talleres de artífices modestos oasis de paz, de serenidad, en medio de estos desiertos de egoísmo, de miseria moral, de abyección y de vileza (ibid.).

Quest for self, self-projection, quest for an ideal—as in Unamuno and Azorín, and as in more northern Romantics of a century earlier, it is extremely difficult to separate them. Baroja's novels offer abundant evidence. Their autobiographical character is well known:

En sus obras reconoce Baroja, explícitamente, su eminente carácter autobiográfico [. . .]. En realidad, toda la obra barojiana es cual una gigantesca representación, desmesurada tanto por la diversidad de sus escenarios como por el número de sus personajes, entre los cuales transita, señera, una criatura singular, encarnación literaria de quien fraguó la tramoya y mueve los hilos que ponen en movimiento la escena; y todo en ella: los paisajes y los personajes, sus ideas y sus emociones, están vistos y relatados a través de ese personaje que no es nadie sino el propio Baroja (Granjel, *Retrato de Pío Baroja*, Barcelona 1953, p. 139).

Fernando Ossorio, in *Camino de perfección* (1902; VI, 7–129), will serve as an example. His quest is basically a quest for self. A family history of emotional instability, divided childhood allegiances and, very especially, an instinct-suppressing religious education have made of him a man '[sin] deseos, ni voluntad, ni fuerza para nada' (20). '¡Si yo supiera para qué sirvo!' (14). Madrid, 'aquella gran capital, con sus chimeneas', is significantly depicted in his painting as a devouring monster (11), and his affair with his aunt Laura serves only to press upon him his own 'angustia brutal' (25). 'Viendo que la intranquilidad y el dolor crecían por momentos', he decides to seek refuge in travel (31). But, initially at least, in landscapes as in people he finds only reflections of his own spiritual desolation. Even a night scene seems to be the image of his own future: 'oscuro, opaco, negro' (32). Inner experience and external experience fuse. What does it matter, he asks, whether his state of mind comes from within or without? 'Además, el mundo de afuera no existe; tiene la realidad que yo le quiero dar' (58). Toledo suggests itself as a possible response to his indefinable longings, but he is disillusioned by his visit: 'Toledo no era ya la ciudad mística soñada por él, sino un pueblo secularizado, sin ambiente de misticismo alguno' (63).[79] 'A los dos meses de estar en Toledo, Fernando se encontraba más excitado que en Madrid' (66). The recollection of a girl he once seduced in Yécora sends him off on another quest, and brings him face to face with another disillusion—and with a reminder of the torments of his childhood education.[80] In Marisparza, a lonely *casa de labor*, he experiences, despite the austere, dismal, desolate landscape, the first signs of regeneration. 'Todo lo que se había excitado en Madrid y en Toledo iba remitiendo en "Marisparza". Al ponerse en contacto con la tierra, ésta le hacía entrar en la realidad. Por días iba sintiéndose más fuerte, más amigo de andar y de correr, menos dispuesto a un trabajo cerebral' (98). But further contact with Yécora convinces him of the need to escape, 'a cualquier parte, con tal de salir de Yécora' (106). In a significantly unnamed 'pueblo encantador' on the way to Alicante—ideal realms are commonly unnamed in Baroja's writing—he finds joy and repose among 'campos de verdura' (109). 'Nunca he sentido, como ahora, el despertar profundo de todas mis energías, el latido fuerte y poderoso de la sangre en las arterias [. . .]. Nunca, nunca ha sido para mis ojos el cielo tan azul, tan puro, tan sonriente; nunca he sentido en mi alma este desbordamiento de energía y de vida' (110). The continuing subjectivity of vision is evident. But even happiness can tire: 'Lo cierto es que hace dos semanas que estoy aquí, y empiezo a cansarme de ser dichoso [. . .]; experimento a veces nostalgia por las ideas tristes de antes, por las tribulaciones de mi espíritu' (111). Don Vicente, an uncle by marriage, will surely be pleased to see him. Ossorio is offended by the initial formality of the family's attitude towards him, but

---

[79] The accompanying details are omitted from the *Obras completas*:

Los caciques, dedicados al chanchullo; los comerciantes, al robo; los curas, la mayoría de ellos con sus barraganas, pasando la vida desde la iglesia al café, jugando al monte, lamentándose continuamente de su poco sueldo; la inmoralidad reinando; la fe, ausente, y para apaciguar a Dios, unos cuantos canónigos cantando a voz en grito en el coro, mientras hacían la digestión de la comida abundante, servida por alguna buena hembra (Should be inserted at the end of Chapter 22, *OC* VI, 63).

[80] Details are again omitted from the *OC* edition. See above, p. 149 n. 57.

the sense of harmony and renewed energy that he experienced in Marisparza and in the unnamed 'pueblo encantador' in Alicante is gradually reinforced by his love for his cousin Dolores and by their subsequent marriage. As aboulia and agitations yield to calm and tranquillity Fernando Ossorio, subjective as ever, sees the world around him with new eyes:

> Aquel baile brutal, salvaje, que antes disgustaba profundamente a Ossorio, le producía entonces una sensación de vida, de energía, de pujanza [. . .]. Era aquel baile una brutalidad que sacaba a flote en el alma los sanos instintos naturales y bárbaros, una emancipación de energía que bastaba para olvidar toda clase de locuras místicas y desfallecientes (125).

Nature, with its invitation to love life, has finally prevailed over the Church, with its exhortations to abhor it. Ossario is resolved that his own son shall be brought up in Rousseauesque harmony with nature.

As my final example I take a poet who became closely associated with the movement of 98 only in its later period, when intellectual notions of determinist causality were yielding to a more emotive view of the fusion of landscape, people and culture. I refer, of course, to Antonio Machado. His dislike of urban existence is well known:

> ¡Este placer de alejarse!
> Londres, Madrid, Ponferrada,
> tan lindos . . . para marcharse (Poem CX).

Like his 'loco' he seeks to escape:

> Huye de la ciudad . . . Pobres maldades,
> misérrimas virtudes y quehaceres
> de chulos aburridos, y ruindades
> de ociosos mercaderes [. . .].
> Huye de la ciudad. ¡El tedio urbano!
> —¡carne triste y espíritu villano!—(XVI).

But Machado has two notably different directions of escape: in his first two books, *Soledades* (1903) and *Soledades, galerías y otros poemas* (1907), he escapes inwards into the galleries of his own soul; in later works, most notably in *Campos de Castilla* (1912), he escapes outwards into the Spanish countryside. The difference is striking and José Luis Cano, in the introduction to his edition of *Campos de*

*Castilla*, has contrasted the 'intimismo trémulo y espiritualmente rico' of the earlier period with the 'poesía más objetiva y realista' of *Campos de Castilla*.[81] The distinction is clearly justified, up to a point. And yet . . . Is the poetry of *Campos de Castilla* objective and realistic? Does it lack the 'intimismo trémulo y espiritualmente rico' of the poet's earlier writings? I suggest that in both cases the broad answer must be 'No', that, like Unamuno, Azorín and Baroja, Machado finds in the landscape, towns and people of Castile a reflection of his own intimate preoccupations, and that he communicates these findings to his reader via an 'intimismo' that, if not 'trémulo', is at least 'espiritualmente rico'. One cannot justify these suggestions in a single paragraph, but the immediately relevant point, I think, is clear: that the main preoccupations underlying Machado's pre-Soria poems underlie also his vision of Castile. In his pre-1907 poems, amidst deserted parks and gardens and ominous, anguished, Chirico-type cities, the poet was obsessed basically by the relentless passage of time and the emptiness and desolation of a passing present poised constantly between 'esperanzas y recuerdos' (XXII), between 'algo que no llegaba' and 'todo lo que ya se fue' (XCIII). Castile, I suggest, is seized upon as a mirror of these same obsessions. Castile, too, is seen as empty and desolate, poised between recollections of the past and hopes for the future, immersed constantly, like the poet himself, in time's passing:

> Castilla miserable, ayer dominadora,
> envuelta en sus andrajos desprecia cuanto ignora.
> ¿Espera, duerme o sueña? ¿La sangre derramada
> recuerda, cuando tuvo la fiebre de la espada?
> Todo se mueve, fluye, discurre, corre o gira;
> cambian la mar y el monte y el ojo que los mira.
> ¿Pasó? Sobre sus campos aun el fantasma yerra
> de un pueblo que ponía a Dios sobre la guerra.
>
> La madre en otro tiempo fecunda en capitanes
> madrastra es hoy apenas de humildes ganapanes (XCVIII).

Decaying buildings and cities, aged, withered trees, the declining day, the cycle of the seasons, the significant empty seat as a pointer to death, and, transposed into spatial transience, *caminos, caminantes, pasajeros*, rivers that flow down to the sea—all recall

[81] Anaya, Salamanca 1970, pp. 12–13.

Machado's earlier insistence on life as time, and present an intensely personal and immediately recognizable view of Castile notably different from Unamuno's immortalizing vision. 'La característica de Machado,' wrote Azorín shortly after the first appearance of *Campos de Castilla*, 'la que marca y define su obra, es la *objetivización* del poeta en el paisaje que describe [. . .]. Paisaje y sentimientos—modalidad psicológica—son una misma cosa; el poeta se traslada al objeto descrito, y en la manera de describirlo nos da su propio espíritu' (1913; II, 809). Objectivization of the poet in the landscape and subjectivization of the landscape in the poet. But further evidence is perhaps unnecessary, for Machado himself has made the essential point in his apostrophe to the 'campos de Soria':

> me habéis llegado al alma,
> ¿o acaso estabais en el fondo de ella? (CXIII)

As his own soul is sad so he finds a soul with which to commune in the sadness of the Castilian countryside:

> ¡Oh tierras de Alvargonzález,
> en el corazón de España,
> tierras pobres, tierras tristes,
> tan tristes que tienen alma! (CXIV)

Moreover, as he brought Soria with him in 1907, so also he bears it away with him six years later:

> En la desesperanza y en la melancolía
> de tu recuerdo, Soria, mi corazón se abreva.
> Tierra de alma, toda, hacia la tierra mía,
> por los floridos valles, mi corazón te lleva (CXVI).

Machado and Soria have fused. As in Unamuno, Azorín and Baroja, so also in Machado the discovery of Spain is a discovery of self. For the most notable figures of the 98 movement Spain—its landscapes, its people, its villages—is basically a self-projection. 'Los lugares,' says Azorín, 'son nuestra sensibilidad' (1916; III, 595).

### (b) *The quest for self through literature*

El signo de la perdurabilidad de la obra de arte es que cada época, cada pueblo, cada clase social, cada contemplador, ve en ella su propio espíritu. Todos ven cosa distinta, y la obra es la misma (1939; Azorín, V, 878).

In the present section I have felt obliged by the complexity of the subject to confine my observations to the two archetypal *noventayo-chistas*, Unamuno and Azorín, both of whom wrote extensively on the writings of others.

As one would expect from the evidence of earlier sections, Unamuno's judgement of works of literature is intimately related to his notion of their faithfulness to the collective spirit of a given period or region and more especially, beyond period and region, of their faithfulness to what he takes to be the collective, time-resistant essence of a given people throughout its history.[82] This is especially true of his response to Spanish literature. Moreover, if, as Unamuno suggests and as I have myself sought to demonstrate, the quest for Spain is also a quest for personal roots, an attempt to 'salvarse como hombre, como personalidad', to 'afirmar en sí al Hombre' (1918; VIII, 408), it follows that any separation between the quest for Spain and the quest for self is artificial. The 'quest for Spain through literature' is merely an aspect of the 'quest for self through literature'. In both cases the author is concerned to find some form of 'roca viva' relevant to himself. In the present section I shall attempt to maintain the distinction by concentrating on those aspects of Unamuno's quest for self that are not obviously contained in his already studied quest for Spain.

In 1890 Unamuno was finding in his correspondence with

---

[82] As Demetrios Basdekis rightly points out in the opening sentence of his excellent study, *Unamuno and Spanish Literature* (University of California Press, 1967), 'Unamuno's idea that literature is the most genuine mirror of the spirit of a nation and its people is central to an understanding of his approach to literature.' Strangely, however, Basdekis makes no comment on the manifest problem of reconciling this statement with Unamuno's 'unequivocal' opinion of Taine as 'uno de los más peligrosos maestros de críticas literaria e histórica' (p. 35). In fact, throughout his study, which embraces Unamuno's criticism up to the year of his death, Basdekis is illustrating a completely Taine-like approach to Spanish literature, both in the emphasis on collective character and in the intensely personal basis of selection and interpretation. It is of course remarkable that Unamuno, such a champion of subjectivity and so opposed to 'professional' critics, should criticize Taine as 'un escritor profundamente subjetivo, pese a su objectivismo profesional' (1907; III, 593). Must one infer that, for Unamuno, critics should reveal an Unamunian subjectivity or none at all? Compare above, pp. 93–5.

Pedro Mugica 'un nuevo solaz y un nuevo consuelo' (MU–PM, 6 May) and informing his friend of the 'calma y reposo' that he found in his visits to his *novia*, 'mi mayor sedativo, el calmante de mis berrinches' (29 April, 26 July). Looking forward to his marriage, he informed another correspondent, 'tendré en quien refugiarme para huir las necedades del mundo' (MU–JA, 18 December 1890). *Solaz, consuelo, calma, reposo, refugio*—they are all characteristic elements in an ideal realm that Unamuno treasures constantly amidst his own agitations and those of the world around him. Hence, in part at least, his delight in travel: 'Mientras arde e incendia la guerra por esa Europa adentro, ¡qué encanto el de vivir en el remanso de paz de este rincón del pequeñito Portugal, lejos de horrores y junto al mar suspirante!' (1914; I, 426). Hence also, in part at least, his delight in literature: '[França Amado] me regaló, entre otras cosas, la vieja crónica del contestable Nunalvares Pereira, y la estoy leyendo. Pero, ¿ cuántos habrá que lean estas cosas, y más en estos días? Y, sin embargo, para limpiarse la vista y los oídos de lo que se lee y se oye de esta guerra, ¿hay algo mejor que leer cosas así?' (1914; I, 430). Unamuno's own images emphasize the similarity: Rueda's books, he declares, are 'ventanas abiertas al campo libre, donde se vive sencillamente, sin segunda intención, bajo la luminosa gracia de Dios, al aire libre' (1900; VIII, 899) and the reading of 'Antón el de los Cantares' is 'un suave sedativo en horas de cansancio de la batalla de la vida [. . .]. Una excursión por sus obras es un día de campo' (1895; I, 166–7).

But Unamuno is ever conscious of the dangers of aboulia, inertia, stagnation. Withdrawal from the conflicts of life, whether it be via nature or via literature, appeals to him more as an unattainable or only momentarily attainable ideal than as a long-term reality. For the rest, it is a preliminary step towards something more positive: self-discovery, meditation and, ultimately, a more clearly structured ideal relevant to the world from which he has escaped. Fray Luis de León suggests himself as a guide. Already in *En torno al casticismo* Unamuno had found in his reading of Fray Luis not only the historicist appeal of one who had succeeded in reconciling eternal, cosmopolitan humanism with Castilian, reason-ridden mysticism, but also the more personal appeal of one who, 'anhelando "luz purísima en sosiego eterno"', had fused feeling for nature ('tan raro en su casta') with Platonic humanism and thereby shown the world of nature—and, indeed, the world of art—as a reflection of an ideal, harmonious realm of 'Salud y Paz' (*ETC*, 847–51). Fray Luis, he declared a few years later, found in La Flecha 'un refugio de verdura y de sosiego, un asiento de paz': 'allí, contemplando lejos la ciudad donde el siglo le movió guerra y le trató con prisiones y sinsabores, fue donde meditó en la miseria de la ley de la guerra, y donde trazó aquel luminoso cuadro del gobierno pastoril, y donde elevó aquel soberano himno a la paz, himno que hinche las más preñadas páginas de *Los nombres de Cristo*' (1902; I, 60, 64). Fray Luis, it seems, is for Unamuno a superb example of productive, idealizing solitude away from the harassments of the 'mundanal ruido'. It is difficult to believe that this did not play an important part in Unamuno's opinion of him as 'acaso nuestro más grande lírico de la edad clásica' (1923; VIII, 506).

Nor does the quest end with the formulation of one's ideal. 'Sólo volveremos a ser capaces de acción robusta y viva, si de ello volvemos a serlo, cuando lo seamos de soñar con ahinco' (1902; III, 959). Unamuno is here referring to Spain but the words are relevant also to the author himself. Momentary withdrawal from life's agitations permits one to 'soñar con ahinco', but it requires 'acción robusta y viva' to realize one's dream. Hence, perhaps, a reason for Unamuno's view of the admired Fray Luis de León as a 'fraile de combate' (1914; VIII, 306); hence, too, it seems, his scant enthusiasm for San Juan de la Cruz's tendency to self-annihilation and his open rejection of Miguel de Molinos's quietist doctrine (albeit with considerable respect for one manifestly preoccupied with 'la nada'). 'La vida es por sí misma un tesoro y hay una misión que cumplir aquí, en la tierra, que es el reino del hombre. Nada de misticismos enfermizos, que incapacitan para la acción, pues este mundo no es sino de los que lo aman' (1912; VII, 490). Two such men, he claims, despite the traditional view of them as pessimists, were Quevedo and Gracián: Quevedo, 'an ascetic who never quite gives in to quietism and "la nada": an ascetic, in short, whose grandiose polemic represents a bitter resistance to the "decadence" of his times: a seventeenth-century Unamuno',[83] and Gracián, exalted by Unamuno for his '¿dónde irá uno que no guerree?", 'porque lo pésimo es la paz de los optimistas, la paz de los pacíficos; la paz de los guerreros es ya

[83] Basdekis, op. cit., p. 45.

otra cosa' (1920; III, 1018). Calderón, somewhat unfavourably presented in *En torno al casticismo* as the incarnation of the local, transitory, distinctive, exclusive aspects of the Castilian spirit, finds new favour when his abstractions are seen to be 'vital realities which are a springboard for "lucha, agonía (ἀγῶνα), vida," all in direct opposition to "abulia"'[84]

Moreover, as Unamuno himself reveals in his article 'Sueño y acción', dream is for him synonymous with dream of glory and thence with 'sed de inmortalidad':

> Sólo el ansia de sobrevivir, de un modo o de otro, ahoga el enervante goce de vivir. En el grandioso drama de Guillén de Castro, *Las mocedades del Cid*—drama que sirvió de modelo a *Le Cid*, de Corneille—exclama al morir Rodrigo Arias: ¡muera yo, viva mi fama! (1902; III, 960).

We are touching, then, on two further criteria of Unamuno's literary judgement: Does the author concern himself with 'el ansia de sobrevivir' (and therefore merit applause), or does he give himself up to 'el enervante goce de vivir' (and therefore deserve neglect or even scorn)? Significantly, Unamuno pays little attention to Pardo Bazán's best-known novels—or, being an idealist, to late nineteenth-century novelists in general[85]—but is enthusiastic about *La quimera*, 'con [sus] vislumbres de hondas inquietudes, con [sus] miradas al más allá', and about its protagonist Silvio Lago, '[que] padeció una gloriosa enfermedad mil veces más atormentadora que la tisis de que murió su cuerpo [. . .]: ansia de inmortalidad [. . .], la raíz misma del quijotismo, como lo tengo mostrado hasta la saciedad en mi *Vida de Don Quijote y Sancho*; dejar nombre en los presentes y en los venideros siglos' (1905; III, 1098-9).[86] As for the 'enervante goce de vivir', one

[84] Basdekis, op. cit., p. 31.

[85] 'maldito lo que debe atraernos lo natural cuando la Naturaleza, sobre todo la humana, es como la que nos rodea, tan tosca, tan rebelde al espíritu, tan inerme, tan garbancera' (1905; III, 1106).

[86] Similarly, what appeals to Unamuno in Rubén Darío are not the 'guitarradas' and the 'princesa está triste' aspects of his poetry but the 'eternas e íntimas inquietudes del espíritu' (Basdekis, op. cit., p. 8) and what attracts him in José Asunción Silva's poetry are not the influential 'artificios' of Silva's modernism but 'la obsesión del más allá de la tumba, el misterio de la muerte', the 'hambre de eternidad' (1908; III, 521-2). Basdekis offers an abundance of complementary evidence: Unamuno's 'inordinate obsession' with our lives as rivers in Jorge Manrique's *Coplas* (p. 20), his emphasis on

wonders whether it is not this—together with the associated 'emphasis on ribaldry and on the sensual'[87]—that explains Unamuno's disregard of such notable works as the *Libro de buen amor* and the *Celestina*. Certainly his puritanical emphasis on the profound seriousness of life appears to have played a considerable part in his scorn of the ivory-tower aesthetes of his own age, with their 'exquisiteces y refinamientos', their 'erotismo blandengue y baboso' and their alleged lack of concern for '[lo] hondamente humano' (1897; IV, 1135-6).

We are far from having reviewed even the major criteria by which Unamuno judges works of literature.[88] The main point, however, seems clear: that one can say of Unamuno's response to literature something very akin to what Jerónimo de la Calzada said of his response to Spanish landscapes: 'Los paisajes que describe [Unamuno] no son en realidad otra cosa que traslados del paisaje de su alma atormentada, agónica, iluminada por su "yo" personal e individual. Unamuno no sólo vive en sus paisajes,

---

'la dolor del desesser' in Auzias March (p. 22), his fondness for the lines 'Viure, viure, viure sempre: /non voldría morir mai' in Joan Maragall (p. 66) ... Similarly, Peter G. Earle has observed two constant principles of inquiry in Unamuno's approach to Shakespeare: '(1) What is man's essence? (2) Is he condemned to spiritual extinction?' (*Unamuno and English Literarure*, New York 1960, p. 60), and in Portuguese literature Unamuno exalts Antero de Quental as 'un alma que puede ponerse junto a las de Thomson (el del siglo pasado), Senancour, Leopardi, Kierkegaard y los más grandes desesperados', 'una de las almas más atormentadas por la sed del infinito, por el hambre de eternidad' (1907; I, 190).

[87] Basdekis, op. cit., p. 25.

[88] On the application of his own stylistic criteria to others, see Basdekis, op. cit., *passim*, especially perhaps in the treatment of Unamuno's contrasting response to the writings of Santa Teresa (pp. 36-9) and those of Zorrilla (pp. 59-60). Here as elsewhere I find myself impressed by the persistence throughout Unamuno's writings of certain basic criteria of judgement. His literary judgements may change, but not, it seems, the criteria by which he seeks to justify those judgements. 'Odio la paráfrasis y la hinchazón,' he wrote in 1890 (MU–PM, 24 June) and again, a few weeks later, 'Yo nada encuentro como escribir en una lengua clara, fuerte, cruda, ruda, sin más que verbos y sustantivos, hecha a hachazos, una historia honda, fuerte, en que palpiten todas las pasiones, en que se rasguen todos los velos, en que brille radiante y desnuda la Verdad, el hombre bruto, con los atracones de la carne, los furores del espíritu, el divino animal no echado aún a perder por la razón' (MU–PM, July). I find nothing in Unamuno's life-long commentary on the style of others that indicates any departure from these basic criteria Whether he always followed them successfully himself is another matter.

sino que tiene necesidad de verse en ellos.'[89] Numerous scholars have made the point. 'Hombre de una pieza, este gran Unamuno arbitrario molió a los clásicos en su personal molino afectivo.'[90] 'Unamuno assimilated and utilized only that which he considered congenial to his own moral and aesthetic principles. Accordingly, there are entire periods of English literature which are of little or no significance to our theme [. . .]. [Unamuno] consistently employed the notions of other authors *out* of their contexts and *within* his own [. . .]. It is not unusual for Unamuno to transform another's work, the sense of which he may have but partially assimilated, into something which is virtually his own creation, e.g. *Robinson Crusoe*, *Sartor Resartus*.'[91] 'As a critic of literature he rarely comes even remotely close to what is properly called "objective criticism" [. . .]. The ultimate result of this blatant, aggressive, personal immersion into a work of Spanish literature is the "second creation" which Wellek and Warren would consider "futile".'[92] As Unamuno himself declared, there is for him no dividing line between criticism and 'producción artística directa' (1911; VIII, 988).

Unamuno's approach to Cervantes's masterpiece will serve as my final and principal illustration. His interpretation of Don Quixote and his adventures in terms of his own preoccupations is well known. From 1895 to 1905 especially, it has been suggested, one finds a host of contradictions and shifts of position that mirror Unamuno's own mental state. In fact the contradictions and shifts of position are less fundamental than it might at first appear. For example, if in one article Unamuno identifies Don Quixote's adventures with Spain's superficial 'españolismo' of conquest (1895; I, 791, 797–8, 807), in another with selfless service to others (1896;[93] VII, 1191–3), in another with merely material progress (1898; I, 944–5) and in yet another with the illusion of a fuller and more appropriate national future (1902; III, 959–61), his call for an end to such adventures (in 1895 and 1898) does not fundamentally contradict his applause of them (in 1896 and 1902). His Quixotic equations have changed, but not

---

[89] 'Unamuno paisajista', in *CCMU* III (1952), 55–6.

[90] Segundo Serrano Poncela, *Del romancero a Machado*, Caracas 1962, p. 126.

[91] Earle, op. cit., pp. 138–9.          [92] Basdekis, op. cit., p. 8.

[93] Dated 15 October 1895 in *OC*; corrected by Diego Catalán to 15 October 1896 (in *CCMU* XVI–XVII, 1966–67, 57).

his underlying ideas. Similarly, I find no basic conflict between Unamuno's 1898 condemnation of Don Quixote the champion of glory (VII, 1194–6) and his 1902 exaltation of Don Quixote the champion of glory (III, 959–61). In the former case we are in a realm of 'gnosis', with emphasis on traditional national glories; in the latter case we are in a realm of 'pistis', with emphasis on the people's hidden potential.[94] Similarly again, I find no conflict between Unamuno's enthusiasm for Dulcinea when she represents 'la estrella que conduce a la eternidad del esfuerzo' (1896; VII, 1193) and his less enthusiastic view of her when she represents only 'la gloria mundana' (1902; VII, 1204). Of course, the shifting symbolism itself may be significant, but the question is complex, with different interpretations coexisting in the same year, and is further complicated by external events which have at times been unduly left out of account.[95] Fortunately the main point immediately relevant to my own study is clear: that throughout this period—as indeed in his later writings—Unamuno is unwavering in his determination to find present relevance in Cervantes's masterpiece: national relevance, referred to in an earlier section, and personal relevance, with which we are here concerned. As in that earlier section I shall base my case on *Vida de Don Quijote y Sancho* (III, 49–256).

'Dejando a eruditos, críticos e historiadores la meritoria y utilísima tarea de investigar lo que el *Quijote* pudo significar en su tiempo y en el ambiente en que se produjo y lo que Cervantes quiso en él expresar y expresó', Unamuno sets out to write 'una libre y personal exégesis del *Quijote*, en el que el autor no pretende descubrir el sentido que Cervantes le diere, sino el que le da él' (61–2).[96] His main emphasis is on Don Quixote himself:

[94] The distinction was already apparent in *En torno al casticismo*, not only in the author's repeated contrasts between Spain's undesirable 'venerandas tradiciones' and the potentials of eternal tradition, but also in his emphasis on the need for 'la fe viva que no consiste en creer lo que no vimos, sino en crear lo que no vemos' (797). In January 1897 he repeated the notion in his article '¡Pistis y no gnosis!': 'creer lo que no vimos, *gnosis* [. . .]; *pistis*, es decir, crear lo que no vemos' (III, 683) and again, with almost identical wording, in 'La fe' (1900; I, 964). Here as in other aspects of Unamuno's development there is currently, I suggest, too much emphasis on the differences and not enough on the underlying sameness.

[95] See above, p. 108, n. 19.

[96] The words quoted are from the 1913 prologue to the second edition. In

> En esto de cobrar eterno nombre y fama estriba lo más de su
> negocio; en ello el aumento de su honra primero y el servicio de
> su república después. Y su honra ?qué era? ¿Qué era eso de la
> honra de que andaba entonces tan llena nuestra España? ¿Qué
> sino un ensancharse en espacio y prolongarse en tiempo la per-
> sonalidad? ¿Qué es sino darnos a la tradición para vivir en ella y
> así no morir del todo? (69)

The thirst for eternal fame, service to one's country and, linking
both, the desire to perpetuate oneself by fusing with the tradition
of one's race. We have noted something similar in *En torno al
casticismo*. 'In probing the historical destiny of Spain, Unamuno
and Ganivet, I suggest—like Taine in his probings of France—
were seeking also to discover their own context and destiny'
(above, pp. 81–2). 'A medida que se pierde la fe cristiana en la realidad eterna, buscase un remedo de inmortalidad en la Historia'
(1898; I, 946). By his intensely personal view of Spain's 'tradición
eterna', I suggested, Unamuno was seeking also a personal
'remedo de inmortalidad'. In the Manchegan knight, then,
Unamuno finds a mirror of himself. The following lines may or
may not be relevant to Cervantes's Don Quixote; they are certainly relevant to Unamuno:

> El ansia de renombre y fama, la sed de gloria que movía a nuestro
> Don Quijote, ¿no era acaso en el fondo el miedo a oscurecerse, a
> desaparecer, a dejar de ser? La vanagloria es, en el fondo, el terror
> a la nada, mil veces más terrible que el infierno mismo. Porque al
> fin en un infierno se es, se vive, y nunca, diga lo que dijere el
> Dante, puede, mientras se es, perderse la esperanza, esencia misma
> del ser. Porque la esperanza es la flor del esfuerzo del pasado por
> hacerse porvenir, y ese esfuerzo constituye el ser mismo (193).[97]

---

1905 and 1906 Unamuno was more outspoken about 'todos los miserables
bachilleres, barberos, curas, canónigos y duques' from whom he sought to
rescue Cervantes's 'inmortal libro' (I, 1227–38; III, 51–9). 'En pocas cosas
se muestra más de relieve que en lo que con el *Quijote* ocurre en España la
tristísima decadencia de nuestro espíritu nacional [. . .]. Lo que se busca es
no tener que escarbar y zahondar en el propio corazón, no tener que pensar
y menos aún que sentir' (I, 1227–8).

[97] For the special autobiographical significance of this passage, compare
the following:

> Nunca, ni cuando era yo un niño, lograron aterrarme con descripciones
> del infierno, por truculentas que ellas fuesen. Siempre me decía: '¡bien!,
> pero, ¿se existe?, ¿se vive?; ¡entonces no es tan malo el infierno; lo
> peor es no ser!' (1905; III, 1101).

'No puede contar tu vida, ni puede explicarla ni comentarla, señor mío Don Quijote, sino quien esté tocado de tu misma locura de no morir' (254).

Moreover, as Don Quixote represents Unamuno so also Sancho Panza represents the anonymous Spanish people, often uncomprehending, frequently incredulous, consistently misled by 'bachilleres' and 'duques' and 'curas' and 'barberos', 'porque esos bárbaros se lo creen tener todo resuelto; para ellos no hay inquietud del alma, pues se creen nacidos en posesión de la verdad absoluta; para ellos no hay sino dogmas, y fórmulas y recetas' (226–7). As the country people of Castile, in *En torno al casticismo*, showed Unamuno the way to the ideal of eternal tradition, so Unamuno invites us to observe 'cómo son los Sanchos, la baja humanidad, los que guían a los héroes al palacio de la Gloria' (158). 'Sancho era la humanidad para Don Quijote, y Sancho, desfallecido y enardeciéndose a veces en su fe, alimentaba la de su señor y amo' (150). But, as we have noted, Unamuno was no democrat. However he might need Sancho ('Porque los vulgares, los rutineros, los Sanchos, pueden vivir sin caballeros andantes, pero el caballero andante, ¿cómo vivirá sin pueblo?', 190), however he might have to cut his way through the 'rastrojos' and 'escurrajas' of what the traditionalists call tradition in order to find 'el alma viva de las creencias del pueblo' (170), Don Quixote must remain the 'amo' and his visiones must be believed (171):

> Y tú, Sancho, no naciste para mandar, sino para ser mandado, y el que para ser mandado nació, halla su libertad en que le manden y su esclavitud en mandar; naciste, no para guiar a otros, sino para seguir a tu amo Don Quijote: y en seguirle está tu ínsula [. . .]. Habrás oído muchas veces, buen Sancho, que hay que ser ambicioso y esforzarse por volar para que nos broten alas, y yo te lo he dicho muchas veces y te lo repito, pero tu ambición debe cifrarse en buscar a Don Quijote: la ambición del que nació para ser mandado debe ser buscar quien le mande y que pueda de él decirse lo que del Cid decían los burgaleses, según el viejo *Romance de mío Cid*:
> 
> ¡Dios, qué buen vasallo, si oviesse buen señor!
> 
> (198–9)

Sanchos Panza keeps Don Quixote's 'sanchopancismo' alive and Don Quixote 'Quixotizes' Sancho, 'sacándole a flor de alma su entraña quijotesca' (150). Don Quixote may eventually die but through Sancho he will live on:

Mira, pobre Alonso Quijano, mira tu pueblo y ve si no sanará de su locura para morirse luego. Molido y maltrecho y después de que allá, en las Américas, acabaron de vencerle, retorna a su aldea. ¿A curar de su locura? ¡Quién sabe! . . . Tal vez a morir. Tal vez a morir si no quedara Sancho, que te reemplazará lleno de fe. Porque tu fe, caballero, se atesora en Sancho hoy (246–7).

The reference to the Disaster, I suggest, is final proof of the parallels I have been proposing: as Don Quixote finds immortality through his 'Quixotizing' of Sancho, so Unamuno looks for immortality through his 'Unamunoizing' of the Spanish people. His apostrophe to Alonso Quijano is also a reassurance to himself.

On 11 December 1904 Unamuno wrote about his new work to Jiménez Ilundain:

Jamás me ha embargado tan por entero trabajo alguno, ni creo haber puesto en nada de lo mío tanta pasión, tanta vehemencia y tanto de mis entrañas [. . .]. Creo que he acertado a hacer mi obra más personal comentando una obra ajena. Por supuesto, el texto cervantino me da pie para todo género de revoloteos, y no es sino un pretexto para verter mi pensamiento y mi sentimiento todo.

A few months earlier he had made the same point to Nin Frías and declared his work to be 'a la vez un ensayo de genuina filosofía española' (August 1904). The equation is significant and brings us round in full circle to the beginning of my brief study of Unamuno's quest for self through literature: the acknowledged artificiality of my division between the quest for Spain and the quest for self. The artificiality is now even more apparent, for what Unamuno finds to be most intense within himself is also what he believes to be most fundamental in Spain's eternal tradition. What is important in the Spanish people, he believes, is the 'instinto de vida', the 'ímpetu de crearnos un mundo a nuestro antojo'. 'Nuestra voluntad nos pide inacabable persistencia, nuestra vida es continuo anhelo de más vida, de sobrevida o trasvida' (1903; III, 1092). It may well be so, but the observation seems to be significantly related to Unamuno's own concerns. Similarly, there is a clear parallel between Unamuno's distaste for pigeon-hole logic—the logic that he despises in so many (Spanish!) 'bachilleres'—and his statement, 'Nuestra filosofía, si así puede llamarse, rebasa de casilleros lógicos' (1903; III, 1091), between his own aim to fuse reality and ideal and his belief in 'nuestro

espiritualismo materialista, esto de tomar el espíritu a lo material'
(1913; I, 403), between his own stern puritanical morality and his
belief that Spaniards are 'austeros y graves', anti-erotic, lacking in
*joie de vivre* (1901; IV, 751). On the other hand, the elements in
Spanish character that Unamuno finds to be undesirable are
precisely those that are foreign to him and thence also, he would
have us believe, to what is fundamental in the Spanish race. Thus,
Zorrilla is notable principally for his 'valor representativo' but
not of 'nuestra casta en el más alto y noble sentido de tal representación'. Zorrilla represents the Spanish race 'en lo que tiene
de más exclusivo, de menos universal, en sus defectos. Zorrilla
es un espejo en que debemos mirarnos, pero para huir de él y de
lo que nos refleja' (1917; III, 1002–3). It is not easy to reconcile
the observation with the range and frequency of Unamuno's
attacks on such defects, or to escape the conclusion that ultimately, for Unamuno, what is desirable in Spain is what he finds
predominant within himself. Spain's eternal tradition, it seems,
whether it be found in travel or in literature, is a projection of
Unamuno himself.

For Azorín as for Unamuno, reading, like travel, is not merely
a means of discovering national and regional character. It is also
a means of finding spiritual comfort. 'El arte,' he says, 'es con-
fortación del espíritu' (1939; V, 878). The title *El oasis de los
clásicos* (1952) is significant and recalls a view that he expresses
repeatedly, most notably perhaps in the prologue to *Al margen
de los clásicos* (1915):

> Cuando nos acercamos al ocaso de la vida y vamos—doloro-
> samente—viendo las cosas en sí, y no en sus representaciones, estas
> lecturas de los clásicos parece que son a manera de un oasis grato
> en nuestro vivir. Durante un momento nos detenemos a reposar.
> El espíritu se explaya como libre de los diarios y apremiantes afanes.
> Allá hacia la lejanía ideal, camina nuestro pensamiento (III, 175).

Reading, then, represents one of Azorín's longed for realms of
'paz y sosiego'. It is an oasis amidst the agitations and ultimate
sterility of daily life, a means of communing with kindred spirits
and of meditating on problems near to his heart. 'Leo por placer,'
he says in the prologue to *Los dos Luises y otros ensayos* (1921), 'y
no por enterarme de las cosas, no por atesorar erudición [. . .].
Hombres de letras, artistas literarios, enamorados de nuestro arte,

*corroboremos nuestros íntimos sentimientos* en la vida de estos dos grandes laboradores' (IV, 143–4; my italics). My aim in the following paragraphs is to show how Azorín himself corroborates his own 'íntimos sentimientos' in his findings on Spanish literature.

I have shown elsewhere how in the opening chapter of *La ruta de Don Quijote* (1905), before he sets out on his Manchegan travels, Azorín reveals four insistent preoccupations and that these recur throughout the rest of the book in his quest for Don Quixote, 'nuestro símbolo y nuestro espejo' (II, 248): dissatisfaction with the present, nostalgia for the past, illusion for the future, and the feeling of life's ultimate inevitability (and inevitable sadness). Moreover, 'in the last chapter of his travels Azorín brings together, as he did at the beginning of the book, [these same] insistent obsessions. But now they are presented not in personal terms but in terms of the land he has been visiting. La Mancha has not changed Azorín, but in projecting around him his own intense, personal vision of life, Azorín has changed La Mancha'.[98] But as I sought to demonstrate in my study, it was not only La Mancha that Azorín interpreted in the light of his own 'íntimos sentimientos'; it was Don Quixote too. Literature, like travel, served Azorín as a mirror of his own concerns.[99]

*Al margen de los clásicos* (1915; III, 175–276) will serve as a further illustration. As the author warns us in his preface, he is concerned with 'la impresión producida en nuestra sensibilidad por un gran poeta o un gran prosista' (175). Since Taine-like erudition plays a significant part in Azorín's sensitivity, we cannot disregard entirely his preoccupation with context: temporal context ('Romances caballerescos, romance moriscos, romances populares: a lo largo de vuestros versos se nos aparece la España de hace siglos', 183), regional context ('*La fuerza de la sangre* nos trae al espíritu la sensación del centro de España', 213) and national context ('Quevedo nos ofrece una visión dura y violenta de España', 240). Azorín is clearly drawn by elective affinity to a writer like José Somoza (252–70) who not only offers documentation on the Spain of his time, but also anticipates Azorín's own

[98] HR, *Azorín's 'La ruta de Don Quijote'*, Manchester University Press, 1966, p. 157.

[99] Within *La ruta de Don Quijote* there is further evidence of Azorín's subjective approach to literature in his reading—and misreading—of the 1575–76 'relación' on Argamasilla de Alba (HR, op. cit., pp. 99–100, 124–8, 218–20).

basically determinist view of the harmony of man and his physical environment:

> Somoza siente en sí la continuidad de la especie, y él, instintiva-mente, trata de establecer una íntima relación entre su persona—tan castellana—y esta vieja casa, esta vieja ciudad, este viejo palacio, ya en ruinas, y este viejo paisaje, todo sobriedad y luminosidad. La obra toda de Somoza responde a esta armonía de un hombre con su medio (254).[100]

But our main emphasis in the present section must be on Azorín's more personal concerns. As a starting-point I take the four basic preoccupations noted in *La ruta de Don Quijote*. To what extent do we find them also in *Al margen de los clásicos*?

Dissatisfaction with the present is heralded in the preface itself, where reading is described as a pleasant oasis, a means of escape from 'los diarios y apremiantes afanes' (175). It subsequently reappears in the evocation of the prisoner in his dungeon, sur-rounded by the delights of nature yet shut off from them except for the singing of a bird (185), in Fray Luis de León's desire for escape from 'los tráfagos y miserias del mundo' (188), in Don Quixote's melancholy, allegedly akin to that of battle-worn modern man with his desire to leave behind all the 'afanes' and 'angustias' and 'anhelos' and 'esperanzas' of city life (204) . . . Nostalgia for the past, too, runs through the work like a *leitmotiv*: the 'cantor del Cid' writes in a village that is the same today as it was then, 'salvo que todo está mucho más viejo, ruinoso' (177); Jorge Manrique evokes happiness and youth that will never return (182); among Spanish *romances* Azorín is attracted especially by those that suggest a 'fuerza rota', an 'impulso interrumpido', a 'vuelo detenido' (183)[101] . . . Azorín's quest for illusion is implied

---

[100] Compare Azorín's own portrait of Don Rafael in *La ruta de Don Quijote* (II, 271–3) or his description of Don Silverio: 'existe una secreta afinidad, una honda correlación inevitable, entre la figura de don Silverio y los muros en ruinas del Toboso, las anchas puertas de medio punto cegadas, los teja-dillos rotos, los largos tapiales desmoronados' (II, 309). Reverting to José Somoza in *Al margen de los clásicos* one may recall also Azorín's observation, 'La idea de evolución—madre del pensamiento moderno—está ya patente en estas páginas [de Somoza]' (260).

[101] Lest the relevance of this last example be questioned—and a host of others could be offered in its place (Garcilaso, Góngora, Cervantes . . .)—I recall the portrait of Don Rafael in *La ruta de Don Quijote* ('Ahora ya no soy nada') and Azorín's associated reflections on the appeal to him of 'esas

in the desire for escape itself, is heralded in the preface ('Allá, hacia la lejanía ideal, camina nuestro pensamiento') and recurs repeatedly in the pages that follow. Thus, the author of the *Poema de Mio Cid* is presented as a rather Quixotic figure, living his peaceful village life but dreaming and writing of a world of heroic action (177–9); the 'Romance del conde Arnaldos' opens up visions of 'el mar proceloso', of 'países de ensueño y de alucinación' (184–5); another *romance* evokes strivings 'por la belleza, por la paz, por el progreso, por el ideal lejano' (186). . . . Finally, life's inevitability, intimately bound up with the inescapable melancholy of human existence, is emphasized in Azorín's comments on Jorge Manrique (182), in his *romance*-inspired reflections on life as 'una perdurable fatiga' (186), in his Fray Luis-prompted concern with time's relentlessness (190–1), with the 'rostro del ser querido [que] ha de ser llevado en la corriente inexorable del tiempo' (194). . . .

This crude listing of examples disguises two important points: the interaction of the indicated preoccupations as integrated elements in a coherent view of life, and the shift of position that Azorín has undergone in the ten years since he published *La ruta de Don Quijote*. I shall devote a single paragraph to each.

As an illustration of the former point I take Azorín's commentary on Bartolomé Argensola's 'Epístola a Eraso' (209–13). Argensola's declared decision, in this 'maravillosa carta', to leave the city for good prompts a three-page gloss by Azorín on the harassments of urban existence, 'esta barahunda, este estrépito, este ir y venir fatigoso, este continuo charlar con gentes que no nos interesan' (209). '¿No es hora ya de que nos retiremos de todo este ir y venir afanoso? ¿Qué más podríamos gozar y comprender? Ya estamos levantando la casa, preparando nuestro equipaje' (211). At this point Azorín changes his emphasis from dissatisfaction with the present to illusion for the future and notes how Argensola himself imagines the peaceful village house where he will live. But will the illusion of peace and happiness become a reality? Argensola himself makes the point and Azorín, 'conmovido', 'perplejo, espiritualmente desorientado' (212), elab-

voluntades que se han roto súbitamente' and on the various unfinished works that one finds in Argamasilla de Alba (II, 271–3). It all forms part of Azorín's Romantic-like emphasis on ruins and fragments of the past. 'Crepúsculo' and 'deslizarse' are key words in *Al margen de los clásicos*.

orates on it. Once away from the city will the poet not regret what he  has left behind? Even in the quest for illusion, one notes, nostalgia threatens. Let us confess, concludes Azorín, that our modern sensitivity—'¡oh Argensola!, ¡oh Baudelaire!'—is inexorably bound up with urban life. In these few pages, then, Azorín reveals the whole range of preoccupations that we have seen to underlie *La ruta de Don Quijote*: dissatisfaction with the present, illusion for the future, nostalgia for the past, and an obsessive awareness of life's inescapable sadness. Like *his* Argensola—like *his* Manrique, like *his* Garcilaso, like *his* Góngora, like *his* Don Quixote, like *his* Bécquer—Azorín bears with him, inexorably, his own 'dolorido sentir'. 'Cervantes tiene una frase suprema hablando de estos personajes del *Persiles*; una frase henchida de melancolía, de fatalidad y de misterio, que nos hace soñar y nos llena de inquietud. "Todos deseaban, pero a ninguno se le cumplían sus deseos", escribe el poeta. Un deseo siempre anheloso, un deseo errante por el mundo, un deseo insatisfecho, un deseo que siempre ha de ser deseo: eso es el libro de Cervantes' (226). 'Preocupado del misterio del mundo y del angustiador problema del tiempo' (261), one can do little more, Azorín suggests, than contemplate life's eternal melancholy, 'la mano en la mejilla' (231), 'la cabeza entre las manos' (242), 'la frente apoyada en la mano' (248).

And in this, precisely, lies the principal change of emphasis from his writings of a decade earlier. It is anticipated in the preface: 'cuando nos acercamos al ocaso de la vida y vamos—dolorosamente—viendo las cosas en sí, y no en sus representaciones, estas lecturas de los clásicos parece que son a manera de un oasis grato en nuestro vivir.' Azorín's increasing emphasis on literature rather than travel as a source of inspiration is itself a recognition that reality does not, and cannot, live up to his own cherished 'representaciones'. As in *La ruta de Don Quijote* so also in *Al margen de los clásicos* Azorín oscillates constantly between oppressive reality and illusioned ideals, but now he has less confidence than formerly that the future can offer any real escape from the oppressions of the present. Even in the quest for illusion the inevitable failure threatens. 'Fray Luis,' says Azorín, 'en esta poesía ['Contra un juez avaro'], hace, al llegar a esta parte, un tránsito, propio del gran artista, de lo trágico remediable a lo trágico irremediable y eterno' (190). I can find no words with which to express more succinctly Azorín's own development: from the angry clamours of his early writings against social injustice ('lo trágico remediable'), through *La ruta de Don Quijote*, to the almost total acceptance, in the second decade of the twentieth century, of life's inevitable and all-pervading sadness ('lo trágico irremediable'). As early as 1902 Antonio Azorín noted the struggle within him of 'el *hombre-voluntad*' with 'el *hombre-reflexión*' and the predominance of the latter (I, 968). By 1905 the *hombre-reflexión* dominated even more clearly, albeit with some of the confidence still of the *hombre-voluntad*: confidence in a better future for himself in his illusioned escapes from Madrid and confidence in a better future for the Spanish people through the eradication of social injustice.[102] A few years later the *hombre-reflexión* prevails almost entirely:

> ¿Dónde está el secreto de la paz espiritual, de la ecuanimidad, de la dicha? En la conformidad, en dejar que las cosas que no podemos remediar sigan su curso lento, inexorable y eterno (1909; II, 525).

Henceforth, Azorín's prime concern is not with man-made evils, 'lo trágico remediable'; it is with something far deeper: 'lo trágico irremediable', time's destruction and the inevitable passing away of youth, happiness and of life itself. In this context even the illusion of a better future bears with it the awareness of inevitable failure:

> ¡Eternidad, insondable eternidad del dolor! Progresará maravillosamente la especie humana; se realizarán las más fecundas transformaciones. Junto a un balcón, en una ciudad, en una casa, siempre habrá un hombre con la cabeza, meditadora y triste, reclinada en la mano. No le podrán quitar el dolorido sentir (1912; II, 696).

The case, I suggest, is clear. In Spanish literature, as in his travels, Azorín looks for a mirror of his own preoccupations. So far I have confined myself to his preoccupations as a man. To complete my brief survey I must consider his preoccupations as an artist. 'Toda defensa de un estilo,' he declares, 'es una confesión personal' (1924; IV, 509). In his response to writers of the past—in what he praises and what he condemns—Azorín is clearly

[102] Cf. HR, *Azorín's 'La ruta de Don Quijote'*, p. 153. Recall also *Los pueblos* (1905), which caused Azorín's fall from favour in *El Imparcial*.

guided by his own stylistic ideals. I shall again draw my evidence
from *Al margen de los clásicos*, with occasional references to other
works. Azorín's stylistic ideals can be epitomized in four words:
*claridad, realidad, idealidad* and *delicadeza*.

'Lo primero en el estilo es la claridad' (1924; IV, 510). Azorín
makes a similar point in his comments on popular Spanish
*romances*: 'el arte supremo es la sobriedad, la simplicidad y la
claridad' (182). It is one of the keys to his enthusiasm for Cervantes—and to his reservations about Lope de Vega and Tirso de
Molina:

> En Cervantes todo es sencillez, limpieza, diafanidad; en Tirso y
> Lope, todo enmarañamiento, profusión, palabrería vacua y
> bambolla (219).

> ¿Por qué unas líneas—dos o tres—de descripción en Cervantes nos
> producen el mismo efecto—o más intenso—que una amplia, deta-
> llada, prolija descripción? 'La noche ere clara; la hora, las once; el
> camino, solo, y el paso, tardo.' (214)

Moreover, for Azorín the great artist is a man who, like the 'cantor
del Cid', mingles with ordinary people and carries over the details
of his real-life experience into his writings: 'nombra los pueblecillos, lugares, campiñas y ríos por donde pasan sus personajes. No
se olvida de que los caballeros echen el pienso a sus caballos'
(178–9). One is reminded, of course, of Azorín himself, 'un
observador que se desentiende de los grandes fenómenos y se
aplica a los pormenores triviales' (1909; II, 460). But the close
observation of reality is not enough. 'No hay poeta grande sin
emoción' (187). The writer must not only observe reality; he must
also feel it and make his reader feel it. Juan Ruiz, for example, 'ha
corrido mucho por campos y ciudades', but he is insensitive to the
'poesía delicada y profunda' of the countryside; he lacks 'el
recogimiento, la emoción delicada y tierna' (180–1). Cervantes,
on the other hand, bears his reader away to a vast uncontoured
realm of mystery and emotion beyond the immediate physical
world:

> La impresión que nos produce la novela de Cervantes [*La fuerza de
> la sangre*] es la de las cosas que perduran y que continúan más allá
> de los deleznables y rápidos gestos de los hombres (216).

> Toda esta parte de la novela de Cervantes [*Persiles y Sigismunda*]
> es de lo más delicado del libro, porque al ambiente de poesía se
> unen detalles de fino y cotidiano realismo (233).

Similarly, in the writings of José Somoza, Azorín finds an underlying 'preocupación trascendente' and comments:

> Esa idealidad trascendente de Somoza tiene una base de fina y viva realidad. No es nuestro autor un abstraccionista; observa la vida cotidiana, y ensamblando pintorescos detalles, nos ofrece una visión de España. Son sencillamente admirables de sobriedad y de plasticidad algunos de los breves cuadros de Somoza (262).

Reality and the ideal—the eternal poles of Azorín's inner world. 'El estilo es la psicología,' he declares (1935; VIII, 637). As in his response to the world around him so also in his stylistic demands —both of himself and of others—Azorín seeks constantly to bridge the gap. Is this line by Juan Ruiz symbolic of the poet's vain quest for 'reposo' and 'olvido'? (181). Is Góngora's rose a symbol of the 'breve esplendor del poeta'? (200). The 'Romance del conde Arnaldos' carries us away to 'países de ensueño y de alucinación' (185). 'Cervantes, en *La fuerza de la sangre*, nos da la sensación de una noche de luna' (213). The opening scene of *La vida es sueño* 'parece un grabado de Durero; hay en ella una ansiedad, un misterio, una melancolía, una vaga inquietud que nos estremece el espíritu' (247). But we must stem the flow of examples. Are these observations all justified by the works in question? Are they justified by Spanish classics in general? 'No son frecuentes en nuestra literatura estas visiones de un romanticismo delicado y misterioso. La luz de nuestra literatura clásica es más violenta y agria' (215). Yet it is precisely the former, minority aspects of Spanish literature—and of a given author's work—that most attract Azorín's attention in *Al margen de los clásicos*. And as he looks for spring-boards to indefinable realms of mystery and emotion so also he looks for a corresponding delicacy of language in the authors and works selected, another minority characteristic of Spanish literature.[103] Jorge Manrique 'es una cosa etérea, sutil, frágil, quebradiza' (181). 'Nada en nuestra lengua más flúido, tenue, etéreo,' says Azorín of one of Garcilaso's *Canciones*. 'No hay fragmento de prosa más flúida y etérea,' he comments on a passage from *Persiles y Sigismunda* (231). 'La poesía de Bécquer es frágil, alada, fugitiva y sensitiva' (271), in marked contrast to the 'poesía

---

[103] 'Nuestra tradición no es la sencillez y la transparencia. Propendemos a lo inextricable y a lo difuso' ([J. Martínez Ruiz], in *Alma Española* 8, 27 December 1903).

oratoria, rotunda y enfática de la misma época' (275). Indeed, it is Bécquer especially, says Azorin, who gives us that indefinable sensation that we are surrounded by unknown, mysterious forces that our limited senses cannot perceive. In doing so, he believes, Bécquer is in touch, as scientists may one day be, with the extraordinary phenomenon of life and thought (175–6).

A final point. We have seen in a previous section that Unamuno and Azorín, in their reading as in their travels, look for the collective spirit of different periods and regions and, beyond periods and regions, for the collective, time-resistant spirit of the Spanish people throughout their history. We have seen also, in the present section, that, by selection and subjective interpretation, they look also for themselves. We have even glimpsed evidence that the two quests are virtually synonymous and that ultimately both writers interpret Spain in the light of their own self-probing. But it is not only Spain that they interpret in this highly subjective way. We have been concerned throughout this study with the consequences of a determinist system torn from its scientific origins by writers eager to impose structure on the bewildering complexity of a world of collapsing values. In so far as they are egolatrists—as Unamuno and Azorín so clearly are—the proposed structure is centred on the individual writer's *yo*. It would be strange, then, if this subjectivity did not reveal itself also in the manipulation of the determinist system itself. And this, indeed, is what we find. 'Todo escritor característico de una época merece un estudio,' declares Unamuno, 'si no por él por la época que caracteriza' (1922; III, 1034). Nevertheless, in his obsession with 'intrahistory' the eternalizing Unamuno is in fact far less concerned with period character than the more historicist, change-conscious Azorín and studies of period character are relatively rare in his writings. Similarly, despite his manifest appreciation of works that throw light on regional character ('*La barraca* o *Cañas y barro* son novelas admirables porque en ellas Blasco nos ha presentado el alma valenciana', 1912; VII, 733) Unamuno, with his concern for universality and his tendency to equate Spain's eternal tradition with that universality, pays considerably less attention than the variety-sensitive Azorín to differences of regional character, emphasizing, instead, works that reveal directly something of Spanish character as a whole. If the main contention of my study

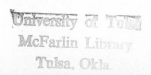

is correct, if in fact evolutionary determinism is accepted as the basic, *underlying* link between the writers of 98, there is much work still to be done on the way in which each individual writer exploits the inherited determinist system in order to make it the bearer of his own intimate concerns.

## 6. EPILOGUE

This has sometimes been called the hypothetico-deductive method, or more often the method of hypothesis, for it does not achieve absolute certainty for any of the scientific statements which it tests; rather, these statements always retain the character of tentative hypotheses, even though their character of tentativeness may cease to be obvious after they have passed a great number of severe tests (Karl Popper, *The Poverty of Historicism*, London 1957, p. 131).

I bring my study to a close with a profound sense of dissatisfaction. My aim in this work has been primarily historical: to emphasize a few basic and often well known characteristics of the so-called 98 Generation and, perhaps more originally, to show these as integrated and mutually complementary aspects in a complex of thought and feeling that extends beyond the mere 'problem of Spain', beyond any clearly definable group of *noventayochistas*, beyond a mere 'generation', and places a host of Spanish writers—historians, essayists, novelists and poets—in an unfailingly recognizable late nineteenth-century European context.

My enthusiasms, however, lie elsewhere: not in what writers great and small have in common with one another, but in what is peculiar to this writer or that writer in his own personal response to the world in which he is immersed; not in the merciless ransacking of texts good and bad for generational or 'movemental' characteristics, but in the delight of confrontation with individual texts; not, in short, in the scholar's contextual approach with which I have here been concerned, but with the critic's evaluative approach: '¿Cómo es *por dentro* esta obra? [. . .] ¿De qué modo suena o disuena a nuestra mentalidad moderna? ¿Qué emoción se produce entre nuestro espíritu y el espíritu del artista pasado?' (Azorín, IX, 967).

But history cannot be evaded. My original work plan, sketched out some twelve years ago, was to prepare a volume of short studies on important Spanish works of the period 1895–1912— some on single works; others comparative (as in Part I of this study)—and to conclude with two general studies in which I proposed to gather my findings together and, in the light of them, to examine the validity of the terms Modernism and 98 Generation. Unfortunately, two of my 'short studies' on single works developed into monographs and the rest threatened to do likewise. Perhaps understandably, reviewers, though extremely kind in their comments on my evaluation of the works studied, noted some disregard of their generational context and significance. But how, in a few paragraphs, does one place a work in a generational context when one feels unable to accept any established definition of the generation in question? Prompted by reviewers and urged on by students I have regretfully accepted time's defeat and, earlier than I should have wished, here developed in print what was to be one of my concluding 'general studies'.

The advantages may well outweigh the disadvantages. Engrossed in one's own ideas one can too easily come to accept one's working hypotheses as indisputable facts. One needs to have them probed by others with a different and possibly more extensive range of relevant reading. Differences between authors passed over in silence, insufficient regard paid to forerunners in Spain itself, the absence of any attempt to define a generational language or even to probe the Generation's basic obsession with time, disregard of the question of the 98 Generation's relationship to Modernism—limitations of space and the desire to preserve a reasonable balance between the three parts of this study can be blamed for much, but doubtless not for everything.[104] More 'refutations' are needed—of this study and of others. Despite a profusion of scholarly works we are surely still far from a proper understanding of the movement of 1898.

---

[104] The investigation of certain of these problems—notably that of the 98's relationship to Modernism—is carried a stage further in a short monograph to be published shortly: HR, *The Spanish 'Generation of 1898'*, The John Rylands University Library of Manchester [1974?].

# BIBLIOGRAPHICAL ABBREVIATIONS

The following list falls into three parts, corresponding broadly to the three main sections of my study: in the first I indicate abbreviations used for works by and on Unamuno and Ganivet; in the second I list works by Taine; in the third I add works by Spanish writers much quoted in my study who reveal significant similarities to Unamuno and Ganivet.

### A. UNAMUNO AND GANIVET

#### 1. *Unamuno*

MU, I–IX   Miguel de Unamuno, *Obras completas.* 9 vols., Escelicer, Madrid 1966–71.

MU, *PE*   Unamuno's contribution to *El porvenir de España* (in MU, III, 635–77).

*ETC*   *En torno al casticismo* (in MU, I, 773–865).

*PG*   *Paz en la guerra* (in MU, II, 87–301).

MU–JA   Letters from Unamuno to Juan Arzadun (in *Sur*, Buenos Aires, Nos. 119–20, September–October 1944).

MU–LA   Letters from Unamuno to Leopoldo Alas (in *Epistolario a Clarín*, Madrid 1941, pp. 33–105).

MU–PJI   Letters from Unamuno to Pedro Jiménez Ilundain (in *Revista de la Universidad de Buenos Aires*, Nos. 331–4, 1948–1949).

MU–PM   Letters from Unamuno to Pedro de Mugica (in *Cartas inéditas de Miguel de Unamuno*, Santiago de Chile 1965).

#### 2. *Ganivet*

AG, I–II   Angel Ganivet, *Obras completas.* 3rd ed., 2 vols., Aguilar, Madrid 1961–62.

AG, *PE*   Ganivet's contribution to *El porvenir de España* (in MU, III, 635–77).

*IE*   *Idearium español* (in AG, I, 147–305).

LSLP   Luis Seco de Lucena Paredes, *Juicio de Angel Ganivet sobre su obra literaria (Cartas inéditas).* Universidad de Granada, 1962.

NML   Nicolás María López, *La Cofradía del Avellano (Cartas íntimas de Angel Ganivet).* Granada 1936.

HR   H. Ramsden, *Angel Ganivet's 'Idearium español'* (*A Critical Study*). Manchester University Press, 1967.

## B. TAINE

[The dates of first editions are indicated in brackets]

ECH　　Essais de critique et d'histoire [1858; 'Préface', 1866]. 4th ed., Paris 1882.

ETL　　Essai sur Tite-Live [1856]. Paris 1856.

HLA　　Histoire de la littérature anglaise [1863–64]. 4th ed., 5 vols., Paris 1877–78.

Int　　De l'Intelligence [1870]. 3rd ed., 2 vols., Paris 1878.

LFF　　La Fontaine et ses fables [1861; an earlier version appeared in 1853]. Cent soixantième mille, Paris 1952.

OFC　　Les Origines de la France contemporaine [1876–93]. 11 vols.: I–II (24th ed., 1902), III–VIII (23rd ed., 1900–01), IX–XI (25th ed., 1906–07), Paris.

PhA　　Philosophie de l'art [Lectures given 1864–69]. 17th ed., 2 vols., Paris 1921.

PhC　　Les Philosophes classiques du xixe siècle en France [1857: a rather different version]. 3rd ed., Paris 1868.

VC　　Sa Vie et sa correspondance [Letters dated 1847–92; published posthumously]. 3rd ed., 4 vols., Paris 1908.

VI　　Voyage en Italie [1866]. 3rd ed., 2 vols., Paris 1876.


## C. OTHER WRITERS

Azorín, I–IX　Azorín, Obras completas. 9 vols.: I–IV (2nd ed., 1959–61), V (1st ed., 1960), VI–VIII (2nd ed., 1962–63), IX (1st ed., 1954), Aguilar, Madrid.

Maeztu, I, II　Ramiro de Maeztu, Obras: I (Autobiografía), Editora Nacional, Madrid 1962; II (Hacia otra España), Rialp, Madrid 1967.

Maeztu, DH　Ramiro de Maeztu, Defensa de la Hispanidad. Ediciones 'Fax', 6th ed., Madrid 1952.

Maeztu, DQ　Ramiro de Maeztu, Don Quijote, Don Juan y La Celestina. Austral, 7th ed., Buenos Aires 1952.

Ortega, I–VI　José Ortega y Gasset, Obras completas. 6 vols., Revista de Occidente, Madrid 1946–47.

PB, I–VIII　Pío Baroja, Obras completas. 8 vols., Biblioteca Nueva, Madrid 1946–51.